W9-BJF-234

Also by COOK'S

**The Cook's Magazine Cookbook**
**Cook's Freestyle Cuisine**

# COOK'S SIMPLE AND SEASONAL CUISINE

EDITED BY

JUDITH HILL

SIMON AND SCHUSTER

NEW YORK LONDON SYDNEY TORONTO TOKYO

Published by Simon and Schuster
A Division of Simon & Schuster Inc.
Simon & Schuster Building
Rockefeller Center
1230 Avenue of the Americas
New York, NY 10020



Designed by Irving Perkins Associates
Manufactured in the United States of America

10 9 8 7 6 5 4 3 2 1

Library of Congress Cataloging-in-Publication Data

Cook's simple and seasonal cuisine.

Includes index.
1. Cookery I. Hill, Judith, date. II. Cook's
magazine. III. Title: Simple and seasonal cuisine.
TX715.C7857 1988 641.5'64 88-4423

ISBN 0-671-62008-8

Seasonal Recipes Color Photo Credits:

*Richard Felber:* Blackened Fish; Bulgur-Stuffed Quail; Cornmeal and Coriander Quesadillas; Deep-Fried Smelt with Tartar Sauce; Shellfish Louisiana. *Vincent Lee:* Apple Charlotte; Champagne-Poached Figs with Heavy Cream; Chiffonade Salad with Tomato-Shallot Dressing; Couscous and Curried Fish with Hot Lime and Cucumber Pickle; Elote con Queso (Corn Custard); Roast Turkey and Garbanzo-Chorizo Stuffing with Salsa Verde; Sesame Sautéed Catfish with Lemon Butter; Shrimp-Guacamole Tostadas; Spinach Wonton Ravioli Soup; The Very Best Angel Food Cake. *Nancy McFarland:* Apple and Cider Soup with Raisins; Avocado Soup with Coriander Salsa; Baked Sweet-Dumpling Squash; Berry Tart; Café à la Mousse; Chicken Mole; Ham and Crab Jambalaya; Mint Marinated Salmon; Poached Peaches with Champagne Sabayon; Roast Goose Stuffed with Cranberries, Apples, and Potatoes. *Jerry Simpson:* Broccoli with Starfruit.

# ACKNOWLEDGMENTS

Of the many people who contributed to this book, we'd especially like to acknowledge Donna Pintek, copy editor extraordinaire, and also Mary Caldwell and Judith Sutton, who wrote the informative sidebars throughout the book. We thank director of photographic styling Sara Barbaris and food stylist Beverly Cox, for their help in making the photographs beautiful, and Sheila Lowenstein and Sally Williams, for their editorial support all along the way. We're grateful to all the writers and chefs who contributed recipes to *COOK'S* magazine and, hence, to this book—particularly Pamela Parseghian and Melanie Barnard, both of whom developed so many fine dishes.

Christopher Kimball
Publisher
*COOK'S* Magazine

Judith Hill
Editor in Chief
*COOK'S* Magazine

# CONTENTS

# INTRODUCTION

At *COOK'S* magazine, we believe in cooking with the seasons. If you use the fruits and vegetables that are at their peak, you get a double dividend: the produce is at its best *and* cheapest. We have, therefore, organized this book according to the seasons. The chapters run from hors d'oeuvre to dessert for ease of use, but within every chapter you will find the recipes arranged by season, spring through winter. This does not mean that you can make the recipes only during their prime time, of course. It does mean that you can be sure of getting peak produce if you do make the dishes during their designated season. Certainly grapes, apples, and zucchini, for example, can be used at off-peak times. All the grilling recipes are in the summer sections, and if you have an indoor grill or live in a warm climate, many of these are year-round possibilities for you.

The recipe methods are divided into sections, most commonly PREPARATION, COOKING, and SERVING. The steps listed under PREPARATION can be completed at least two hours ahead, in the afternoon for an evening party, for instance, and often earlier. The very occasional exceptions are noted. The preparation will often include some cooking that can be done in advance, and sometimes an entire recipe will fall under this heading, when the dish can be completed hours before serving. The COOKING section includes the final steps to be completed shortly before the meal, and SERVING outlines our suggestions for arrangement on the plate.

The recipes range from up-to-date ideas, such as Tortellini with Parsley-Caper Sauce, Stuffed Trout with Tomato-Cumin Sauce, and Sweet Cherry Gratin, to all-time favorites, like Cream of Asparagus Soup, Pennsylvania Dutch Chicken with Dumplings, and the Very Best Angel Food Cake. The recipes are not overly complicated but rather are practical dishes for today's home cook. We all want simpler, lighter food that still tastes good, and that's what we emphasize both in *COOK'S* magazine and in this book.

Christopher Kimball
Publisher
*COOK'S* Magazine

Judith Hill
Editor in Chief
*COOK'S* Magazine

CHAPTER 1

# HORS D'OEUVRE AND FIRST COURSES

**SPRING:**

Baked Asparagus Mousse with Tomato Sauce
Panfried Shad Roe with Bacon and Peas

**SUMMER:**

Tomatoes Filled with Curried Cream Cheese
Individual Salmon Mousse with Cucumber
Mozzarella with Tomatoes and Basil

**FALL/WINTER:**

Grilled Bolete Caps with Mint
Kale Timbales with Sautéed Radishes
Shrimp-Guacamole Tostadas
Smoked Salmon on Parsnip Pancakes

**ALL SEASON:**

Skewered Scallops *Chinoise*
Yellow Potatoes and Scallops
Cornmeal and Coriander Quesadillas
Asian Pasta and Vegetables with Ham
Phyllo Stuffed with Goat Cheese and Prosciutto
Tortellini with Parsley-Caper Sauce

SIDEBARS
Peas
Mint
Boletes

# SPRING

## Baked Asparagus Mousse with Tomato Sauce

An elegant but simple mousse from chef Steve Christianson of Lion's Rock in New York City.

**1 pound tomatoes**
**White pepper**
**1 pound asparagus**
**2 eggs**
**½ teaspoon chopped basil leaves *or* ⅛ teaspoon dried**
**Pinch nutmeg**
**¼ teaspoon salt**
**Basil leaves for garnish**

**PREPARATION:** Peel, seed, and chop the tomatoes. Put tomatoes in a saucepan and cook over low heat for 20 minutes. Pour tomatoes into a food processor and purée with white pepper to taste. Return to pan.

Peel the asparagus. Cook asparagus in salted boiling water until tender, about 6 minutes. Drain. Chop asparagus, reserving 8 whole tips for garnish. Purée chopped asparagus in food processor until smooth. Add eggs, 1 at a time, to food processor. Add basil, nutmeg, salt and a pinch of white pepper.

Lightly butter four 4- to 5-ounce ramekins. Pour asparagus purée into prepared ramekins.

**COOKING:** Heat oven to 350°F. Set ramekins in a pan with 1 inch hot water. Cover with plastic wrap and foil and bake in preheated oven until just set, about 30 minutes. Remove from oven and let sit, covered, for 5 minutes. Reheat sauce.

**SERVING:** Spoon sauce onto 4 plates. Unmold mousse onto sauce and garnish with reserved asparagus tips and basil leaves.

**YIELD:** 4 servings

## Panfried Shad Roe with Bacon and Peas

This traditional seasonal combination can be prepared in less than 45 minutes. For those who can't get enough shad roe during spring, double the quantities and serve it as a main course.

- **2 pairs shad roe (about 1 pound total)**
- **1 tablespoon lemon juice**
- **½ cup shelled green peas (about 5 ounces in the shell)**
- **4 slices bacon**
- **Butter if needed**
- **3 tablespoons flour**
- **Salt and pepper**
- **½ cup fine dry bread crumbs**
- **¼ teaspoon grated lemon zest**
- **1 egg**
- **¼ cup white wine**
- **½ cup heavy cream**
- **4 lemon slices**

**PREPARATION:** In a pot simmer shad roe in salted water with lemon juice until it begins to firm, about 5 minutes. Trim membranes and cut each roe pair into 4 pieces so that you have 8 pieces total. Drain well.

Shell peas and cook in boiling salted water until tender, about 5 minutes. Drain. Dice the bacon and sauté it

### PEAS

Clarence Birdseye didn't do it on purpose, of course, but it was he who ended "pea time." In the nineteenth century, the phrase referred to those verdant months of late spring and summer when native green peas were in the markets, in the North and Midwest. By 1929 Birdseye had perfected a commercial technique for freezing food to which peas adapted well. By the 1950s less than ten percent of the crop, the second largest vegetable crop in the U.S. (just after corn), was sold fresh.

Fortunately, peas have survived the attempt to can or freeze every last one of them. Technology may bring us the best possible frozen peas, but fork into a buttery pile of tender garden peas and the difference speaks for itself.

Peas can be early or late varieties, tall or dwarf, small or large pod, and with smooth or wrinkled seeds. The essential thing to know is that wrinkled seeds are sweeter than smooth. As the seeds of any variety of garden pea mature, they become higher in starch and lower in sugar, so smaller peas of a given type are generally better. Since varieties vary in size, however, a larger one that's at 80 percent of its full size will be sweeter than a smaller one that has reached full growth. Fresh peas should be stiff and crisp and squeak or "sing" when two are rubbed together. Like corn, peas should be used as quickly as possible since the natural sugars begin to wane as soon as they're picked. Older, starchier peas are best cooked and puréed.

*Petits pois,* a kind of garden pea with particularly small, sweet seeds, became the special domain of the French in the eighteenth century. Today *petits pois* are still common in French markets but, although easily cultivated, are seen here only in farmers' markets and specialty shops.

Snow peas, also called Chinese peas, are prized for their flat, crisp, edible pods; the peas inside are tiny. A cross between the garden pea and the snow pea called the Sugar Snap pea was developed in this country and introduced to the market in 1979. It combines a sweet, edible pod with full, firm peas. The best of both worlds.

in a frying pan until crisp. Drain bacon and reserve drippings in pan. There should be about 4 tablespoons; if necessary add enough butter to make 4 tablespoons.

In a shallow dish combine flour with salt and pepper. In another shallow dish combine bread crumbs with lemon zest. In a third shallow dish beat egg lightly. Dip roe into flour and shake off excess, then dip them into egg, and finally into bread crumbs to coat.

**COOKING:** Fry roe in reserved drippings over medium heat, turning once, until browned and crisp, about 5 minutes. Transfer roe to warm plates.

Add wine to pan and scrape bottom with a wooden spoon to deglaze. Add cream and simmer until slightly thickened, 2 to 3 minutes. Add peas and salt and pepper to taste and simmer until heated through.

**SERVING:** Spoon sauce over roe and garnish with reserved bacon and lemon slices.

**YIELD:** 4 servings

# SUMMER

## Tomatoes Filled with Curried Cream Cheese

This is an hors d'oeuvre with flair—red tomatoes filled with yellow curried cream cheese and set on a bed of curly greens. A pastry bag is a near-necessity for making this recipe.

- **20 yellow *or* red cherry tomatoes (about 1 pint)**
- **½ pound cream cheese**
- **1 tablespoon vegetable oil**
- **1 tablespoon curry powder**
- **1 teaspoon mustard seeds**
- **1–2 tablespoons heavy cream**
- **Salt and pepper**
- **1 tablespoon minced chives for garnish**
- **Bed of curly parsley *or* chicory leaves**

**PREPARATION:** Stem cherry tomatoes and slice in half. Using a small spoon or your finger, scoop out seeds. Drain halves upside down. Bring cream cheese to room temperature.

In a small frying pan warm the oil over medium-low heat. Add curry powder and mustard seeds and stir to toast lightly, about 1 minute. Cool to room temperature. Beat spice mixture into softened cream cheese. Add cream as needed to make mixture soft enough to pipe through a pastry bag. Season to taste with salt and pepper.

Turn tomato halves cut side up and sprinkle lightly with salt and pepper. Fit a pastry bag with a small star tip, fill bag with cream cheese mixture, and pipe into shells. Sprinkle chives over filled tomatoes.

**SERVING:** Make a bed of the curly parsley or chicory leaves on a serving platter. Arrange tomatoes on top. (If put on a flat surface, they will not stand upright.)

YIELD: 40 hors d'oeuvre

## INDIVIDUAL SALMON MOUSSE WITH CUCUMBER

The smooth, pinky-orange mousse looks beautiful on a bed of crunchy, pale green cucumber.

- **1 English cucumber *or* 2 regular cucumbers**
- **Salt**

SALMON MOUSSE

- **½ pound skinned salmon fillet**
- **4 egg whites**
- **Salt and white pepper**
- **5 dashes hot red-pepper sauce**
- **¼ cup minced chives *or* scallion tops**
- **4 teaspoons minced dill *or* 1½ teaspoons dried**
- **1 cup heavy cream**
- **4 teaspoons lemon juice**
- **Black pepper**
- **1 tomato**

**PREPARATION:** If using regular cucumbers, peel and seed them. Grate cucumber, toss with 1 teaspoon salt, and set in a strainer for 15 minutes.

FOR THE MOUSSE: Heat oven to 350°F. Butter four 4-

ounce ramekins. Make sure all mousse ingredients are very cold. Purée salmon in food processor for 10 seconds. Add egg whites and process 10 seconds. Add 1 teaspoon salt, ¼ teaspoon white pepper, red-pepper sauce, 2 tablespoons chives, and ½ the fresh dill or all the dried dill and process to blend. Add cream and process briefly to combine. Mixture should be smooth and thick.

Divide among prepared ramekins and rap the ramekins sharply on work surface to get rid of air bubbles. Cover ramekins with plastic wrap and top with foil. Set them in a baking pan and pour in hot water to reach halfway up sides of ramekins. Bring water to a simmer on top of the stove. Transfer to preheated oven and bake until mousse is set and springy, about 20 minutes.

Meanwhile, rinse and drain cucumbers and toss with lemon juice and black pepper to taste. Cut tomato into 8 wedges.

**SERVING:** Arrange beds of cucumber and tomato wedges on 4 plates. Unmold mousse onto prepared plates and sprinkle with remaining 2 tablespoons chives and 2 teaspoons fresh dill. Serve warm, room temperature, or slightly chilled.

**YIELD:** 4 servings

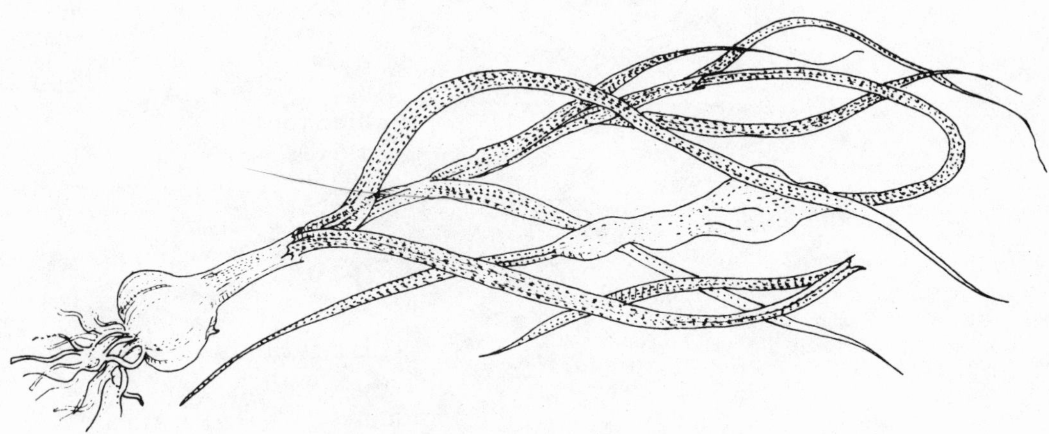

# MOZZARELLA WITH TOMATOES AND BASIL

The quality of the cheese is paramount in this dish, but you might vary the type. Experiment with smoked mozzarella, fontina, or provolone, either smoked or plain.

- **½ pound whole-milk mozzarella**
- **½ red onion**
- **2 plum tomatoes**
- **¼ cup shredded basil**
- **1 tablespoon red-wine vinegar**
- **1 tablespoon olive oil**
- **Salt and coarse black pepper**

**PREPARATION:** Cut the mozzarella into 2-inch-long, ¼ -inch wide sticks. Mince the onion. Core, quarter, and seed the tomatoes and cut into thin wedges. Combine all the ingredients in a large bowl and toss gently. Taste and add more salt and pepper as needed.

**SERVING:** Serve at room temperature or slightly chilled.

**YIELD:** 4 servings

# FALL/WINTER

## Grilled Bolete Caps with Mint

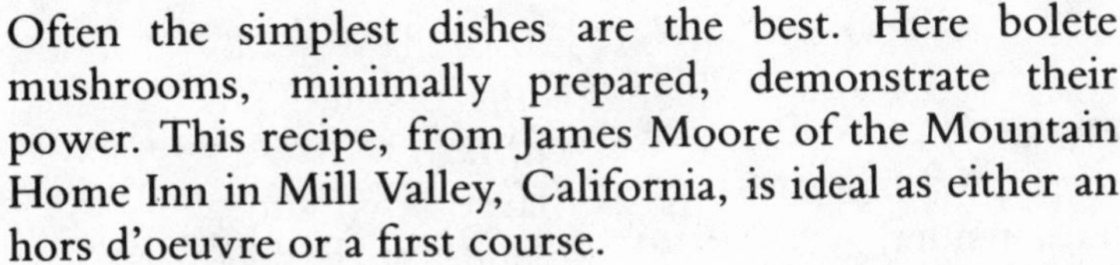

Often the simplest dishes are the best. Here bolete mushrooms, minimally prepared, demonstrate their power. This recipe, from James Moore of the Mountain Home Inn in Mill Valley, California, is ideal as either an hors d'oeuvre or a first course.

**1 pound boletes**
**¼ cup light olive oil**
**Mint sprigs for brushing**
**Salt**
**2 tablespoons shredded mint**

**PREPARATION:** Trim the mushrooms. If mushrooms are large, cut into thick slices. Otherwise, leave caps whole and cut stems in half lengthwise.

**COOKING:** Heat grill or broiler. Coat mushrooms lightly with oil. Grill over medium-hot fire until heated through, about 4 minutes. Baste frequently with oil, using mint sprigs as a brush. Transfer to a warm plate. Season with salt, sprinkle with shredded mint, and serve.

**YIELD:** 4 servings

### MINT

Since mint asks almost nothing but a little space in the ground, even the most neglectful gardener can have a thriving patch. The types you're most likely to grow or see in the produce section are peppermint, with deep green, pointed leaves, and its slightly narrower-leaved cousin, spearmint. More exotic varieties include pineapple mint, apple mint, and orange-bergamot mint.

When buying cut mint, look for a healthy, green color and firm, small, tender leaves. Store fresh mint in the refrigerator crisper, first wrapped in moist paper towels and then put in a plastic bag.

Fresh mint is delicate and tends to lose its flavor when cooked for a long time; it's best to mince it and add just before serving. Mint does not mix well with herbs other than the ever-congenial parsley.

# KALE TIMBALES WITH SAUTÉED RADISHES

If you don't have timbale molds, custard cups work equally well for this unusual appetizer.

- **¾ pound kale**
- **3½ tablespoons butter**
- **1 clove garlic**
- **½ cup milk**
- **¼ cup heavy cream**
- **¼ cup fresh bread crumbs**
- **1 egg**
- **1 egg yolk**
- **Salt and pepper**
- **1 shallot**
- **32 radishes**

**PREPARATION:** Remove the ribs from the kale. Bring a large saucepan of salted water to a boil and cook kale until tender, 8 to 10 minutes. Drain, plunge into cold water, and squeeze dry, removing as much water as possible. Chop. In a large frying pan melt 2 tablespoons butter over medium-high heat. Add kale and cook, stirring occasionally, until all liquid has evaporated, 3 to 5 minutes. Remove from heat.

Crush the garlic. In a small saucepan bring milk, cream, and garlic almost to a boil over medium-high heat. Remove from heat, cover, and let sit for 5 minutes. Discard garlic. Add bread crumbs and set aside.

Butter four ½ -cup timbale molds. Butter 4 pieces of foil to cover molds.

In a bowl combine egg, extra yolk, milk mixture, kale, and salt and pepper. Divide mixture among prepared molds and cover with prepared foil. Chop the shallot. Slice the radishes.

**COOKING:** Heat oven to 350°F. Put molds in a baking pan and fill pan with hot water to come halfway up the molds. Bring water to a simmer on top of the stove.

### BOLETES

To many wild mushroom mavens, the bolete—with its sweet, clean, woodsy flavor and meaty texture—is the best of all. You may be familiar with the bolete *(Boletus edulis)* by one of its other names: king bolete, cèpe, porcini, or Steinpilz. Up in the Rockies, the season for this convex-capped mushroom is midsummer, and it's most often found a week or so after a torrential thunderstorm; in the Sierra, the season is late summer or early fall; and along the West Coast, boletes pop up in late fall or early winter.

Boletes in peak condition range in size from that of a fat grape to almost two pounds. A perfect bolete (which may be dark brown, pale brown, or almost white if it has never broken through the forest duff) resists firm hand pressure. When you slice the cap with a sharp knife, the flesh should be almost crunchy and shouldn't shred. Bolete stems tend to be more fibrous than the caps, but the fibers are almost unnoticeable in very young (not necessarily small) boletes. Perfect young boletes are completely edible and can be eaten cooked or raw.

Transfer to preheated oven and bake until timbales are just firm, about 20 minutes.

In a large frying pan melt remaining 1½ tablespoons butter over medium-high heat. Add shallot and cook until soft, 3 to 4 minutes. Add radishes and cook, stirring constantly, until they are coated with butter and hot through, no longer than 2 minutes. Remove from heat and season with salt and pepper.

**SERVING:** Unmold timbales. Surround with sautéed radishes and serve.

**YIELD:** 4 servings

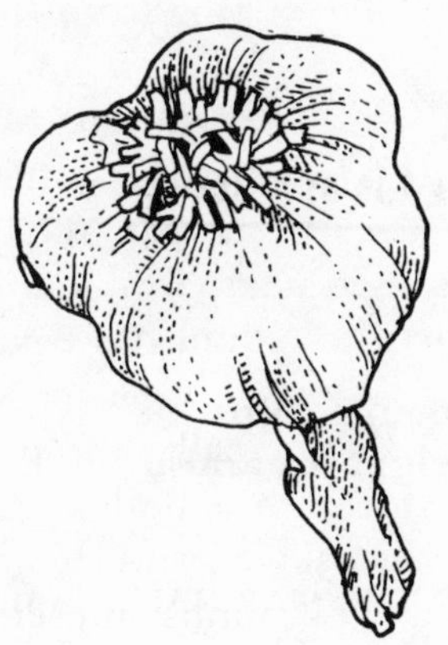

Older boletes are still desirable. They will be spongier than young ones, and the tube mouths under the cap may be slimy or taste bitter—remove them before cooking the mushrooms. Chop the stem to whatever size you want, or "string" it, pulling or slicing it apart with the grain to get fine strands like noodles. These strands, slowly sautéed in butter, make a nice nest for the sautéed cap slices. Mature cap slices, when cooked in the same manner but for less time, will be sweet and nutty.

For boletes of any age, keep the seasoning subtle and don't waste them in tomato or spicy sauces, which would overwhelm their flavor. Don't sauté the mushrooms past golden brown or they're likely to become bitter.

Dried boletes are used primarily as a flavoring—taste and aroma are great; texture is poor, visual appeal, zero. Avoid boletes or any other mushrooms that have been dried over a wood fire. This is a frequent practice, unfortunately, and completely overpowers the flavor. Don't buy mushrooms that smell like a fireplace. Good dried boletes develop an earthy, toasted nut flavor, with a subtle, almost chocolate accent.

# SHRIMP-GUACAMOLE TOSTADAS

A time-honored taste combination in miniature. Cooling coriander is matched with hot jalapeño and smooth guacamole with crunchy tortilla chips.

## LIME-CORIANDER MARINADE

**1 lime**
**1 small clove garlic**
**1 tablespoon chopped coriander**
**¼ cup vegetable oil**
**1 teaspoon Dijon mustard**
**¼ teaspoon ground cumin**
**Salt and pepper**

**12 shrimp**

## GUACAMOLE

**1 plum tomato**
**1 fresh *or* pickled jalapeño pepper**
**1 lime**
**2 ripe avocados**
**Salt and pepper**

**24 round corn tortilla chips**
**Coriander sprigs for garnish**

**PREPARATION:** FOR THE MARINADE: Squeeze the lime to make 2 tablespoons juice. Crush the garlic. Combine the lime juice, coriander, garlic, oil, mustard, cumin, ½ teaspoon salt, and ¼ teaspoon pepper in a bowl.

In a pot of boiling salted water cook the shrimp until they turn pink, about 2 minutes. Drain, wait until cool enough to handle, and shell. Cut in half lengthwise through the back and remove vein, if any. Combine warm shrimp with marinade, cool to room temperature, and refrigerate at least 1 hour.

FOR THE GUACAMOLE: Peel, seed, and mince the tomato. Mince the jalapeño. Squeeze the lime to make 2 tablespoons juice. Peel the avocados. In a bowl mash the avocados with a fork or potato masher. They shouldn't be perfectly smooth. Combine avocados, tomato, jalapeño, lime juice, and salt and pepper to taste. If not using immediately, press plastic wrap directly on surface of guacamole.

**SERVING:** Heat oven to 350°F. Put tortilla chips on a baking sheet and heat in preheated oven until they are crisp and golden, about 5 minutes. Cool slightly. Drain shrimp. Spoon 2 teaspoons guacamole on each tortilla chip. Put a shrimp half, cut side down, on top of guacamole. Garnish each with a small sprig of coriander.

**YIELD:** 24 tostadas

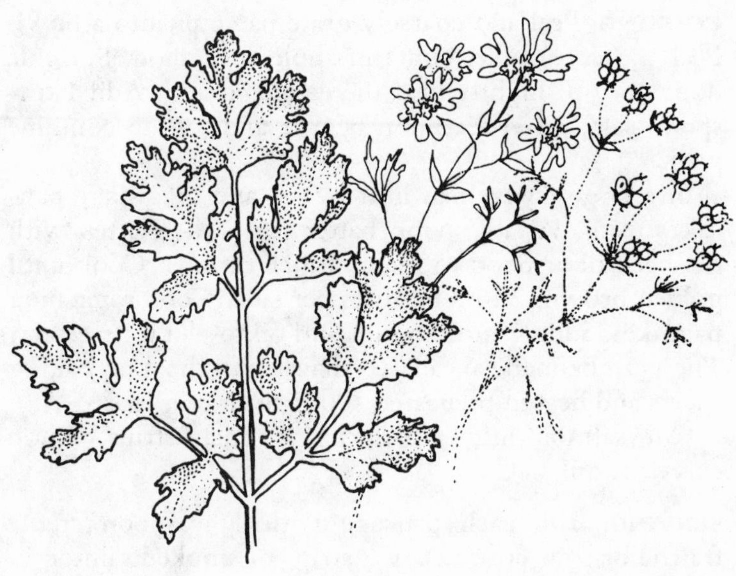

# SMOKED SALMON ON PARSNIP PANCAKES

The concept of potato pancakes gets a reworking by substituting parsnips and garnishing with smoked salmon.

- **3 parsnips (about ¾ pound total)**
- **¼ tart apple**
- **¼ small onion**
- **⅓ cup flour**
- **2 eggs**
- **Salt and pepper**
- **2 tablespoons butter**
- **¼ cup vegetable oil**
- **¼ pound smoked salmon**
- **Chives *or* dill sprigs for garnish**
- **¾ cup crème fraîche *or* sour cream**

**COOKING:** Peel and coarsely grate parsnips into a bowl. Peel and core apple. Grate in apple and onion. Sprinkle flour on top. Lightly beat the eggs and add. Add 1 teaspoon salt and ¼ teaspoon pepper and toss to combine well.

In a large frying pan heat butter and oil. Make pancakes using ½ tablespoon batter for each. Flatten with the back of a spoon to make 2-inch rounds. Cook until golden brown, 2 to 3 minutes per side. Cook remaining pancakes, adding more butter and oil to pan if necessary. They can be made ahead. To reheat, put them on baking sheets and heat in preheated 400°F. oven until crisp.

Cut salmon into 1-inch by ¼ -inch strips. Chop chives or dill.

**SERVING:** Top each pancake with 1 teaspoon crème fraîche or sour cream. Lay 2 strips of smoked salmon in a cross on top and sprinkle with chives or dill.

YIELD: about 35 hors d'oeuvre

# ALL SEASON

## SKEWERED SCALLOPS *CHINOISE*

Sweet tangerines balance the spicy peppers and ginger in this Chinese-inspired hors d'oeuvre.

**½ clove garlic**
**1 small fresh hot red pepper *or* ½ teaspoon hot red-pepper flakes**
**3 tangerines**
**1 pound sea scallops**
**3 tablespoons peanut oil**
**1 teaspoon minced gingerroot**
**2 tablespoons rice-wine vinegar**
**1 tablespoon honey**
**¾ teaspoon salt**
**¼ teaspoon black pepper**
**15–20 snow peas**
**2 scallions**

**PREPARATION:** Mince the garlic and fresh red pepper, if using. Squeeze 1 of the tangerines to get ¼ cup juice. Peel and section remaining 2 tangerines. Cut sections in half if large. Trim scallops and cut into ¾-inch chunks if large.

In a saucepan warm the oil over low heat. Add garlic, gingerroot, and red pepper and sizzle for 30 seconds.

Add vinegar, tangerine juice, honey, salt, and pepper. Heat to a simmer, stirring to dissolve honey. Add scallops and cook, tossing gently, for 2 minutes. Pour scallops and marinade into a bowl and cool to room temperature. Cover and refrigerate at least 1 hour.

In a pot of boiling salted water cook snow peas until just tender, about 1 minute. Refresh under cold running water, drain, and pull pods apart lengthwise.

Mince scallions. Wrap 1 piece of tangerine and 1 scallop in a snow pea half and skewer with a toothpick. Dip 1 side in minced scallion. Cover and refrigerate if not serving immediately.

**SERVING:** Arrange on a platter and serve just slightly chilled.

**YIELD:** 30 to 40 hors d'oeuvre

## YELLOW POTATOES AND SCALLOPS

Yellow-fleshed Finnish potatoes have exceptional flavor and are increasingly available. If you can't get them, any other firm boiling potato will work well in this recipe contributed by chef Fred Bramhall of Dudley's in Denver, Colorado.

**1 pound Finnish (about 2) *or* new potatoes (about 4)**
**1 pound sea scallops**
**2 onions**
**2 sweet red peppers**
**1 cup olive oil + more if needed**
**¼ teaspoon cayenne**
**¼ teaspoon ground cardamom**
**¼ teaspoon ground cumin**
**⅛ teaspoon ground cloves**
**Salt and pepper**
**¼ cup sherry vinegar *or* other mild vinegar**
**2 bunches watercress (about ¾ pound total)**

**PREPARATION:** Put potatoes in a saucepan with cold salted water to cover. Cover and bring to a boil. Uncover, reduce heat to a simmer, and cook until done, about 30 minutes (15 minutes for new potatoes). Drain and cool.

Trim scallops. Halve onions and cut crosswise into thin slices. Halve, seed, and cut peppers into thin slices.

**COOKING:** Heat 2 tablespoons olive oil in a large frying pan. Add onions and peppers and sauté over medium-low heat until browned and very tender, stirring occasionally, about 20 minutes. Add cayenne, cardamom, cumin, and cloves and cook 3 minutes. Set aside.

Cut potatoes into ¼-inch slices. Heat 3 tablespoons olive oil in a large frying pan. Add as many potato slices as will fit in 1 layer, season with salt and pepper, and sauté over high heat until lightly browned on both sides, about 5 minutes. Transfer potatoes to a bowl. Repeat procedure for remaining potatoes, adding more oil as needed. Put scallops in the same pan, adding 1 tablespoon olive oil if necessary. Season scallops with salt and pepper and sauté quickly over high heat until they just test done, about 4 minutes. Add scallops to potatoes.

Heat remaining olive oil in pan over medium-high heat for 1 minute. Add vinegar and swirl to combine. Season with salt and pepper.

**SERVING:** Put watercress on plates. Center a spoonful of the red-pepper mixture on top and arrange potato slices and scallops around edge. Pour warm oil and vinegar over all.

**YIELD:** 4 servings

# CORNMEAL AND CORIANDER QUESADILLAS

These quesadillas are excellent served whole as a first course or cut into wedges as an hors d'oeuvre. We provide a recipe for cornmeal tortillas, but you can also use the store-bought soft flour or cornmeal variety.

CORNMEAL TORTILLAS

**1½ cups flour**
**½ cup cornmeal**
**1 teaspoon salt**
**1 tablespoon minced coriander**
**2 tablespoons vegetable shortening**
**½ cup warm water**

CHEESE FILLING

**2 ounces shredded Monterey Jack cheese (about ½ cup)**
**2 ounces shredded sharp Cheddar cheese (about ½ cup)**
**2 ounces shredded whole-milk mozzarella cheese (about ½ cup)**
**2 tablespoons grated Parmesan cheese**
**½ teaspoon ground cumin**
**Salt**
**4 scallions**
**3 tablespoons minced coriander leaves**

**Jalapeño pepper for garnish, optional**

**Butter and oil for frying**

**½ cup sour cream**
**Coriander sprigs for garnish, optional**

**PREPARATION:** FOR THE TORTILLAS: Sift the flour. Combine flour, cornmeal, salt, and coriander in a mixing bowl and cut in shortening until mixture resembles coarse crumbs. Add water and stir until mixture comes together in a ball. Cover with plastic wrap and let rest for 1 hour. Divide dough into 8 balls. Roll into thin 7½ - to 8-inch circles. If not using immediately, stack with plastic wrap between each tortilla and wrap well.

FOR THE CHEESE FILLING: Mix the cheeses, cumin, and ½ teaspoon salt. Mince scallions, including half of the green part, and add with coriander to the cheese mixture.

Spread the filling on 4 tortillas, leaving a ½-inch margin. Top with remaining tortillas and press edges together. Cut jalapeño pepper into thin slices, if using.

**COOKING:** Heat 2 large frying pans or a griddle over medium-high heat. Add 2 teaspoons each butter and oil to prevent quesadillas from sticking. Cook, turning once, until quesadillas begin to brown, about 3 minutes total.

**SERVING:** Serve quesadillas whole or cut into wedges and garnish with sour cream and, if desired, jalapeño pepper and coriander sprigs.

YIELD: 4 servings

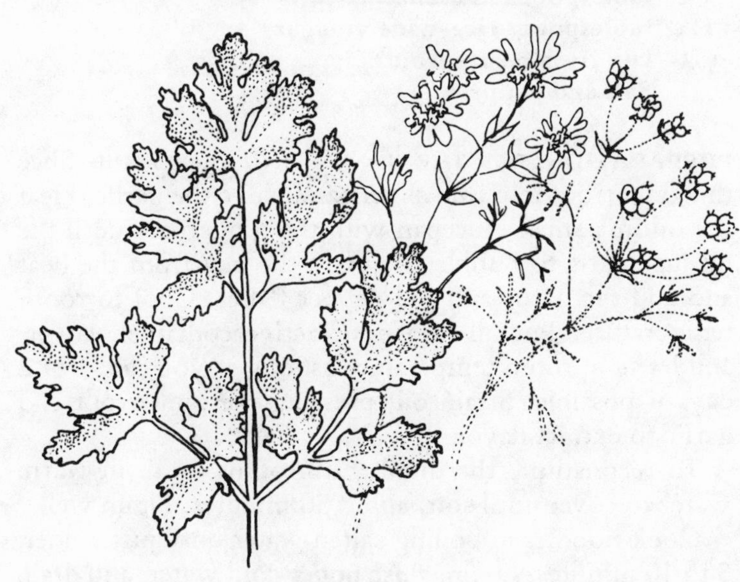

# ASIAN PASTA AND VEGETABLES WITH HAM

This flavorful pasta salad can be made a day ahead. We recommend preparing the dressing well ahead to let its flavors develop, or, if you have only a short time, doubling the quantities of the ingredients that flavor the oil—ginger, garlic, and hot pepper.

GINGER AND PEPPER OIL

**2 inches gingerroot**
**2 cloves garlic**
**½ cup peanut oil**
**¼ teaspoon red-pepper flakes, *or* to taste**

**⅛ ounce dried mushrooms, such as tree ears, optional**
**½ pound dry Chinese egg noodles *or* vermicelli**
**¼ pound snow peas (about 1½ cups)**
**1 carrot**
**2 scallions**
**½ pound sliced smoked ham**
**1½ tablespoons soy sauce**
**1½ tablespoons rice-wine vinegar**
**1 cup fresh bean sprouts**
**Salt and pepper**

**PREPARATION:** FOR THE GINGER AND PEPPER OIL: Slice the gingerroot into thin slivers and halve the garlic. Heat the oil in a small saucepan with the gingerroot until the oil just starts to bubble. Remove the pan from the heat and add the garlic and red-pepper flakes. Cool to room temperature. Put oil in a nonreactive container, cover, and let sit at room temperature as long as you can, 1 or 2 days if possible. Strain oil, pressing the gingerroot and garlic to extract flavor.

To reconstitute the dried mushrooms, soak in warm water to cover until soft, about 30 minutes. Drain well.

Cook noodles in boiling salted water until just tender, 5 to 10 minutes. Drain, rinse under cold water, and drain thoroughly. Toss the noodles with a little of the oil to coat.

Trim the snow peas and cook in boiling salted water until just tender, about 2 minutes. Drain and rinse under cold water. Cut lengthwise into thin strips. Shave thin strips off the carrot with a vegetable peeler. Cut the scallions diagonally into ¼-inch slices. Cut the ham into thin julienne strips.

In a large bowl whisk together the soy sauce, vinegar, and remaining steeped oil. Add the noodles, snow peas, carrot, scallions, ham, mushrooms, and bean sprouts. Toss well and season to taste with salt and pepper. Serve at room temperature or slightly chilled.

**YIELD:** 4 servings

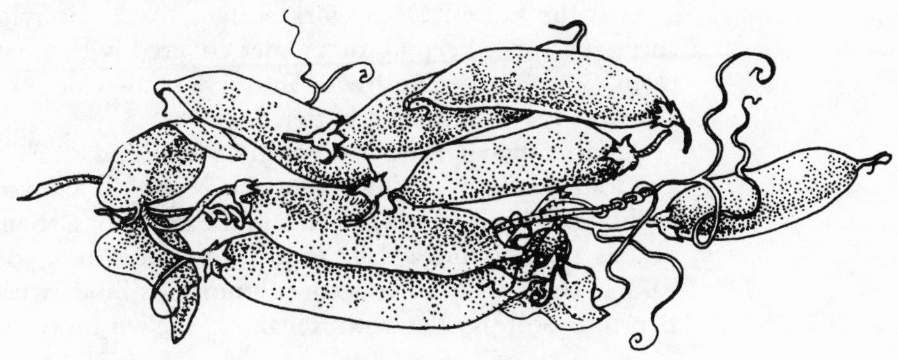

# PHYLLO STUFFED WITH GOAT CHEESE AND PROSCIUTTO

The stuffing for phyllo triangles, outlined here, can vary infinitely. Try crab and cream cheese with a touch of mustard or perhaps fine strips of Oriental vegetables sautéed and seasoned with soy and a splash of vinegar.

**½ pound medium-sharp soft goat cheese**
**3 tablespoons cream cheese**
**½ cup cottage cheese**
**2 teaspoons chopped thyme *or* ½ teaspoon dried**
**Black pepper**
**2 eggs**
**3 ounces prosciutto**
**¼ pound butter**
**½ pound fresh phyllo dough, approximately**

**PREPARATION:** In a food processor blend cheeses with thyme, pepper, and eggs until smooth. Cut prosciutto into ⅛-inch by ½-inch strips. Stir into cheese.

Melt the butter. On a work surface, lay out phyllo 1 sheet at a time, keeping remainder covered with a damp cloth. Cut sheet lengthwise into 1¾-inch-wide strips. Brush strips with melted butter.

Put less than 1 teaspoon of filling at 1 end of a strip and fold corner over filling to make a triangle. Continue folding phyllo from side to side in the shape of a triangle just as you would a flag. Put, seam side down, on a baking sheet. Repeat procedure until all filling is used. Brush tops of pastries with remaining melted butter.

**COOKING:** Heat oven to 400°F. Bake phyllo triangles in preheated oven until golden brown, about 15 minutes.

**YIELD:** 50 to 60 triangles

# Tortellini with Parsley-Caper Sauce

This do-ahead hors d'oeuvre is based on ready-made tortellini, which we find can be of high quality. Try a number of brands until you find the one you like best.

**½ pound small fresh *or* frozen meat or cheese tortellini**
**Olive oil, if necessary**

Parsley-Caper Sauce

**1 ounce Parmesan cheese**
**1 clove garlic**
**2 tablespoons sunflower seeds**
**2 tablespoons capers**
**¾ cup tightly packed flat-leaf parsley**
**½ cup olive oil**
**Salt and pepper**

**PREPARATION:** In a large pot of boiling salted water cook tortellini until just done, about 8 minutes. Drain, rinse with cold water, and toss with a little olive oil if not serving at once.

FOR THE SAUCE: Grate the cheese. Drop garlic clove into a food processor and chop 10 seconds. Add sunflower seeds, cheese, capers, and parsley and process to a coarse purée. With machine running, add olive oil in a thin stream. Or to make by hand, crush garlic and capers to a paste. Grate the cheese, mince the sunflower seeds and parsley, and add to garlic/caper paste. Whisk in the oil. Season to taste with salt and pepper.

**COOKING:** Put cooked tortellini in a pot. Pour in the sauce, toss to coat and heat through. Pour into a warm shallow bowl.

**SERVING:** Skewer several tortellini with toothpicks or small skewers and provide additional picks or skewers on the side for the remaining tortellini.

YIELD: about 50 tortellini

CHAPTER 2

# SOUPS

**SPRING:**
Spinach Wonton Ravioli Soup
Cream of Asparagus Soup

**SUMMER:**
Corn Soup with Tomato Relish
Chilled Cream of Chervil Soup

**SUMMER/FALL:**
Avocado Soup with Coriander Salsa

**FALL/WINTER:**
Parsnip Soup with Coriander
Simple Wild Mushroom Soup
Banana-Squash/Apple Soup
Squash, Leek, and Sweet Potato Soup

**ALL SEASON:**
Chicken Stock
Chicken Consommé
Chicken Soup with Almonds
New Bedford Baked Seafood Chowder
Ham and Crab Jambalaya

SIDEBARS
Avocado
Coriander
Winter Squash

# SPRING

## Spinach Wonton Ravioli Soup

It's simple to make ravioli with Oriental wonton skins. Available in packages of one hundred, wonton squares cost about a penny apiece and freeze well. Here, they are filled with an Italian spinach stuffing, shaped into ravioli, floated in chicken stock, and garnished with an Oriental touch—sliced scallion tops. Thin slices of radish are added at the last minute for colorful crunch and taste. It's an international combination that works.

Ravioli Filling

**5 ounces spinach**
**1 small clove garlic**
**1½ tablespoons chopped *pancetta or* bacon (about 1 ounce)**
**1 teaspoon heavy cream**
**Salt and pepper**

**1 egg yolk**
**24 wonton skins**
**4–5 radishes**
**3 scallions**
**4 cups Chicken Stock (page 49)**
**Salt and pepper**

**PREPARATION:** FOR THE FILLING: Trim and wash the spinach, put it in a pot with just the water clinging to the leaves, and cook over medium-high heat for 1 minute. Drain, squeeze dry by the handful, and chop.

Mince the garlic. In a large frying pan cook *pancetta* over low heat until crisp. Remove with a slotted spoon and drain. In fat rendered from *pancetta* sauté garlic over medium heat 1 minute. Add spinach and cook, stirring, until all moisture evaporates, about 2 minutes. Remove from heat and add *pancetta* and cream, tossing to combine well. Season to taste with salt and pepper and set aside to cool.

Beat the egg yolk with 1 teaspoon water for egg wash. Fill wonton skins, keeping unused skins between layers of damp towels so that they won't dry out. Put 12 skins on a work surface and put 1 teaspoon filling in the center of each. Brush edge of each skin with egg wash and put another skin on top. Using your fingers, firmly press edges together. With a ravioli cutter or a 2-inch round cookie cutter, cut away excess skin and discard.

Halve the radishes and cut into thin slices. Cut the scallion tops into diagonal slices.

**SERVING:** Bring stock to a simmer. Cook ravioli in stock until they float to the top, about 1 minute. Reduce heat, add radishes and scallion tops, and simmer 2 minutes. Season to taste with salt and pepper and serve.

YIELD: 4 servings

## CREAM OF ASPARAGUS SOUP

Developed by Bruce Naftaly and Robin Sanders, owners of Le Gourmand in Seattle, this beautiful pale-green soup is the essence of springtime. It can be served either hot or cold.

**2 pounds asparagus**
**2 cups Chicken Stock (page 49)**
**2 cups heavy cream**
**¼ cup chopped chervil *or* parsley**
**Salt and white pepper**
**Nutmeg**

**PREPARATION:** Snap tough ends off asparagus and cook spears in boiling salted water until tender, about 5 minutes. Drain. Reserve 4 tips for garnish and purée the remaining asparagus in a food processor. Strain.

Heat the asparagus purée over low heat. Add stock, cream, and chervil or parsley. Heat and season with salt, white pepper, and nutmeg.

**SERVING:** Reheat if necessary and taste for seasoning. Top each serving with reserved asparagus tips.

YIELD: 4 servings

# SUMMER

## Corn Soup with Tomato Relish

It's hard to believe that anything as simple as this soup can be so wonderful. Alice Waters of Chez Panisse in Berkeley, California, concocted the recipe to make the most of corn, tomatoes, and basil—all at their height of flavor during summer.

**6 ears corn**
**4 tablespoons butter**
**Salt and pepper**
**3 cups spring water**
**4–6 tablespoons heavy cream, if necessary**

Tomato Relish

**1–2 ears corn**
**1 ripe tomato**
**6–8 basil leaves**
**Salt and pepper**

**PREPARATION:** Scrape 6 ears of corn with the dull side of a knife. You should have about 3¾ cups of fairly liquid corn. Melt butter in a heavy pot. Add corn and salt and pepper. Toss over medium heat for 3 minutes. Add water and cook over low heat, stirring occasionally, for 15 minutes. Cool slightly.

In a food processor process soup until smooth. Press through a fairly fine sieve. Add cream if necessary. (This will depend on the milkiness of the corn.)

**FOR THE RELISH:** Cut (do not scrape) ¾ cup kernels from the ears of corn. Peel, seed, and dice the tomato. Chop the basil. Stir corn, tomato, basil, and salt and pepper together in a bowl. Let stand a few minutes.

**SERVING:** Heat soup until just hot. Stir in tomato relish.

**YIELD:** 4 servings

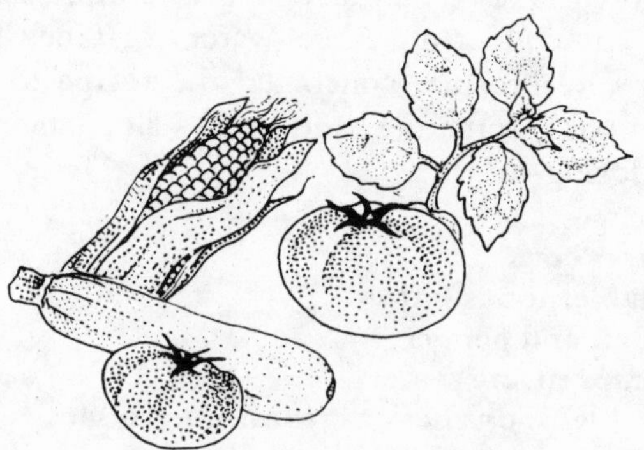

# CHILLED CREAM OF CHERVIL SOUP

Chervil's slight anise taste is heightened by Pernod in this cool and creamy soup. It's an especially rich version of vichyssoise and is best served as a first course in relatively small portions.

- **5 small potatoes (about ½ pound total)**
- **4 scallions**
- **3 tablespoons butter**
- **1 cup loosely packed chervil leaves + more for garnish**
- **½ cup parsley leaves**
- **2 tablespoons Pernod**
- **1 cup Chicken Stock (page 49)**
- **¾ teaspoon salt**
- **⅛ teaspoon white pepper**
- **1 cup heavy cream**
- **Milk, cream, *or* stock, if necessary**

**PREPARATION:** Peel potatoes and put in a saucepan with cold salted water to cover. Bring to a boil, reduce heat to a simmer, and cook, covered, until tender, about 10 minutes. Drain.

Chop scallions. Melt butter in a saucepan. Add scallions and sauté over medium heat until soft, about 3 minutes. Add chervil and parsley and sauté 1 minute. Add Pernod, stirring with a wooden spoon to deglaze pan. Add stock, potatoes, salt, and white pepper. Stir to combine. Purée mixture in a blender or food processor until smooth. Stir in cream and chill.

**SERVING:** If the soup seems too thick, thin with a little milk, cream, or stock. Adjust seasoning to taste. Garnish with chervil leaves.

**YIELD:** 4 servings

# SUMMER/FALL

## AVOCADO SOUP WITH CORIANDER SALSA

### AVOCADO

The combination of buttery texture and subtly nutty flavor in a perfectly ripened avocado has no peer. How to find that perfect avocado is the problem. Until recently, the choice often seemed to be between a rock-hard fruit that rotted before it ripened and a mushy, already spoiled specimen. But now that both consumers and marketers have become more knowledgeable, the quest is easier.

There are many varieties of avocado grown in the United States, but the two major types come from Florida and California. (Some avocados are grown in Texas, but they represent only a small percentage of the crop.) The skin of almost all avocados is some shade of green, ranging from light to very dark, and the surface may be smooth or pebbled. Florida avocados are usually larger than those from California. Shiny, bright green,

This beautiful soup is an ideal way to begin a summer dinner. And if you have chicken stock in the freezer, the recipe couldn't be simpler—there's not even any cooking involved.

**2 small avocados**
**4 teaspoons lemon juice**
**4 teaspoons lime juice**
**2 cups Chicken Stock (page 49)**
**1⅓ cups light cream**
**Salt and pepper**

CORIANDER SALSA

**2 small tomatoes**
**1 2-inch piece cucumber**
**½ red bell pepper**
**1 jalapeño pepper**
**2 scallions**
**1 small clove garlic**
**1 tablespoon minced coriander**
**Pinch cumin**
**Salt**

**PREPARATION:** Pit and peel the avocados. Purée the avocados in food processor or food mill with lemon and

smooth-skinned Florida specimens do make an impressive display, but they tend to be almost watery and to have less appealing taste and texture than the California varieties. There are smooth-skinned California avocados as well, but anyone who has tried the smaller, pebbly-skinned, black Hass "alligator pear" knows that it is truly superb, the most flavorful and creamy of all. Florida avocados are available from midsummer through the winter and may be the only type found in some markets during the winter. The Florida varieties are also frequently cheaper than those from California. California avocados are becoming available year-round but are more prevalent during the summer and fall (when the prized Hass is in season).

An avocado is perfectly ripe when it yields all over to very gentle pressure. Interestingly enough, avocados, unlike most fruits, will never become perfectly ripe while still on the tree. You can allow an avocado to ripen at room temperature, or you can speed up the process by placing it in a paper bag in a warm, dark place, where it will ripen in a few days. Adding a tomato to the bag further hastens the process due to the gas released by the tomato. An avocado that has been stored in the refrigerator will never ripen further, so, if it is already ripe, you can hold it there for a day or two.

A ripe avocado can be sliced and dressed with a light vinaigrette, made into ever-popular guacamole, or, as we have done, puréed with lemon and lime juice as the base of a chilled soup accompanied by a coriander salsa (page 42). The rich but unobtrusive taste makes it an excellent complement to the familiar ingredients of Southwestern cooking such as jalapeños, garlic, cumin, and coriander. If you are using an avocado in a hot dish, be careful not to overcook it or it will become bitter.

The flesh of an avocado turns brown on exposure to air, but dousing the slices with lemon or lime juice or keeping them in acidulated cold water helps to prevent this reaction. To store part of an avocado, leave the pit in place, coat the flesh with lemon juice, and wrap tightly in plastic wrap; it will keep in the refrigerator for a few days. (One footnote: It is very easy to grow an avocado plant from a seed, but not if the avocado has been in the refrigerator—a refrigerated pit is unlikely to germinate.)

lime juices. Add the stock, cream, and salt and pepper. Blend well. Chill at least 20 minutes.

FOR THE SALSA: Peel, seed, and chop the tomatoes and cucumber. Seed and chop bell pepper. Carefully remove seeds and ribs from the jalapeño and mince the flesh. Mince the scallions and garlic. Combine all salsa ingredients in a bowl. Or, mince garlic and jalapeño in food processor, add remaining ingredients, and process to combine. Let stand at least 15 minutes at room temperature.

**SERVING:** Serve soup with a spoonful of salsa in the center of each bowl.

YIELD: 4 servings

# FALL/WINTER

## Parsnip Soup with Coriander

> **CORIANDER**
>
> With the increasing interest in Indian, Mexican, and Chinese cuisines—as well as in the cooking of the American Southwest—fresh coriander leaves have become as familiar to Americans as the powdered seeds. Coriander is also known as cilantro or Chinese parsley, and, with its long stems and flat, jagged leaves, it does look somewhat like Italian parsley. Its smell, however, is distinctive, a pungent, anise-y aroma that some people find a little off-putting at first; others are immediately addicted. Like other herbs, fresh coriander is most widely available in the late spring through the fall, but it can usually be found year round in ethnic groceries and some specialty stores.
>
> Fresh coriander keeps exceptionally well if you put the bunch in water just like a bouquet

Invented by teacher, author, and caterer Martha Stewart, this soup must be the easiest possible introduction to the glories of the parsnip. Even those who are less than enthusiastic about root vegetables will like sweet parsnips combined with an even sweeter pear and accented with fresh coriander.

**1 shallot**
**1 small pear**
**1 potato**
**1 pound parsnips**
**2 tablespoons butter**
**1 teaspoon ground coriander**
**4 cups Chicken Stock (page 49)**
**¾ cup heavy cream**
**1 tablespoon minced coriander**
**Salt and pepper**

**PREPARATION:** Mince the shallot. Peel, seed, and cut the pear into chunks. Peel and cut the potato and parsnips into chunks.

Melt butter in a heavy saucepan. Sauté shallot for 3 minutes. Add ground coriander, pear, and potato and cook over low heat for 10 minutes. Add parsnips and stock and simmer until potatoes are very tender, about 45 minutes.

Transfer mixture, 1 to 2 cups at a time, to a food processor. Process until smooth. Or push mixture through fine plate of a food mill. Add ½ cup cream. Whip remaining ¼ cup cream for garnish.

**SERVING:** Heat the soup and season with 2 teaspoons minced coriander and salt and pepper to taste. Serve with a small dollop of whipped cream in the center of each bowl and a sprinkling of remaining minced coriander.

**YIELD:** 4 servings

and refrigerate it. It does not freeze terribly well. You can preserve it, like basil, by chopping it, combining with water or oil, and freezing the mixture, but the fresh herb is preferable. Dried coriander leaves have little taste.

Fresh coriander loses much of its pungency during cooking, lending more subtle flavor than the raw leaves. Once you have become an aficionado, you may want to use more coriander in recipes in which it is to be cooked—or add some chopped fresh leaves at the last minute. The pungent roots of the plant can also be used to good effect in cooking.

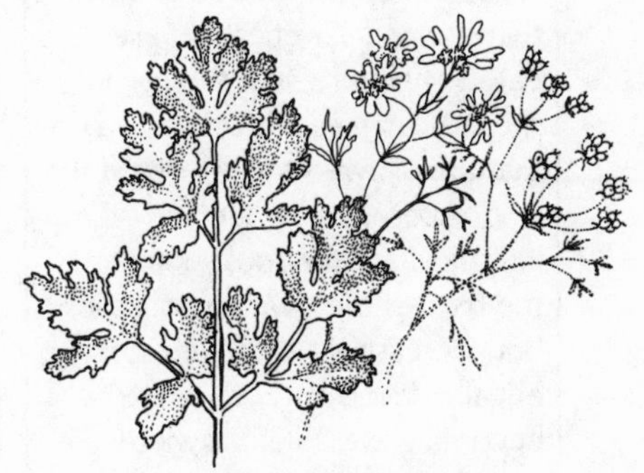

## Simple Wild Mushroom Soup

This basic soup recipe is a fitting showcase for any variety of mushroom.

- **¾ pound chanterelles or shiitake mushrooms *or* 2 ounces dried mushrooms**
- **1 shallot**
- **2 tablespoons butter**
- **Salt and white pepper**
- **1 quart Chicken Stock (page 49)**
- **4–6 tablespoons heavy cream, sour cream, *or* crème fraîche**

**PREPARATION:** Trim and wash the mushrooms or, if using dried, reconstitute in water to cover for 30 minutes. Chop the shallot.

In a large saucepan melt butter over medium-low heat. Add mushrooms and cook gently for 2 minutes. Add shallot and cook until soft, about 5 minutes. Season to taste with salt and white pepper. Add stock and simmer 10 minutes.

Remove mushrooms from stock and put them in a

food processor. Process very briefly to chop fine (rather than reduce to a paste) and return to pot.

**SERVING:** Bring soup to a simmer and adjust seasoning. Reduce heat, add cream, and heat through.

**YIELD:** 4 servings

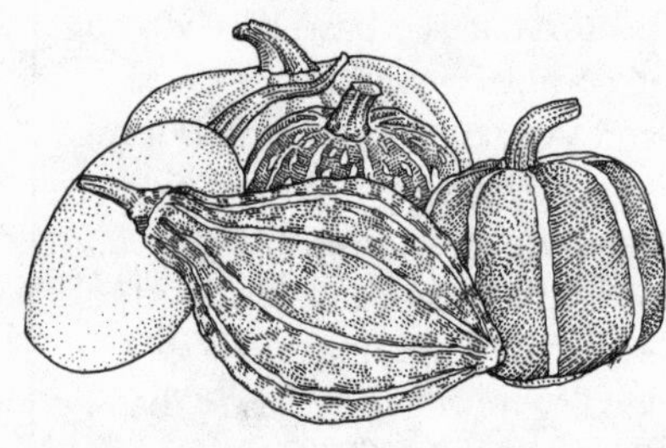

## BANANA-SQUASH/APPLE SOUP

The enormous banana squash is available year round and is usually sold for convenience in pre-cut chunks. Despite its name, it is a large, smooth oval. Its skin is a mottled, ivory-to-peach color, and its flesh a vivid yellow-orange.

In this soup, the banana squash's slight natural sweetness is augmented by that of an apple and caramelized onions. The garlic is optional. Dedicated alliomaniacs can add handfuls of whole garlic cloves, allowing them to caramelize gently with the onions for an unexpectedly nutty effect.

**1–1½ pounds banana squash**
**2 onions**
**2 cloves garlic, optional**
**3 tablespoons butter**
**1½ teaspoons oil**
**½ teaspoon sugar**
**3 cups Chicken Stock (page 49)**
**¼ pound Monterey Jack cheese *or* mild Swiss**
**1 tart apple, such as Granny Smith**
**⅛ teaspoon ground mace**
**½ cup half-and-half**
**Salt and pepper**

**PREPARATION AND COOKING:** Cut squash into chunks and steam or boil until fork-tender, 20 to 25 minutes. Scoop out enough pulp to measure 1½ cups. Purée in a

### WINTER SQUASH

Now that acorn squash is available year round and you can buy zucchini in January, the terms *summer squash* and *winter squash* have lost their descriptive value. However, they are still the usual designations for the two main types of squash: the soft-shelled, thin-skinned varieties that are eaten immature, and the hard-shelled varieties with inedible skin that are allowed to mature on the vine. Acorn, butternut, and Hubbard are the most popular of the hard-shelled winter squashes, but, increasingly, more unusual and equally delicious varieties are becoming available. Spaghetti squash, for example, has become familiar, and the *kabocha,* a Japanese import, is now grown in California and is no longer limited to Oriental food stores. Other types you may encounter include the banana, buttercup, sweet dumpling, delicata, Mediterranean, golden nugget, and turban squash—and, of course, the familiar pumpkin, now in miniature as well as standard size.

blender or food processor. Chop onions. Mince the garlic if using.

In a large frying pan combine butter and oil. Cook onions in butter/oil mixture, covered, over medium-low heat until wilted, about 10 minutes. Add optional garlic halfway through. Uncover pan, lower heat, and sprinkle with sugar. Sauté until onions and garlic caramelize to a golden brown, stirring and scraping frequently, 30 to 35 minutes. Add stock. Shred the cheese.

**SERVING:** Peel, core, and dice the apple. Add diced apple and mace to the stock and simmer until apple bits just lose their crispness, about 5 minutes. Stir in squash, cheese, and half-and-half. Warm just until cheese melts, being careful not to boil. Season to taste with salt and pepper and serve.

**YIELD:** 4 servings

## Squash, Leek, and Sweet Potato Soup

With its trio of vegetables, this soup speaks strongly of fall. The serving size given here corresponds to featuring the soup as the centerpiece at an autumn lunch or supper. Figure on 6 servings as a first course.

- **2 large leeks**
- **1 small onion**
- **2 cloves garlic**
- **2 tablespoons butter**
- **¾ teaspoon chopped gingerroot**
- **¾ teaspoon saffron threads, optional**
- **1 sweet potato**
- **¾ pound Hubbard *or* butternut squash**
- **4 cups Chicken Stock (page 49)**
- **½ teaspoon sugar**
- **Pinch cinnamon**
- **¼ teaspoon ground ginger**
- **Salt and pepper**
- **1 cup heavy cream**

While it is true that many winter squashes are available throughout the year, late fall and winter are the peak times to buy them; then you will find the greatest variety and the best choices. Winter squashes vary in color from light gold spaghetti squash to dark green acorn; some varieties are mottled or even two-toned. Acorn squash is often flecked with orange, and the orange-red turban squash is slashed with green and white. (Unfortunately, turban squash looks better than it tastes.) In general, choose those with the richest, most intense hues.

All winter squashes should feel heavy for their size; if they seem light, they are probably dried out. Look for squashes with the stems still attached. Some of the larger types are sold in pieces. Hubbard squash, which may weigh as much as ten pounds, is most often found this way and so is the banana squash. Cut squash must be stored in the refrigerator, where it will keep for up to a week. A whole winter squash, however, has an impressively long shelf life; most varieties will keep in a cool place for anywhere from 3 to 6 months and some even longer. In fact, many varieties become more flavorful over time.

**PREPARATION:** Cut the well-washed leeks (all of the white and some green) into thin slices. Cut the onion into thin slices. Crush the garlic.

In a large pot melt butter over medium heat. Add leeks, onion, garlic, and gingerroot. Cover and cook over low heat until leeks and onion are soft, 20 to 30 minutes.

Toast the saffron threads in a 350°F. oven for 3 minutes and powder them. Peel and slice the sweet potato. Peel, seed, and cut the squash into 1-inch chunks. You should have 3 cups.

In a bowl dissolve saffron in a little stock. Add sweet potato and squash to the pot with the leek/onion mixture. Add stock, including that with the saffron, the sugar, cinnamon, ground ginger, and salt and pepper to taste. Cook, partially covered, over medium heat until squash and sweet potato are tender, 20 to 25 minutes.

Transfer mixture to a food processor or blender and purée. Add cream.

**SERVING:** Reheat. Taste for seasoning.

**YIELD:** 4 servings

# ALL SEASON

## Chicken Stock

If we had to rely on just one stock, it would be chicken, hands down. The most flexible of stocks, it is good with virtually all flavors from vegetables to meat and even with fish. It's also the easiest stock to keep on hand. Simply save stray chicken parts in the freezer until enough accumulate for a batch of stock, put them in a pot (no need to defrost), and simmer with vegetables. When the stock is made, pour it into small containers and freeze until needed. With good chicken stock in the freezer, you're only minutes away from a multitude of superb soups, as this chapter demonstrates.

**1 large onion**
**3 whole cloves**
**4 cloves garlic**
**2 ribs celery**
**2 carrots**
**4 pounds chicken bones and parts, such as carcasses, wing tips, necks, and gizzards (no liver)**
**1 bay leaf**
**4 whole peppercorns**
**½ teaspoon dried thyme**
**6 sprigs parsley**
**Salt**

**PREPARATION:** Halve the onion and stick the cloves in it. Peel the garlic. Chop the celery and carrots.

Put all ingredients except thyme and parsley in a large stockpot and add cold water to cover bones and vegetables completely. Salt very lightly. Bring water to a boil, skimming any foam. Add thyme and parsley. Simmer, partially covered, about 3 hours. Strain stock and reduce to 2 quarts. Cool, chill, and remove fat.

YIELD: 2 quarts

## CHICKEN CONSOMMÉ

Nothing makes a better start for a fine meal than consommé. Strong-flavored yet light, consommé rouses the appetite without quelling it. And the obvious care taken to make beautifully clear consommé promises more good things to come.

- **2 ounces lean beef**
- **¼ pound lean white chicken meat**
- **1 large carrot**
- **1 small leek**
- **2 ribs celery**
- **6 cups Chicken Stock (page 49)**
- **¼ cup chopped parsley**
- **3 egg whites**
- **3 egg shells, optional**
- **Salt and pepper**

VEGETABLE GARNISH

- **2 carrots**
- **2 leeks**
- **2 ribs celery**

**PREPARATION:** Grind or mince the beef and chicken. Chop the carrot, leek, and celery.

Degrease surface of chilled stock thoroughly. Whisk beef, chicken, carrot, leek, celery, parsley, egg whites, and optional shells into cold stock. Bring to a boil, whisking constantly. Lower heat to a simmer. Egg whites and other solid ingredients will coagulate and rise to the surface. Gently push egg whites away from center, leaving a hole large enough for a ladle to fit through. Simmer, undisturbed, for 35 minutes. Strain stock by gently ladling it into a sieve lined with cheesecloth and set over a bowl. Add salt and pepper to taste.

FOR THE VEGETABLE GARNISH: Slice the carrots into paper-thin rounds. Cut the leeks (white and pale green parts only) into very narrow 1-inch-long strips. Peel the celery and cut into thin slices. Cook each vegetable separately in boiling water until tender and drain. Plunge each into ice water to retain color.

**SERVING:** Reheat consommé, ladle into bowls, and add the garnish.

YIELD: 4 servings

## Chicken Soup with Almonds

This is a delicious first-course soup that can be made in half an hour—and almost entirely ahead of time. Double the recipe to use it as a main dish.

**4 tablespoons butter**
**1 large clove garlic**
**¾ pound boneless chicken**
**6 tablespoons olive oil**
**½ cup sliced almonds (3 ounces)**
**¾ cup parsley sprigs**
**3 tablespoons minced chives *or* scallion top**
**1 tablespoon lemon juice**
**Salt and pepper**
**¼ cup grated Parmesan cheese**
**4½ cups Chicken Stock (page 49)**
**¼ cup uncooked *tubettini or* other small dried pasta**

**PREPARATION:** Bring butter to room temperature or soften in a microwave oven. Mince the garlic. Cut the chicken into bite-size pieces.

Heat 4 tablespoons oil in a large frying pan and sauté the almonds over medium-low heat until golden, about 2 minutes. Add garlic and cook 1 minute. Remove and reserve ½ the almonds and garlic. Transfer remaining almonds and garlic and the oil from the frying pan to a food processor. Wipe and reserve frying pan. Add the parsley, chives or scallions, lemon juice, ¼ teaspoon salt, and butter to processor and purée coarsely. Add the cheese and process briefly to blend.

In reserved frying pan heat remaining 2 tablespoons olive oil. Season the chicken with salt and pepper and sauté over medium-high heat until golden, about 3 minutes.

**SERVING:** Bring stock to a boil and cook pasta in it until tender, about 8 minutes. Add the chicken, puréed almond mixture, and reserved almonds and garlic. Season with salt and pepper to taste.

**YIELD:** 4 servings

# New Bedford Baked Seafood Chowder

A tried and true recipe from New Bedford, Massachusetts, the fishing capital of the East Coast for over a hundred years. This recipe was contributed by the United Fishermen's Wives of New Bedford.

- **2 carrots**
- **1 rib celery**
- **3 potatoes**
- **2 onions**
- **1 teaspoon chopped dill**
- **Salt**
- **3 peppercorns**
- **1 whole clove**
- **1 bay leaf**
- **2 tablespoons butter**
- **2 cups water**
- **1½ pounds fish fillets, such as cod, flounder, haddock, *and/or* pollack**
- **6 tablespoons dry white wine *or* milk**
- **⅔ cup light cream**
- **4 teaspoons flour**
- **4 teaspoons chopped parsley**

**PREPARATION:** Heat oven to 375°F. Cut the carrots and celery into ½-inch pieces. Peel and cut the potatoes into 1-inch cubes. Chop the onions.

In a large ovenproof pot combine carrots, celery, potatoes, onions, dill, salt, peppercorns, clove, bay leaf, and butter. Add water and bring to a boil. Cover and put in preheated oven for 40 minutes. Cut the fish into 1½-inch pieces.

Remove peppercorns and clove. Add fish and wine or milk. Stir, cover, and bake 20 minutes.

In a bowl combine cream and flour, whisking until smooth. Whisk in a little of the hot chowder broth. Slowly add cream mixture to chowder over low heat, stirring constantly but gently so fish pieces won't break.

Heat until chowder thickens. Do not boil. Season to taste.

**SERVING:** Reheat chowder if necessary and serve sprinkled with parsley.

**YIELD:** 4 servings

## HAM AND CRAB JAMBALAYA

Because the base for this soup is made with chicken stock, it complements almost any set of ingredients. Rather than ham and crab, you might try chicken and fresh sausage, or duck and smoked sausage, or ham with either crayfish or fresh sausage—or anything else that strikes your fancy.

**1 shallot**
**½ rib celery**
**1 clove garlic**
**Salt and pepper**
**2 tomatoes *or* 2 canned Italian plum tomatoes**
**1 green pepper**
**¼ pound smoked ham**
**⅓ pound crab meat *or* ⅓ pound peeled shrimp**
**1½ teaspoons oil**
**⅓ cup uncooked rice**
**2 teaspoons tomato paste**
**1 tablespoon minced flat-leaf parsley**
**2½ cups Chicken Stock (page 49)**
**¼ teaspoon cayenne**

**PREPARATION:** Mince the shallot and celery. You should have 1 tablespoon shallot and ¼ cup celery. Mash the garlic with 1 teaspoon salt. Peel and seed the tomatoes or, if using canned, cut into ½-inch chunks. Roast the pepper over a gas flame or charcoal grill or under a broiler until skin is blackened. Remove skin, stem, seeds, and ribs. Cut the pepper into ¼-inch strips. Cut the ham into ¼-inch-thick strips. Cut the crab meat into bite-size pieces.

Heat oven to 350°F. In a large heavy pan heat oil over medium-high heat. Add rice and stir. Cook until rice is coated with oil. Stir in shallot and celery. Cook until shallot wilts, about 2 minutes. Add garlic/salt paste, tomatoes, and tomato paste and stir well. Add parsley, green pepper, stock, ¼ teaspoon black pepper, and cayenne. Bring to a simmer.

Cover and put in preheated oven for 17 minutes. Stir in ham and crab or shrimp and return to oven for 3 minutes.

**SERVING:** Reheat if necessary, covered, just until heated through. Season to taste with salt and pepper and serve.

**YIELD:** 4 servings

CHAPTER 3

# SALADS

**SPRING:**

Chiffonade Salad with Tomato-Shallot Dressing
Dandelion Salad
Asparagus and Morel Salad with Red-Wine Vinaigrette

**SUMMER:**

Tomato Salad with Tricolor Pepper Vinaigrette
Portuguese Green Bean Salad
Grilled Scallion and Potato Salad
Cucumber and Plum Salad with Goat Cheese
Cucumber and Cabbage Slaw with Brie

**FALL/WINTER:**

Vegetable Macedoine
Pepper and Endive with Salsa Vinaigrette
Endive, Watercress, and Orange Salad
Warm Noodle/Spaghetti Squash Salad with Chinese Dressing

**ALL SEASON:**

Hot Papaya Salad
White Bean Salad with Thyme
Warm White and Black Bean Salad with Sausage
Knotted Bean Salad

SIDEBARS
Peppers
Cucumbers
Belgian Endive

# SPRING

## Chiffonade Salad with Tomato-Shallot Dressing

This pretty red and green salad was developed by Dean Fearing when he was at The Verandah Club in Dallas, Texas. He's now chef/owner of his own well-regarded restaurant, Mansion on Turtle Creek, also in Dallas.

You can vary the greens. Butter lettuce and watercress or romaine and curly endive are both good combinations.

- **½ cucumber**
- **½ pound spinach**
- **2 heads radicchio**

Tomato-Shallot Dressing

- **1 tomato**
- **1 large shallot**
- **5 tablespoons white-wine vinegar**
- **4 teaspoons safflower oil**
- **1 teaspoon salt**

**PREPARATION:** Peel the cucumber, halve lengthwise, and seed. Cut lengthwise into thin slices and then crosswise into 2½-inch pieces. Put cucumber in a bowl of cold water and refrigerate for several hours to crisp. Cut the spinach and radicchio into thin shreds (chiffonade).

FOR THE DRESSING: Peel, seed, and chop the tomato. Mince the shallot. Combine tomato, 3 tablespoons vinegar, oil, salt, and shallot in a food processor. Blend until smooth.

**SERVING:** Toss spinach and radicchio with remaining 2 tablespoons vinegar. Spoon dressing on 4 chilled salad plates. Drain cucumber thoroughly. Mound spinach/radicchio mixture in center of plates and top with drained cucumber.

YIELD: 4 servings

## Dandelion Salad

The first dandelion greens of spring are the best. Pick them right out of your lawn before they flower and become bitter. Hothouse dandelion leaves are now available and can be enjoyed for a longer season.

**¼ cup walnuts**
**1 quart dandelion greens**

Garlic Vinaigrette

**1 clove garlic**
**1 tablespoon wine vinegar**
**Salt and coarse black pepper**
**3 tablespoons walnut oil**

**PREPARATION:** Chop the walnuts. Tear the greens into manageable pieces.

FOR THE VINAIGRETTE: Mince the garlic. In a bowl whisk together vinegar, garlic, and salt and pepper to taste. Whisk in oil.

**SERVING:** Add dandelion greens to bowl, tossing well to coat each leaf with dressing. Divide among plates and top each serving with walnuts. Serve immediately.

YIELD: 4 servings

# ASPARAGUS AND MOREL SALAD WITH RED-WINE VINAIGRETTE

Asparagus and morels, harbingers of spring, are a perfect flavor combination. They unite here in an extravagant first-course salad.

**¾ pound asparagus**
**¼ pound fresh morels *or* other mushrooms**
**2 tablespoons olive oil**

RED-WINE VINAIGRETTE

**1 lemon**
**1 tablespoon red-wine vinegar**
**Salt and pepper**
**5 tablespoons olive oil**

**2 tablespoons chopped chives**

**PREPARATION:** Trim asparagus and cut into 1-inch pieces. Cook asparagus in a pot of boiling salted water until bright green and tender, about 6 minutes. Drain, rinse with cold water, and drain thoroughly. Set aside to cool.

Trim morels and gently brush off any dirt. Heat 2 tablespoons olive oil in a small frying pan, add the morels, and sauté until just tender, about 3 minutes. Set aside to cool.

FOR THE VINAIGRETTE: Grate zest from lemon or remove in thin strips with a citrus zester and whisk together with vinegar, 1 tablespoon juice from the lemon, and salt and pepper. Whisk in the olive oil.

**SERVING:** Combine the asparagus, morels, and chives and toss gently with dressing.

YIELD: 4 servings

# SUMMER

## Tomato Salad with Tricolor Pepper Vinaigrette

Alice Waters of Chez Panisse in Berkeley, California, developed this simple salad with all the color and taste of summer.

Tricolor Pepper Vinaigrette

- **2 shallots**
- **½ green pepper**
- **½ yellow pepper**
- **½ red pepper**
- **1½ tablespoons red-wine vinegar**
- **1½ tablespoons balsamic vinegar**
- **Salt and pepper**
- **½ cup olive oil**
- **5 tomatoes**

**PREPARATION:** FOR THE VINAIGRETTE: Cut the shallots and peppers into ⅛-inch dice. In a bowl whisk together the vinegars and salt and pepper. Whisk in the oil. Stir in the shallots and peppers and let stand a few minutes. Adjust seasoning with salt and pepper to taste.

**SERVING:** Slice the tomatoes, arrange on a platter, and pour the vinaigrette over them.

**YIELD:** 4 servings

### PEPPERS

The green bell pepper is not alone any more. These days bell pepper hues include red, yellow, brown, and even purple. As peppers ripen on the vine, they turn gold, red, or brown and become sweeter and milder in flavor; the flesh also becomes a little softer. Unlike tomatoes, peppers do not continue ripening once they have been picked. Both green and purple bell peppers are underripe and would turn red if left on the vine. Purple peppers turn green when cooked. Fully ripe peppers have a shorter shelf life than their green counterparts and are almost always sold at higher prices.

You'll find domestic bell peppers in the market throughout the year, although the season peaks in late summer to early fall. Imports, many from the Netherlands and Mexico, can be found most of the year. Buy peppers that are bright-colored, shiny, smooth, and firm and store them in the refrigerator.

The sweet pepper category encompasses more than just bells. The heart-shaped *true pimiento,* most readily available in late summer and early fall, is somewhat smaller and meatier than the bell but has a similar flavor. Narrow, light green *Italian peppers,* typically roasted or fried, have thinner flesh than the bell and a sweet, very intense flavor. Long yellow sweet peppers, alternately known as *banana peppers* or *Hungarian wax peppers,* are also available, but be forewarned: these sweet peppers have a lookalike hot counterpart. A bright red or yellow relative of the *Hungarian* peppers, the *Cubanelle* or *Cuban pepper,* is also sweet. In late summer and early fall, you might find curved *bull's horn (corno di toro) peppers* and thick-fleshed *lamuyo peppers* in your market.

Cooked peppers are more palatable with their skin removed. French chefs often take it off with a vegetable peeler just as you'd peel a potato. In America we generally roast the peppers, which adds good flavor, too. Char them on a grill, over a gas flame, or close to a broiler's heat source.

# PORTUGUESE GREEN BEAN SALAD

When green beans are prime at local produce stands, this salad is a memorable first course. Or you might cut the proportions somewhat and serve it as a side dish with a plain entrée such as roast chicken. Although coriander is the authentic Portuguese flavoring, basil can be substituted for a milder, sweeter taste.

**2 pounds tender, young green beans**

WINE-VINEGAR DRESSING

**1 clove garlic**
**2 shallots**
**1 lemon**
**¼ cup wine vinegar**
**Salt and pepper**
**½ cup olive oil**
**1 tablespoon minced parsley**
**1 teaspoon chopped chives**
**1 teaspoon chopped coriander *or* basil**

**2 whole pimientos**
**3 hard-cooked eggs**
**¼ pound cured ham**
**12 anchovy fillets**
**1 tablespoon capers**

**PREPARATION:** Trim the beans. Cook beans in boiling salted water until just tender, 5 to 7 minutes. Drain, refresh immediately under cold water, and drain well.

FOR THE DRESSING: Crush the garlic to a paste. Chop the shallots. Put both in a large bowl. Grate ½ teaspoon lemon zest and squeeze 2 tablespoons juice. Add to the bowl along with the vinegar and salt and pepper. Whisk together and whisk in olive oil. Whisk in parsley, chives, and coriander or basil.

Combine beans with dressing. Cover and refrigerate for 2 hours. Cut the pimientos into strips. Quarter the eggs. Cut the ham into small dice.

**SERVING:** Drain beans, reserving dressing. Put beans on a large platter or on individual plates. Arrange pimientos, eggs, and anchovies over beans and scatter capers and ham over all. Drizzle some of the reserved dressing over salad and serve with remaining dressing on the side.

**YIELD:** 4 servings

## Grilled Scallion and Potato Salad

A great picnic dish, this salad keeps for hours without refrigeration and provides the delicious taste of grilled food without having to lug along the barbecue and charcoal.

- **4 red potatoes (about 1 pound total)**
- **4 scallions**
- **6 tablespoons olive oil**
- **Salt and pepper**
- **2 tablespoons white vinegar**

**PREPARATION:** Heat the grill. Slice unpeeled potatoes into ⅛-inch rounds. Toss potatoes and whole scallions with 2 tablespoons olive oil, 1 teaspoon salt, and ½ teaspoon pepper. Grill potatoes and scallions, turning once, until they test done and are golden brown, about 8 minutes. Grill in batches if necessary.

Whisk together the remaining 4 tablespoons olive oil and vinegar in a large bowl. Cut the scallions and potatoes into bite-size pieces. Toss potatoes and scallions with the oil and vinegar mixture. Season to taste with salt and pepper.

**SERVING:** Serve warm or at room temperature. The salad is better if it's not refrigerated. It will keep at room temperature for several hours.

**YIELD:** 4 servings

Turn the peppers so that the skin blackens all around, and, when they are completely charred, set them aside until they're cool enough to handle. The skin will pull off easily.

As an added bonus for gardeners, pepper plants, with their starry white flowers and shiny pointed or heart-shaped leaves, are pretty as well as productive. In fact, when Christopher Columbus first introduced peppers to Europe, the plants were preferred for ornamental rather than culinary use. For anything and everything else you might want to know about peppers, sweet or hot, we recommend the beautifully illustrated *Peppers: The Domesticated Capsicums* by Jean Andrews (University of Texas Press, 1984).

# CUCUMBER AND PLUM SALAD WITH GOAT CHEESE

Cucumbers, plums, and goat cheese—an unusual combination that works. Prune plums are recommended because they're firmer than juicy red and purple plums, although any firm plum can be used.

**8 pickling *or* 4 regular cucumbers**
**Salt**
**3 prune plums**

GOAT-CHEESE DRESSING WITH HERBS

**½ clove garlic**
**Salt and pepper**
**¼ pound mild fresh goat cheese**
**¼ cup heavy cream, approximately**
**1–2 tablespoons lemon juice**
**Pinch sugar**

**1 tablespoon shredded mint**
**1 tablespoon minced chives**
**1 tablespoon chopped coriander**
**Mint leaves *or* chive flowers for garnish, optional**

**PREPARATION:** Peel cucumbers, score with a fork, and halve lengthwise. Seed and cut into ¼-inch diagonal slices. In a large bowl toss cucumbers with 2 tablespoons salt. Add a few ice cubes and cold water to cover. Set aside for 30 minutes, rinse well, and drain thoroughly. Halve, pit, and slice the plums.

FOR THE DRESSING: Mash garlic with a pinch of salt. In a large bowl mash goat cheese with a fork. Stir in enough cream to make mixture the consistency of yogurt. Add lemon juice to taste, garlic/salt mixture, sugar, shredded mint, chives, coriander, and salt and pepper. Combine well.

Combine cucumbers and plums. Add dressing, tossing gently. Chill at least 30 minutes but not more than a few hours.

**SERVING:** Serve garnished with mint leaves or chive flowers.

**YIELD:** 4 servings

## CUCUMBERS

It is unfortunate that waxing cucumbers for longer shelf life has become so much the rule that some consumers think cucumber skin is naturally waxy. It certainly is not, and unwaxed cucumbers are worth seeking out.

There are three main types of cucumber: the smooth-skinned garden variety; the long, thin, almost seedless type often called English or European (or burpless); and the small yellowish-green, bumpy-skinned pickling Kirby cucumbers. The least attractive, the pickling cucumbers, are nonetheless the most flavorful. Furthermore, they are never waxed and are more likely to be fresh. English cucumbers are shrink-wrapped in plastic rather than waxed, but they are usually more expensive and sometimes have less flavor than the other varieties.

Cucumbers are coated with paraffin for two reasons. First, marketers think consumers find shiny vegetables more appealing. Second, waxing helps seal in moisture. Cucumbers have a high moisture content; they dehydrate quickly after picking and become wrinkled and limp. Select cucumbers that are dark green (except, of course, when buying pickling cucumbers), firm, small, and thin. Large, fat cucumbers may be bitter and have tough seeds. In both regular and English

*Shrimp-Guacamole Tostadas, page 22*

*Cornmeal and Coriander Quesadillas, page 28*

*Spinach Wonton Ravioli Soup, page 36*

*Avocado Soup with Coriander Salsa, page 42*

*Ham and Crab Jambalaya, page 54*

*Chiffonade Salad with Tomato-Shallot Dressing, page 58*

*Shellfish Louisiana, page 90*

*Mint Marinated Salmon, page 102*

*Couscous and Curried Fish with Hot Lime and Cucumber Pickle, page 116*

*Sesame Sautéed Catfish with Lemon Butter, page 110*

*Deep-Fried Smelt with Tartar Sauce, page 114*

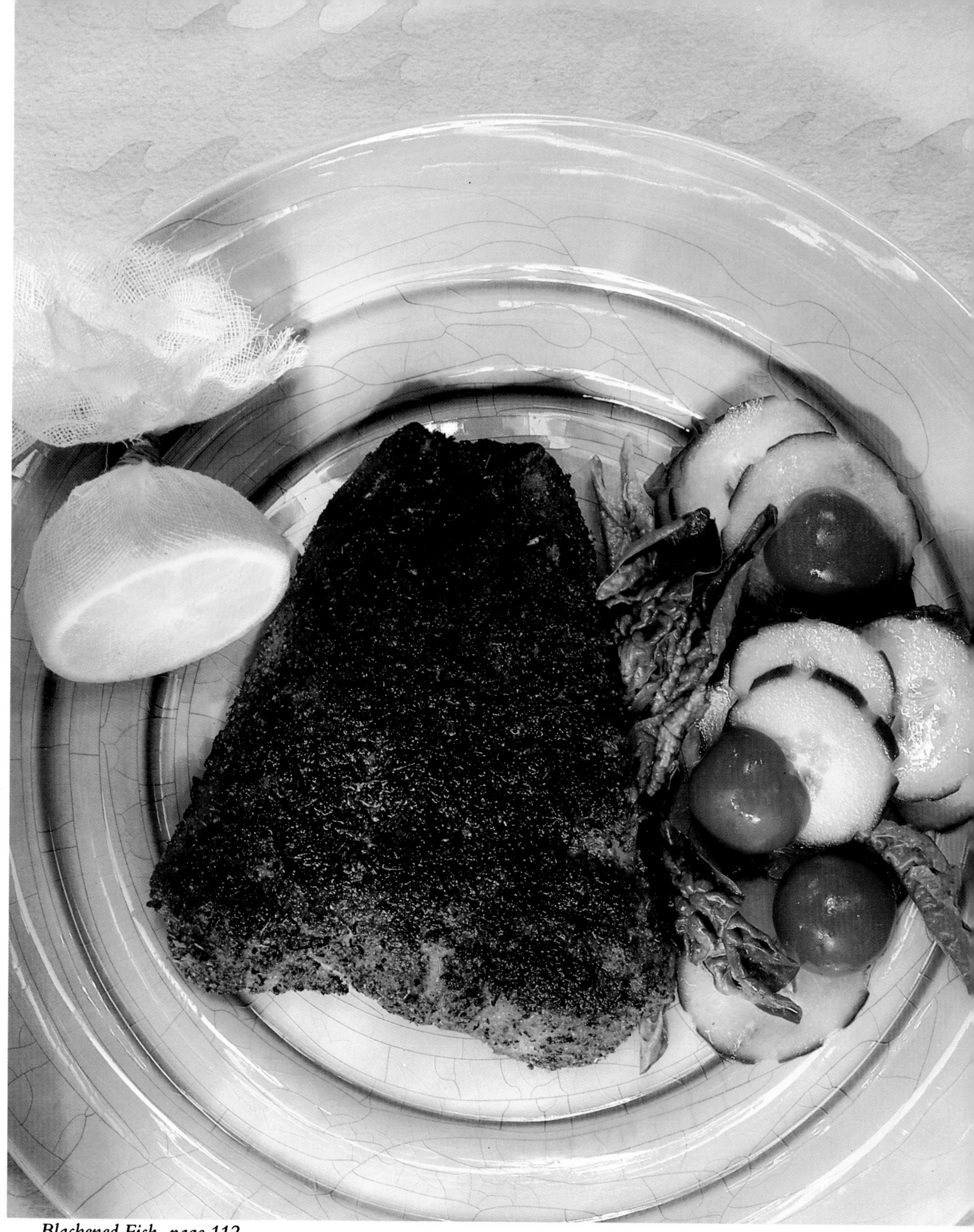

*Blackened Fish, page 112*

*Roast Turkey and Garbanzo-Chorizo Stuffing with Salsa Verde, page 136*

# Cucumber and Cabbage Slaw with Brie

This delicious slaw is dotted with peas and carrots and is a good use for the less-than-perfect Brie often found in our markets. The salad can be made well ahead of serving.

**½ cup shelled peas, fresh *or* frozen (5 ounces unshelled)**
**½ savoy *or* Napa cabbage**
**1 small carrot**
**2 pickling cucumbers *or* ½ English cucumber**
**½ pound Brie**

Red-Onion Vinaigrette

**½ small red onion**
**4 teaspoons balsamic vinegar**
**½ teaspoon lemon juice**
**Salt and pepper**
**3 tablespoons oil**

**PREPARATION:** Cook peas in boiling salted water until tender, about 5 minutes. Drain. Core the cabbage and cut into thin strips. If desired, score carrot with a channel knife to make a flower/star design when the carrot is cut. Slice the carrot into paper-thin rounds. Halve the cucumbers lengthwise and slice very thin. Cut the Brie into small pieces.

FOR THE VINAIGRETTE: Halve and cut the onion into thin slices. In a bowl whisk the vinegar, lemon juice, and salt and pepper together. Whisk in oil. Add the onion and set aside.

Toss the peas, cabbage, carrot, cucumbers, and Brie with the dressing. Season to taste with salt and pepper.

**SERVING:** Serve at room temperature.

**YIELD:** 4 servings

cukes, yellowing indicates aging. Pickling cucumbers are more likely to be shriveled because they are not waxed so choose carefully.

If you are limited to waxed cucumbers, peel them before using; hot or boiling water will remove some, but not all, of the paraffin coating. There is no need to peel unwaxed cucumbers; scoring their skins with a fork adds a decorative touch. Bitterness usually is not a problem with today's cucumbers, but large, seedy cukes are the most likely candidates and so are better peeled and seeded as a matter of course. Yet much of the flavor resides in the seeds—another reason to choose small cucumbers with tender seeds.

While cucumbers are popular raw in salads, they are equally good cooked. Anyone who has never had sliced cucumbers sautéed in butter and sprinkled with fresh herbs is in for a treat—it's like discovering a new vegetable.

# FALL/WINTER

## VEGETABLE MACEDOINE

This updated macedoine (the traditional version includes only carrots, peas, and celery root) can stand on its own as a first course—as macedoine does in many French restaurants—or can be used to fill tomatoes. This adaptation is from Waldy Malouf, executive chef at La Crémaillère in Banksville, New York.

- **1 carrot**
- **1 turnip**
- **1 small celery root**
- **¼ pound green beans**
- **½ cup shelled peas, fresh *or* frozen (5 ounces unshelled)**
- **2 pickling *or* 1 regular cucumber**
- **1 tablespoon minced tarragon *or* chives**
- **1 tablespoon minced watercress**
- **¼ cup shredded radicchio *or* spinach**
- **⅔ cup mayonnaise**
- **Salt and pepper**

**PREPARATION:** Cut carrot, turnip, and celery root into ⅓-inch dice. In a pot of boiling salted water blanch them until tender, about 5 minutes. Drain and cool under cold running water. Cut the green beans into ⅓-inch lengths. Blanch beans and peas until tender, about 4 minutes. Drain and cool under cold running water. Peel and seed the cucumber. Scoop out pea-sized balls or cut into ⅓-inch dice. Blanch the cucumber 20 seconds. Drain and cool under cold running water.

Combine blanched vegetables with tarragon, watercress, and radicchio and mix in mayonnaise and salt and pepper.

**SERVING:** Serve at room temperature or slightly chilled.

YIELD: 4 servings

## PEPPER AND ENDIVE WITH SALSA VINAIGRETTE

A Mexican inspiration, this red and green winter salad is especially appropriate at Christmastime.

SALSA VINAIGRETTE

- **1 clove garlic**
- **1 small fresh mild green chili *or* 1 ounce canned chili**
- **3 tablespoons red-wine vinegar**
- **Salt**
- **⅓ cup virgin olive oil**
- **1 tablespoon minced onion**
- **2 tablespoons minced tomato**

- **2 heads Belgian endive**
- **1 red bell pepper**
- **1 small head Boston *or* red-leaf lettuce**

**PREPARATION:** FOR THE VINAIGRETTE: Mince the garlic. Peel, seed, and mince the fresh chili or mince the canned chili. In a bowl whisk together the vinegar and salt. Whisk in oil, onion, and tomato. Let sit for at least 30 minutes.

Cut endive lengthwise into strips. Cut the red pepper into long slivers.

**SERVING:** Toss endive and pepper with dressing. Line a bowl with lettuce leaves and top with endive and pepper.

YIELD: 4 servings

### BELGIAN ENDIVE

Belgian endive is expensive not only because most of it is imported but also because it is a time-consuming, labor-intensive crop. It was discovered accidentally only in the last century by a Belgian farmer who found that the chicory roots he was storing had sprouted tasty white leaves. To grow Belgian endive, the chicory roots are forced and then grown in darkness so that they don't turn green. Much hand labor is required, one of the reasons the cultivation of this plant has not spread to the technology-oriented United States.

Endive is available twelve months of the year, but it is at its peak in the winter and early spring. Quality may not be quite as good during the warmer months. A slightly bitter tang is part of its appeal, but shopping carefully and treating it well are important in avoiding an unpalatable taste. The heads are shipped wrapped in paper to protect them from light, which will turn the leaves brown and too bitter. Choose those that have been well treated, although some tinges of brown on a few outer leaves may be inevitable. Also, leaves that are tipped with green rather than yellow are likely to be more bitter. Look for short, plump heads that seem firm and fresh.

It's best to use endive as soon as possible after buying it, but it will remain fresh for a day or two stored in a plastic bag in the refrigerator. In light of the price, it's reassuring that there is little or no waste with a head of endive. One or two outer leaves may have to be discarded and the core removed for some dishes, but each head provides a surprising number of compact leaves. It's important to avoid soaking endive in water, which makes it really bitter, but the careful handling heads receive means that they are quite clean when they reach the market. Merely wipe the outer leaves with a damp cloth and the endive is ready to use.

Endive can be cooked and often is. We prefer it raw in salads. For one thing, this is more economical, since cooking reduces it considerably. Even more important, cooking brings out the bitterness, in contrast to the crisp and refreshing raw leaves with their hint of bitter character.

# ENDIVE, WATERCRESS, AND ORANGE SALAD

Sweet oranges temper the bite of watercress and endive in this salad developed by Jimmy Schmidt when he was at the London Chop House in Detroit. The talented young chef is now with The Rattlesnake Club in Denver.

WALNUT VINAIGRETTE

**2 ½ tablespoons white-wine vinegar**
**Salt and pepper**
**6 tablespoons walnut oil**
**1 tablespoon safflower oil**
**1 tablespoon light cream**
**1 small red onion**

**4 heads Belgian endive**
**2 large bunches watercress**
**2 oranges**

**PREPARATION:** FOR THE VINAIGRETTE: Whisk together vinegar and salt and pepper. Whisk in oils and then cream. Dice the onion. Put onion on the corner of a kitchen towel and gather towel to form a pouch. Wring towel and onion to squeeze out juice. While still in towel, rinse onion under cold water. Wring out excess moisture and add onion to dressing. Set aside for 2 to 3 hours.

Cut off tips of endive leaves 2 inches from the top. Trim stems of watercress 2 inches from top. Peel the oranges and cut into thin slices.

**SERVING:** Toss endive, watercress, and oranges with vinaigrette. Or arrange ingredients in concentric circles on a serving plate; the oranges around the edge, then the endive, tips outward, and the watercress in the center. Spoon dressing over all.

YIELD: 4 servings

# Warm Noodle/Spaghetti Squash Salad with Chinese Dressing

In this innovative salad, noodles, spaghetti squash, and smoked meat are tossed with bright peas and oranges in a colorful tangle dressed with Oriental flavors. Spaghetti squash hit the market initially as a novelty, but the lemon-yellow ovals have remained popular. The name describes the profusion of long pale-yellow strands the cooked flesh separates into when scraped out with a fork. The salad can be served at room temperature, slightly chilled, or warm.

Chinese Dressing

**1 ½ tablespoons sesame seeds**
**1 tablespoon Szechuan peppercorns *or* 1 teaspoon other peppercorns**
**2 scallions**
**2 tablespoons minced coriander**
**1 tablespoon sesame oil**
**½ cup peanut oil**
**½ cup rice-wine vinegar**
**2 tablespoons brown-rice vinegar *or* other rice vinegar**
**2 tablespoons soy sauce**
**Salt**

**¾ cup snow peas or Sugar Snap peas *or* broccoli florets**
**¾ cup fresh mandarin orange *or* tangerine sections**
**1 cup roasted or smoked duck, cured ham, *or* smoked chicken**
**2 pounds spaghetti squash**
**½ pound dry Chinese noodles *or* vermicelli**
**Salt**

**PREPARATION:** FOR THE DRESSING: Toast the sesame seeds in a 325°F oven until golden, about 5 minutes. Crush the peppercorns. Cut scallions, including 2 inches of green part, into ¼-inch slices. Whisk all dressing ingredients together.

Remove strings from peas if using. Chop the orange or tangerine sections. Cut the meat into slivers.

**COOKING:** Heat oven to 350°F. Pierce squash in at least 12 places with a sturdy fork. Bake until skin can be pierced easily, about 45 minutes. When done, cut squash in half and remove seeds. Scrape out long strands of squash with a fork. Measure out 2 cups. Meanwhile, cook peas or broccoli florets in boiling salted water until just done, about 10 minutes for peas, 5 minutes for broccoli. In a large pot of boiling salted water cook noodles until just barely done, about 6 minutes.

Toss warm squash with noodles, peas or broccoli, chopped orange or tangerine, and slivered meat. Toss with about ½ the dressing and season with salt.

**SERVING:** Put salad on plates and pass remaining dressing separately.

**YIELD:** 4 servings

# ALL SEASON

## HOT PAPAYA SALAD

Tart lime juice, hot peppers, and pungent coriander over sweet and mellow papayas—a delectable combination. Serve as a first course, as a side salad with Mexican or Indian food, or with plain grilled meat or poultry.

**2 jalapeños**
**¼ cup minced coriander**
**Salt**
**Juice of 2 limes**
**2 firm ripe papayas**
**Coriander sprigs for garnish**

**PREPARATION:** Seed and mince jalapeños. Add jalapeños, coriander, and salt to lime juice.

Peel, halve, and seed papayas. Put papaya halves on a cutting surface, cut side down. Starting ½ inch from stem, cut papayas lengthwise into ⅛-inch slices attached at the stem end.

**SERVING:** Spread each papaya on individual plates, gently fanning them out. Pour lime juice mixture over papayas and garnish with coriander sprigs.

**YIELD:** 4 servings

# WHITE BEAN SALAD WITH THYME

Sparked with flecks of red pepper and tomato, this salad is nearly a meal in itself. Just add bread and a few slices of salami or ham. A reduced portion of the same combination makes a nice first course. Or serve the salad as a picnic or buffet side dish.

**½ pound dried Great Northern beans (about 1¾ cups)**
**1 onion**
**1 carrot**
**1 rib celery**
**1 clove garlic**
**3 tablespoons olive oil**
**1 tablespoon minced flat-leaf parsley + 3 sprigs**
**½ bay leaf**
**2 cups Chicken Stock (page 49)**
**Salt and pepper**
**2 tablespoons chopped thyme + optional sprigs for garnish *or* 2 teaspoons dried**
**1 lemon**
**¼ cup dry white wine**
**4 scallions**
**½ red pepper**
**2 plum tomatoes**

**PREPARATION:** Soak beans overnight in water to cover. Or bring to a boil, remove from heat, and let sit, covered, for 1 hour. Drain.

Quarter the onion and chop carrot and celery. Mince the garlic. In a large saucepan heat 2 tablespoons olive oil and add onion, carrot, celery, and garlic. Cook over medium-low heat until vegetables begin to soften, about 5 minutes. Add parsley sprigs, bay leaf, stock, beans, and water to cover if needed and bring to a boil. Reduce heat, cover, and simmer until beans are tender, about 1 hour. Add salt halfway through cooking.

Remove and discard bay leaf and parsley sprigs. Drain beans, reserving both beans and liquid. Return liquid to pan, bring to a boil, and reduce over high heat to ½ cup, about 15 minutes. Squeeze lemon juice into pan, add wine, salt and pepper, chopped thyme, and minced parsley, and heat through. Pour mixture over beans and chill.

Mince scallions and red pepper. Peel, seed, and chop tomatoes. Sauté scallions, red pepper, and tomatoes in remaining 1 tablespoon olive oil over medium heat until just wilted, about 3 minutes. Stir into salad and season to taste with salt and pepper.

**SERVING:** Serve at room temperature, garnished with thyme sprigs if desired.

YIELD: 4 servings

# WARM WHITE AND BLACK BEAN SALAD WITH SAUSAGE

This satisfying warm salad was developed in COOK'S test kitchen to serve as a main dish, though it can be cut down to make an admirable first course. The combination of white and black beans gives this Italian classic a new look.

**¾ cup dried Great Northern beans**
**¾ cup dried black beans**
**1 rib celery**
**1 white onion**
**2 bay leaves**
**Salt and pepper**
**1 red onion**
**3 tablespoons red-wine vinegar**
**1 red pepper**
**¾ pound sweet Italian sausage *or* other sausage**
**3 tablespoons olive oil, approximately**
**½ cup Chicken Stock (page 49)**
**½ cup chopped flat-leaf parsley**

**PREPARATION:** Soak beans separately overnight in water to cover. Or bring each to a boil separately, remove from heat, and let sit, covered, for 1 hour. Drain.

Halve the celery and the white onion. Put the beans in separate pans with fresh water to cover well. Put ½ the celery, white onion, and 1 bay leaf in each pan. Bring to a boil, lower heat, and simmer until tender, about 1 hour. Add salt halfway through cooking. Drain beans and discard the vegetables and bay leaves.

Mince the red onion and put into a large bowl with the vinegar. Dice the red pepper.

**COOKING:** Heat oven to 375°F. Cook sausage in preheated oven until just done, about 25 minutes. Slice sausage diagonally, drain, and keep warm. Reserve about 3 tablespoons sausage drippings. Add enough olive oil to make 6 tablespoons.

Warm beans in stock. Drain beans and put into the bowl with the onion and vinegar. Add the reserved sausage drippings and olive oil, red pepper, and parsley. Toss and season to taste with salt and pepper.

**SERVING:** Put the beans on plates and arrange sausage slices alongside or around them.

**YIELD:** 4 servings

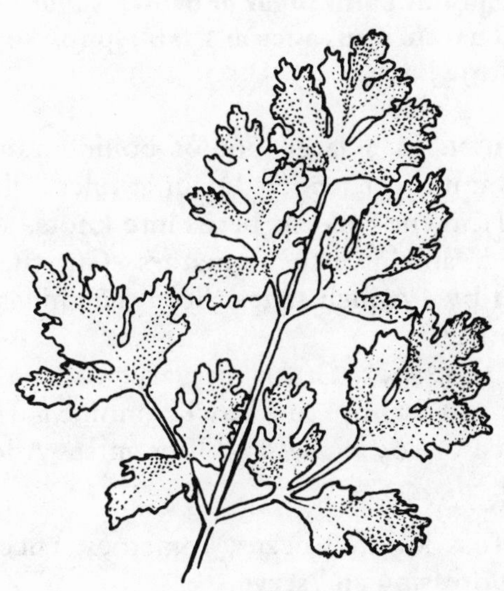

# KNOTTED BEAN SALAD

Slightly chewy Chinese long beans are a foot in length or even longer. Susan Feniger and Mary Sue Milliken, co-owners of Border Grill and City Restaurant, both in Los Angeles, use them here in a striking salad. Of course, it can be made with regular green beans, too.

- **1 pound Chinese long beans**
- **2 tomatoes**
- **1 small zucchini**
- **5 serrano *or* 2 jalapeño chilies, see note, below**

PEANUT DRESSING

- **3 cloves garlic**
- **1 cup roasted peanuts**
- **½ cup dried shrimp**
- **2 tablespoons palm sugar *or* brown sugar**
- **¼ cup Thai shrimp sauce *or* 1 tablespoon soy sauce**
- **¼ cup lime juice**

**PREPARATION:** In a large pot of boiling salted water cook beans until just tender. Drain at once. Plunge into ice water. Trim ends and tie beans into knots.

Peel, seed, and dice the tomatoes. Cut the zucchini into ⅛-inch by 1½-inch strips. Seed the chilies, remove ribs, and mince.

FOR THE DRESSING: Crush the garlic to a paste. Chop the peanuts and shrimp. In a bowl combine garlic, sugar, shrimp sauce or soy sauce, and lime juice. Add peanuts and shrimp.

**SERVING:** Toss knotted beans, tomatoes, zucchini, and chilies with dressing and serve.

YIELD: 4 servings

NOTE: For a milder salad, decrease number of chilies.

CHAPTER 4

# SHELLFISH

# SPRING

## Soft-Shell Crabs with Mustard Greens and Vermicelli

A pretty and quick first course, this dish can be turned into an entrée by doubling all quantities except the fat for frying the crabs. The pasta with mustard greens and walnuts would complement nearly any seafood; from fried oysters to broiled or sautéed red snapper to boiled lobster.

- **½ pound mustard greens**
- **¼ pound vermicelli *or* other fine pasta**
- **5 tablespoons butter**
- **2 tablespoons olive oil**
- **2 tablespoons chopped walnuts**
- **½ cup grated Romano cheese**
- **Salt and pepper**
- **Oil for frying**
- **4 soft-shell crabs**
- **Flour for dredging**
- **2 tablespoons chopped parsley**

**PREPARATION:** Wash mustard greens, trim, and chop into 1-inch pieces.

### SPRING GREENS

The profusion of spring greens begins as early as February or March. *Dandelion greens* are among the first. They have a refreshing, undeniably bitter taste that combines well with walnut or other intense oils. They are best known as the base for the popular French salad made with bacon, croutons, and a dressing of warm bacon fat and vinegar. You can gather dandelion greens right out of the lawn, but they must be picked before they flower to avoid toughness and unpalatable bitterness. Dandelion greens tend to be gritty, so clean them well in several changes of water just before you plan to use them. Larger-leafed cultivated varieties have less flavor, but many people consider this an advantage since

**COOKING:** Cook pasta in boiling salted water until tender. Drain and toss lightly with 1 tablespoon butter and the olive oil. Add all but 1 teaspoon walnuts.

In a large frying pan heat 2 teaspoons butter and ½ cup water over medium heat and add the mustard greens. Simmer until tender, about 5 minutes. Add the pasta and heat through. Add cheese and toss. Season to taste with salt and pepper.

Meanwhile, heat ½ cup oil and remaining 2 tablespoons butter in a large frying pan over medium-high heat. Season the crabs with salt and pepper and dredge them in flour. Put crabs in pan and fry until golden, 3 to 4 minutes per side.

**SERVING:** Put pasta on individual plates and sprinkle with remaining nuts and parsley. Put a fried crab at the side of each serving of pasta.

**YIELD:** 4 servings

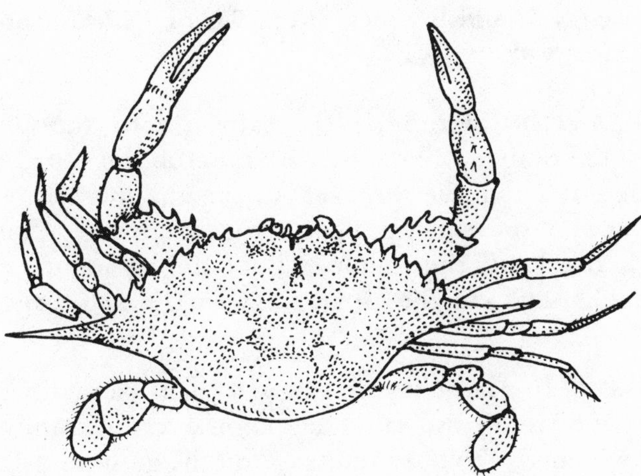

the greens are not so bitter. They are also available year-round.

Two other types of greens that have a real bite to them are *mustard* and *turnip greens.* Although tiny mustard leaves are occasionally added to salads, both these greens are usually cooked. They are more popular in the South, where they are the basis of a "mess of greens." There are many types of mustard greens, of varying color and texture, but those typically available in the marketplace are frilly and bright green. Turnip greens are paler than mustard greens and have narrower leaves. The turnip greens used in cooking are those of the white turnip, but they are rarely sold with the root vegetable still attached. Choose the small- to medium-size leaves of each plant. Like other greens, these should be stored in plastic bags in the refrigerator; turnip greens are hardier and will keep a few days longer than mustard greens.

*Sorrel* is a sour, lemony green that is still far more popular in Europe than in the United States. Yet its pronounced taste is a perfect complement to fish or chicken. Wild sorrel is as abundant as a weed in the countryside, but the cultivated varieties have larger, fleshier leaves that are easier to prepare. In some markets, sorrel is called sour grass. Its leaves are arrowhead-shaped; look for those that are 6 to 8 inches in length, bright green, and smooth, with the thinnest stems. Store sorrel in plastic bags in the refrigerator, and wash it thoroughly before using. You may want to remove the larger, tougher stems, just as you would with spinach, before cooking the leaves. Sorrel is usually used in moderation, but bear in mind that a whole pound will cook down to about half a cup. Cooking sorrel automatically turns it into a purée, a characteristic that opens a range of recipe possibilities.

Another green that is usually cooked is *Swiss chard.* Chard is at its peak slightly later than the other spring greens, but, as with many of the others, it is now available all year. It has large flat green leaves and white or reddish ribs. Chard can be used raw in salads or can be cooked. The leaves and ribs of the larger plants are usually cooked separately, and the ribs served as a vegetable in themselves like celery or asparagus.

*Spinach* is obviously the best known of the spring greens. It is available year-round but is at its best in the spring. Its high water content makes it more perishable during the hotter months. Most of the spinach sold on the East Coast has crinkly leaves, but a flat-leaf variety is prevalent in California and other parts of the West. Prepackaged spinach is rarely a good buy; it is more expensive than loose leaves and often includes rotting leaves and tough stems. Before using spinach, remove the tough stems by folding

# QUICK PAELLA WITH ASPARAGUS

Based on the famous Spanish seafood dish, this version is quick and makes a perfect centerpiece for a spring luncheon or supper. The addition of asparagus is untraditional but a departure worth making. Peeling the asparagus makes it more tender and faster cooking. For a quick fish stock, use ⅔ bottled clam juice and ⅓ water.

**⅛ teaspoon saffron threads, optional**
**⅓ cup white wine**
**1 onion**
**1 large clove garlic**
**12 littleneck clams**
**12 mussels**
**12 large shrimp**
**½ pound smoked sausage**
**1 pound asparagus**
**3 tablespoons olive oil**
**1 cup rice**
**Salt and pepper**
**⅛ teaspoon cayenne**
**1 ⅔ cups Shellfish Stock (page 90) or Chicken Stock (page 49)**

**PREPARATION:** Crumble the saffron into the wine. Chop the onion. Mince the garlic. Scrub the clams and mussels and remove the beards from the mussels. Peel and devein the shrimp. Cut the sausage into ½-inch slices. Break off the tough ends of the asparagus, peel the stalks, and cut the asparagus into 1½-inch diagonal pieces.

**COOKING:** In a large frying pan or a paella pan with a lid heat the olive oil and sauté the onion over medium heat until softened, about 4 minutes. Add the garlic and sauté 1 minute. Add the rice and stir briefly. Add salt, black pepper, and cayenne. Add the stock and the saffron/wine mixture and bring to a boil. Cover the pan, lower the heat, and simmer 10 minutes. In another frying pan sauté the sausage over medium-low heat until lightly browned, about 4 minutes. Drain.

Push the clams into the rice. Cover the pan and simmer 5 minutes. Add the mussels and shrimp and push into the rice. Scatter asparagus over the top. Cover and simmer 5 minutes. Add the sausage, stir, and simmer, covered, until rice and asparagus are done, clams and mussels are open, and sausage is heated through, about 5 minutes.

**YIELD:** 4 servings

each large leaf in half lengthwise and zipping off the stem. Spinach is notoriously gritty, so wash it in several changes of cold water. Once it has been washed, it should be used as soon as possible or wrapped in paper towels and stored for a brief time in the refrigerator. Leave it longer than several hours, and you will find it sadly wilted. Finally, don't cook it in an aluminum pot, which will turn it grayish rather than dark green.

# SUMMER

## SOFT-SHELL CRAB WITH TOMATO PILAF

### SHELLFISH SEASONS

The taboo against eating oysters in the summer months is related to spawning cycles, which affect the texture and the taste of these bivalves. While spawning, they're softer and less sweet. The warm months (those without an R) are the breeding period for oysters, and so traditional wisdom is reasonably correct. Oysters from cold waters are best from fall through early spring. There is less variation in Southern oysters because the warm water encourages year-round spawning.

*Clams, mussels,* and *scallops,* are all edible, and available, year-round. The spawning season for clams and mussels is summer, and so both of these bivalves tend to be plumper and more flavorful from September to May.

*Lobsters* can be found in the marketplace throughout the year but are at their peak from the late

Grilled soft-shell crabs and tomato-flavored rice make a simple but special meal. Add a salad and a fruit dessert for a summer feast.

MARINADE

**1 lemon**
**3 shallots**
**1 small clove garlic**
**2 teaspoons chopped marjoram**
**¼ cup minced parsley**
**Pinch ground coriander**
**½ cup white wine**
**Salt and pepper**
**½ cup olive oil**

**12 soft-shell crabs**

TOMATO PILAF

**4 large tomatoes**
**1 onion**
**¼ teaspoon saffron threads, optional**
**Salt**
**Pinch cayenne**
**Pinch sugar**

**6 tablespoons olive oil**
**3 tablespoons butter**
**1 cup rice**

**PREPARATION:** FOR THE MARINADE: Grate ⅛ teaspoon zest from the lemon and put in a large nonreactive bowl. Squeeze the lemon juice into the bowl. Chop the shallots and garlic and add. Stir in remaining marinade ingredients. Coat the crabs with marinade and marinate for at least 30 minutes.

FOR THE TOMATO PILAF: Peel, seed, and chop the tomatoes. Mince the onion. Soak the saffron threads in 2 tablespoons hot water if using. In a saucepan cook tomatoes with salt, cayenne, and sugar in 3 tablespoons olive oil over medium-high heat, until almost dry, about 5 minutes.

In another saucepan sauté onion in butter and remaining 3 tablespoons olive oil until soft. Add rice and stir over medium heat until grains are opaque, about 2 minutes. Stir in saffron, if using, with its liquid, 1½ cups water, and 1 teaspoon salt. Bring to a full boil, boil for 1 minute, and turn heat to very low. Add tomatoes and cook, tightly covered, for 20 minutes.

**COOKING:** Heat grill or broiler. Put marinated crabs on grill and cook, basting occasionally with marinade, until top shell is brick red, 1 to 3 minutes per side.

**SERVING:** Fluff pilaf with a fork, season to taste, and put on plates. Arrange crabs around pilaf.

**YIELD:** 4 servings

spring through the early fall. The female lobster is considered to have more flavor than the male, and, according to some gastronomes, the meat of female lobsters is most delectable after the eggs have been formed but before they have been laid.

*Crayfish,* long a favorite in the southern United States, has gained popularity with the craze for Cajun and Creole cuisines. Domestic supplies come from two primary sources—Louisiana and California. Louisiana's high season is spring to early summer and California's from late spring to early fall.

Americans can choose from many types of *crabs*, but most of those available at the fishmonger's are blue crabs. Crabs should be sold live, for they deteriorate quickly. In general, they are at their best in the summer months. Soft-shells crabs that have just molted, are a seasonal delicacy and molting usually takes place in late June and early July. You can still find them throughout August and even into early September, but after that you will have to wait for next year.

# LOBSTER AND ZUCCHINI CONSOMMÉ

Nothing is more elegant than consommé. This recipe makes use of every last bit of lobster flavor, even from the shells, and stretches two small lobsters into a first course for four. A long simmering time is needed, but all the cooking can be done ahead.

- **2 1½-pound lobsters**
- **2 quarts + 1 cup water**
- **3 tomatoes**
- **2 scallions**
- **1 rib celery**
- **½ cup parsley stems, approximately**
- **8 cloves garlic**
- **1 small onion**
- **½ teaspoon dried thyme**
- **1 bay leaf**
- **1½ teaspoons coarse-ground black peppercorns**
- **Salt**
- **2 cups white wine**
- **3 egg whites**
- **1 zucchini**
- **Parsley leaves for garnish**

**PREPARATION:** Put lobsters in a pot with 1 cup of water and steam, covered, until bright red, about 7 minutes. Remove lobsters and cool. Strain and reserve lobster cooking liquid. Remove meat from lobster shells and save both meat and shells. First twist off the claws. Twist off the tail from the thorax. Spread the tail flat, rounded shell up, and cut through lengthwise. Remove the vein and pull out the meat. To remove the claw meat in 1 piece, move the "thumb" from side to side and pull it off. Gently crack the claws with the dull side of a chef's knife and slide the claw meat from the cracked shell. Halve thorax lengthwise with a large chef's knife and remove and discard the gelatinous sac behind the eyes. Chop thorax into quarters.

### ZUCCHINI

To a summer gardener, zucchini is what there's always too much of—those two or three innocuous-looking plants take over the whole plot and just keep on producing. In contrast to winter squash, zucchini and the other summer squashes (such as crookneck and pattypan) have a soft, edible skin and are harvested and eaten immature before the seeds toughen. Mid-summer through early fall is the prime time for zucchini, but now it is available year-round.

Zucchini is also commonly called green squash, but recently a beautiful bright yellow variety has appeared on the market. Small, firm zucchini of good color, with shiny, unblemished, tender skin, are the most flavorful. Choose those that feel heavy for their size. Zucchini that is too old may be bitter, and oversized squash with dull skin is no bargain. In general, you will want to select those that are no more than 6 inches in length. However, the larger squash are suitable for stuffing, and the flesh of giant-sized zucchini is salvageable if peeled and seeded.

Zucchini has a high water content, which means it should be kept in a plastic bag to prevent dehydration. Like all summer squashes, it should be stored in

Core and quarter tomatoes. Chop the scallion bulbs. Slice the scallion tops on an angle into very thin strips and reserve separately. Chop the celery, parsley stems, garlic, and onion.

In a large pot combine the lobster shells, tomatoes, chopped scallion, celery, parsley stems, garlic, onion, thyme, bay leaf, 1 teaspoon peppercorns, 1 teaspoon salt, white wine, remaining 2 quarts water, and reserved lobster cooking liquid. Bring to a boil, lower heat, and simmer for 2 hours, skimming froth. Strain and chill.

Whisk the egg whites and add to the chilled stock. Slowly bring to a simmer over low heat, stirring until egg whites coagulate and begin to rise to the surface. Gently push egg whites from center, leaving a hole large enough for a ladle to fit through. Cook for 30 minutes. Gently strain the stock by ladling it through a sieve with several layers of cheesecloth (or through a coffee filter). Strain again if not absolutely clear. Season to taste with salt. This can be done 1 day ahead.

Meanwhile, scrape away any white substance the lobster meat has given off, so that it won't cloud the consommé. Cut the meat into bite-size pieces, leaving the claws whole if desired.

Cut the zucchini into ¼-inch dice and cook in boiling salted water until tender, about 3 minutes. Drain.

**SERVING:** Reheat consommé. Add the zucchini, remaining ½ teaspoon peppercorns, and lobster meat and heat through. Sprinkle with reserved scallion tops and parsley leaves.

**YIELD:** 4 servings

the refrigerator. Zucchini's high moisture content also means that it may become mushy during cooking if some of this water is not removed first. Salt the squash, allow it to drain in a colander for about half an hour, and then squeeze out as much water as you can before proceeding with the recipe. You may find this unnecessary with sliced or cubed zucchini, but grated zucchini is always better this way.

# FALL/WINTER

## Oysters with Golden Caviar

This delectable combination—crisp-fried oysters and shoestring potatoes with a creamy sauce and a final fillip of golden caviar—is worth the trouble of last-minute frying. Preparations are not lengthy, and they can be done ahead of time, leaving only the frying for the last minute. The recipe is from Susumu Fukui of La Petite Chaya in Los Angeles, California

- **24 oysters**
- **1 cup Chicken Stock (page 49)**
- **¾ cup heavy cream**
- **4 potatoes**
- **Oil for frying**
- **Salt and pepper**
- **1 cup flour, approximately**
- **1 tablespoon butter**
- **4 teaspoons minced chives**
- **¼ cup golden caviar**

**PREPARATION:** Shuck oysters if in the shell, and reserve liquor.

Cook the oyster liquor and fish stock over high heat until reduced to 2 tablespoons. Add the cream and simmer until slightly thickened, about 10 minutes.

Just before frying, peel the potatoes and cut into fine

julienne. To cut the potatoes ahead of time, either keep them in cold water and drain thoroughly on paper towels before frying. Or blanch the cut shoestrings for 30 seconds in boiling salted water and drain well.

**COOKING:** Heat oil to 375°F. Deep-fry the potatoes until crisp and golden, about 5 minutes. Drain on paper towels. Sprinkle with salt and pepper. Keep warm. Flour oysters lightly and deep-fry until crisp on the outside, about 2 minutes. Drain on paper towels. Sprinkle with salt and pepper. Meanwhile, reheat the sauce. Whisk in the butter and add chives.

**SERVING:** Pour the sauce onto plates. Mound the crisp potatoes on the sauce. Put oysters on top of the potatoes and garnish with caviar.

**YIELD:** 4 servings

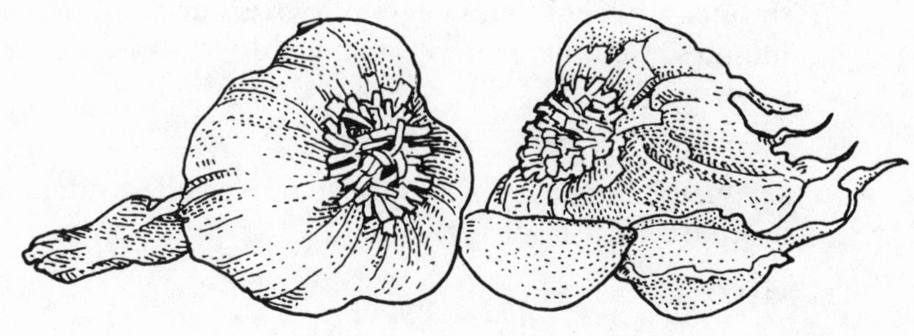

# OYSTER-THYME PAN ROAST

This traditional American dish is not what it sounds like. It's kin to oyster stew, but in a pan roast the creamy bivalves are usually served over toast. Here thyme is an added accent.

**1 shallot**
**½ rib celery**
**24 oysters**
**6 tablespoons butter**
**¾ cup heavy cream**
**2 tablespoons white wine**
**¼ teaspoon hot red-pepper sauce**
**2 teaspoons minced thyme *or* ¾ teaspoon dried**
**Salt**
**Cayenne**
**4 slices bread**

**PREPARATION:** Mince the shallot and celery. Shuck the oysters, if in the shell, and drain them, reserving liquor.

**COOKING:** Sauté shallot and celery in butter over medium-low heat for 1 minute. Stir in cream, oyster liquor, wine, red-pepper sauce, thyme, and oysters. Bring to a simmer and cook until edges of oysters just curl, about 2 minutes. Remove from heat and add salt and cayenne to taste.

Toast the bread.

**SERVING:** Put toast in soup plates and ladle oysters and broth over the toast.

YIELD: 4 servings

# ALL SEASON

## Sautéed Shrimp with Garlic

Chef Wayne Ludvigsen of Ray's Boathouse in Seattle developed this recipe for those wonderful Northwestern spot shrimp.

**3 cloves garlic**
**1½ lemons**
**6 tablespoons olive oil**
**1 pound unshelled shrimp**
**Salt**
**Minced parsley for garnish**

**PREPARATION:** Mince the garlic. Cut 1 lemon into wedges.

**COOKING:** In a large frying pan heat the oil with the garlic. Add shrimp, toss, and sauté for 30 seconds. Squeeze ½ lemon over the shrimp. Season with salt and cook until shrimp are done, about 3 minutes.

**SERVING:** Garnish shrimp with parsley. Serve with lemon wedges and provide finger bowls of warm water and plenty of napkins.

**YIELD:** 4 servings

## SHELLFISH LOUISIANA

To call this creamed fish on toast would be an injustice, though it does have the straightforward appeal of that old favorite. Luxurious shellfish, butter-crisped croutons, and a hint of Cajun seasonings lift the dish to special status. If you use crab meat, ask your fishmonger for some shells and heads from crabs or other crustaceans so that you can make stock. Most fish shops are happy to give them away. These proportions serve four as a first course. For a main course, double all ingredients and pass the extra croutons as needed.

**2 pounds crayfish *or* 1 pound shrimp *or* 1½ pounds crab meat**

SHELLFISH STOCK

**½ onion**
**½ rib celery**
**½ carrot**
**¼ pound shellfish shells**
**1 sprig parsley**
**2 peppercorns**
**2½ cups water**

CROUTONS

**5 slices white bread**
**2 tablespoons oil**
**2 tablespoons butter**

**2 slices bacon**
**1 scallion**
**2 tablespoons butter**
**2 tablespoons flour**
**½ cup heavy cream**
**¼ teaspoon hot red-pepper sauce**
**Pinch thyme**
**Pinch oregano**
**Salt and pepper**
**2 teaspoons minced parsley**

**PREPARATION:** Bring a pot of water to a boil and add shellfish. Return to a boil and cook crayfish for 30 seconds, shrimp for 1 minute, or lobster for 10 minutes. Drain and cool. If using crayfish, set aside 4 for garnish. Remove meat from shells, save shells for stock, and dice shrimp or lobster. Leave crayfish tails whole.

FOR THE STOCK: Put all ingredients in a large pot. Bring to a boil and skim the foam. Lower heat and simmer, uncovered, for 2 hours. Strain. You should have 1¼ cups. Reduce by boiling or add water if necessary.

FOR THE CROUTONS: Remove the crust from the bread and quarter each slice diagonally. Heat 1 tablespoon oil in a large frying pan over medium heat. Add 1 tablespoon butter and let melt. Fry half the triangles until golden on both sides. Heat remaining oil and butter and fry the rest of the triangles.

Dice the bacon. Mince the scallion.

**COOKING:** In a heavy saucepan cook bacon over low heat until crisp, about 5 minutes. Remove bacon and pour out all but a thin film of fat. Raise heat to medium and add butter. Sauté shellfish and scallion for 30 seconds. Remove with a slotted spoon. Add flour to frying pan and stir well. Cook roux over medium heat, stirring, until golden, about 3 minutes. Gradually stir in 1¼ cups shellfish stock, cream, red-pepper sauce, thyme, oregano, and salt and pepper to taste. Bring to a boil and simmer over medium heat, stirring often, for 2 minutes. Return bacon, shellfish, and scallion to frying pan and stir well. Taste for seasoning.

**SERVING:** Arrange 5 croutons in a star pattern on each plate and put the shellfish in the center. Sprinkle with parsley and garnish with whole reserved crayfish if desired.

YIELD: 4 servings

# SHRIMP IN PERNOD

This recipe provides lots of rich sauce, so serve it with plain rice on the side or toss the shrimp and sauce with thin noodles such as fettuccine or linguine. The shrimp butter in this recipe is useful to know. You can always turn extra shells from lobster, crab, shrimp, or crayfish into shellfish butter and use it to enrich sauces or soups or to top broiled fish.

**1½ pounds unshelled shrimp**

SHRIMP BUTTER

**Shells from shrimp, above**
**¼ pound butter**

**2 shallots**
**2 scallions**
**2 tablespoons lemon juice**
**1½ cups Chicken Stock (page 49)**
**1½ cups Pernod**
**3 tablespoons Dijon mustard**
**2 tablespoons oil**
**½ pound butter**
**Salt and pepper**

**PREPARATION:** Peel the shrimp, reserving the shells.

FOR THE SHRIMP BUTTER: Put shells in a saucepan with ¼ pound butter: Cook over medium heat, turning frequently, until shells turn pinkish brown, 5 to 7 minutes.

Transfer shells and butter to a food processor and process until shells are well pulverized. Strain butter through a cheesecloth-lined sieve. Gather up edges of cheesecloth and twist as tightly as possible to get all the butter. Discard shells and refrigerate butter until ready to use.

Mince the shallots. Chop the scallions, green tops included.

**COOKING:** Heat 1 tablespoon shrimp butter in a heavy saucepan. Add shallots and sauté over medium heat until soft. Add lemon juice, stock, and Pernod, turn heat to high, and bring to a boil. Boil until mixture is reduced to 1 cup, 10 to 15 minutes. Stir in mustard.

Heat 2 tablespoons shrimp butter with the oil in a large frying pan. Add shrimp and sauté over medium-high heat until they turn pink on both sides, about 3 minutes.

Whisk ½ pound butter into the Pernod mixture, 1 tablespoon at a time, over the lowest possible heat. The butter should soften to form a creamy sauce but should not melt completely. You may have to move pan off and on heat to maintain proper temperature. Whisk in remaining shrimp butter in the same way. Add shrimp and season to taste with salt and pepper.

**SERVING:** Put shrimp on warm plates and sprinkle with scallions. Serve immediately.

**YIELD:** 4 servings

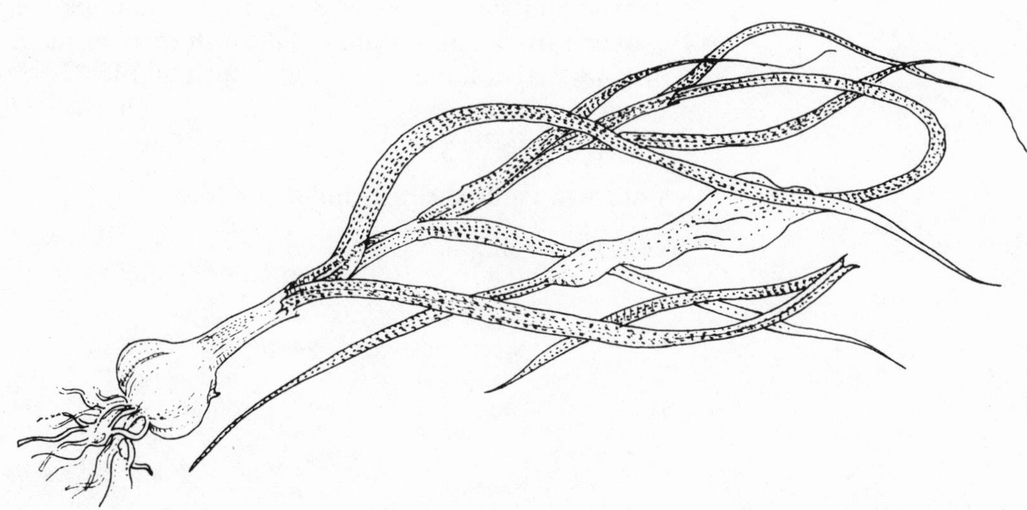

# SCALLOPS IN WHITE WINE, SHALLOTS, AND HERBS

This is another recipe from Wayne Ludvigsen. Again he uses the very best products—in this case, the tiny pink scallops available in the Northwest—and prepares them simply. We love mussels made this way, too.

**1 pound unshelled pink scallops *or* mussels**
**1 shallot**
**¼ cup white wine**
**4 tablespoons butter**
**Pinch thyme**
**1 broken bay leaf**
**Pepper**

**PREPARATION:** Scrub the scallops or mussels. Remove beards from mussels. Chop the shallot.

**COOKING:** Bring the wine, butter, shallot, thyme, bay leaf, and pepper to a boil. Add the shellfish, cover tightly, and steam over low heat until scallops are just cooked through and begin to fall from their shells, 2 to 3 minutes. If using mussels, cook just until they open, about 5 to 10 minutes. Strain stock through a sieve lined with a cheesecloth or through a coffee filter.

**SERVING:** Ladle shellfish and broth into bowls.

**YIELD:** 4 servings

CHAPTER 5

# FISH

**SPRING:**

Broiled Salmon with Sorrel

**SUMMER:**

Grilled Fish with Browned Butter and Fried Parsley

Trout with Tomato

Grilled Salmon with Corn, Tomato, and Basil Relish

Stuffed Trout with Tomato-Cumin Sauce

Grilled Catfish with Smoked Peppers

Mint-Marinated Salmon

**SUMMER/FALL:**

Smoked Fish Cakes with Green-Tomato and Red-Pepper Relish

**FALL/WINTER:**

Mushroom-Stuffed Trout

Sautéed Sole in Cream Sauce

Sesame-Sautéed Catfish with Lemon Butter

Halibut Blackened in Soy and Lemon with American Caviar

Blackened Fish

**ALL SEASON:**

Deep-Fried Smelt with Tartar Sauce

Couscous and Curried Fish with Hot Lime and Cucumber Pickle

SIDEBARS

Parsley

Basil

Lemons and Limes

# SPRING

## Broiled Salmon with Sorrel

Sharp sorrel complements rich salmon in this quick, elegant dish from Rosellini's the Other Place in Seattle.

- **3 shallots**
- **2 lemons**
- **3 tablespoons white-wine vinegar**
- **4 salmon fillets (about 6 ounces each)**
- **4 teaspoons oil**
- **Salt and pepper**
- **½ pound butter**
- **⅓ cup chiffonade of sorrel + more for garnish**

**PREPARATION:** Mince the shallots.

Squeeze ¼ cup lemon juice into a small heavy saucepan. Add vinegar and shallots and cook over medium-high heat until liquid is reduced to 1 tablespoon, about 15 minutes.

**COOKING:** Heat the broiler. Brush salmon with oil and sprinkle with salt and pepper. Reheat reduced liquid and then whisk in the butter, 1 tablespoon at a time, over very low heat, so that it softens to form a creamy sauce but does not melt completely. Stir in ⅓ cup (cut crosswise into thin strips for chiffonade) sorrel and season with salt and pepper. Remove from heat but keep warm.

Broil salmon on a rack in preheated broiler 4 to 6 minutes, depending on thickness of fish.

**SERVING:** Spoon sauce over fish and garnish with remaining sorrel chiffonade.

**YIELD:** 4 servings

# SUMMER

## Grilled Fish with Browned Butter and Fried Parsley

Frying parsley briefly in browned butter makes an easy year-round fish sauce. In winter simply move the cooking of the fish from the grill to the broiler. Use curly parsley for frying because it retains its shape better than flat-leaf.

**2 cups parsley sprigs**
**2 1-pound trout *or* 1½ pounds 1-inch thick salmon, swordfish, tuna, *or* shark steaks**
**Olive oil for brushing**
**Salt and pepper**
**½ pound butter**
**Lemon wedges for garnish**

**PREPARATION:** Remove large stems from parsley and rinse small sprigs. Pat dry. Brush fish with oil and sprinkle with salt and pepper.

**COOKING:** Heat grill. Cook trout on hot grill until just done, about 4 minutes per side. Cook 1-inch steaks 3 minutes per side.

Heat butter in a saucepan over medium heat until it just starts to brown. (Don't let it get too brown at this point, or it will burn by the time the parsley is cooked.) Add parsley and salt and pepper to taste and stir until crisp, about 1 minute.

**SERVING:** Put fish on plates and pour sauce on top. Serve with lemon wedges on the side.

**YIELD:** 4 servings

### PARSLEY

In decades past, fresh herbs—save one—were a novelty at American tables. The lone exception was parsley, which was liberally sprinkled over almost everything. Even now that fresh basil, chervil, coriander, and a host of other herbs are commonplace, parsley is still a kitchen staple and serves the cook honorably. Besides being a pretty and sturdy garnish, parsley has a fresh, mild taste, good on its own and compatible with many other herbs. In the French kitchen, parsley combines with bay leaf and thyme for the classic bouquet garni and with chervil, chives, and tarragon for the traditional *fines herbes* mixture. In addition to its use as a supplementary flavor, parsley can be served as a salad green or can be sautéed as a vegetable.

There are three commonly grown parsley strains and many varieties of each. The ubiquitous curly parsley comes in over thirty varieties. Flat-leaf or Italian parsley has a slightly stronger taste. In general, you can use curly or flat-leaf interchangeably, although you may want to use more of the curly because its flavor is milder. A third type is usually grown for its root, which has a flavor that hints of celeriac. It goes by several names—Hamburg parsley, parsley root, or turnip-rooted parsley.

Parsley will stay fresh for a week in the refrigerator. Rinse it well and dry it, allowing some moisture to cling to the leaves. Put the parsley in a glass of water, stems down and leaves billowing above the rim, and refrigerate.

Parsley is inexpensive and plentiful all year long, so there is no need to resort to invariably flavorless dried or frozen. Recipes most commonly call for parsley's tender leaves, although the tough stems, which can be strained out later, add good flavor to a stock.

# TROUT WITH TOMATO

Try this recipe with other thin fish fillets, too. It's from chef Wally Watley of Leslee's Restaurant in Evanston, Illinois.

**5 ½ tablespoons butter**
**Salt and pepper**
**1 teaspoon cayenne**
**2 shallots**
**½ clove garlic**
**¼ cup olive oil**
**1 tomato**
**1 lemon**
**4 trout fillets (¼ to ⅓ pound each)**
**¼ cup dry white wine**
**¼ cup chopped herbs, such as parsley *and/or* basil + more for garnish**

**PREPARATION:** Bring butter to room temperature or soften in a microwave oven. Mix 1 teaspoon salt, 1 teaspoon black pepper, and cayenne together. Mince shallots and garlic. Mix shallots, garlic, olive oil, and 4 tablespoons butter together.

Peel, seed, and chop the tomato. Cut lemon into wedges.

Put trout fillets on a baking sheet, skin side down. Sprinkle with ⅔ of salt and pepper mixture. Turn trout over, skin side up, and top with shallot mixture. Sprinkle with wine.

**COOKING:** Heat oven to 450°F. Bake in preheated oven, turning once, until fish just tests done, 4 to 6 minutes total. Transfer trout fillets to plates and keep warm. Scrape drippings into a small saucepan. Reduce cooking liquid slightly over high heat, about 2 minutes. Add tomato and ¼ cup herbs. Bring to a boil. Season to taste using the remainder of the salt and pepper mixture. Remove from heat and whisk in remaining 1½ tablespoons butter.

**SERVING:** Serve sauce around or atop trout. Garnish with remaining herbs and lemon wedges.

**YIELD:** 4 servings

## GRILLED SALMON WITH CORN, TOMATO, AND BASIL RELISH

This relish, the epitome of summertime, is simplicity itself, yet makes a special dish of plain grilled fish. Also good with swordfish, it can be served hot, cold, or at room temperature.

CORN, TOMATO, AND BASIL RELISH

- **3 ears corn**
- **3 beefsteak tomatoes**
- **¼ cup shredded basil**
- **Salt and coarse black pepper**

- **4 1-inch-thick salmon *or* swordfish steaks (about 6 ounces each)**
- **Olive oil**
- **Salt and pepper**
- **Basil sprigs for garnish**

**PREPARATION:** FOR THE RELISH: Cook the corn in boiling salted water until just tender, about 5 minutes. Cool. Cut the kernels from the cobs. You should have 1½ cups. Core, peel, seed, and dice the tomatoes. Combine the tomatoes, corn, and basil. Season the relish to taste with salt and pepper.

**COOKING:** Heat the grill. Brush the fish with oil and season to taste with salt and pepper. Cook on hot grill, turning once, until fish just tests done, about 6 minutes total.

**SERVING:** Put grilled fish and relish on plates and garnish with basil sprigs.

**YIELD:** 4 servings

### BASIL

Pesto may be passé among the trend-conscious, but basil remains hugely popular—and no wonder, for it is one of the most delicious and versatile of all herbs. It is a major ingredient in Italian cooking, of course, and it is also featured in Provençal and Thai cuisines.

There are dozens of different kinds of basil, but most of them fall into one of two basic groups: sweet basil, by far the most common, and the spicy varieties. Bright green sweet basil is the type most often found in the marketplace. The purple-leaved plant sometimes referred to as ornamental basil actually has just as much of the characteristic pungent aroma and flavor. Other varieties that fall into the sweet-basil category include tiny French fineleaf, bush, *piccolo verde fino,* and lettuce-leaf basil. However, these are more likely to be found in the backyard of a devoted gardener than at the greengrocer's. Among the spicy basils are varieties that hint of clove, cinnamon, and licorice; these tend to hold up well during cooking and are good in poaching syrups for fruit or in palate-cleansing sorbets. And then there are certain types that don't seem to fit in either category—such as lemon basil, which does belong in this family but tastes a lot more like lemon than basil.

Basil is at its peak and most widely available from May through the early fall. Keep cut basil, stem down, in a glass of water. You may find it likes this treatment so well that roots sprout. Be careful not to keep it at too cold a temperature or it will turn black.

Basil loses most of its flavor when dried, but fortunately (it's too good to be limited to the summer months) there are other successful methods of preserving it. One of the easiest and quickest ways is just to cover the leaves with olive oil and then use both oil and leaves in cooking. Or, wash and thoroughly dry the leaves, seal them in plastic, and freeze them. Once frozen, basil cannot be "reconstituted"—the leaves will shrivel and blacken upon thawing—but its flavor will still be evident, and it can be used in cooked dishes perfectly well. The Italians often keep basil by layering it with coarse sea salt in a tightly sealed jar. And, finally, you can purée basil leaves with a bit of oil in a processor blender and freeze this mixture in small packages or containers. (Or, you can pour the mixture into an ice tray until it freezes and then keep basil cubes ready for use.) The basil-oil purée can be used as the base in a

# STUFFED TROUT WITH TOMATO-CUMIN SAUCE

Don't let the long ingredient list fool you. This crisp-coated stuffed trout is quick to make.

**1 onion**
**2 scallions**
**1 rib celery**
**3 slices day-old French bread**
**5 tablespoons butter**
**2 tablespoons chopped ham**
**1 cup corn kernels (cut from 2 ears corn *or* frozen)**
**Salt and pepper**
**¼ teaspoon cayenne**
**¼ teaspoon hot red-pepper sauce**
**1 egg**
**⅓ cup heavy cream**
**4 whole boneless trout (about 6 ounces each, boned weight)**
**⅓ cup flour**
**⅓ cup cornmeal**
**2 tablespoons oil**
**½ cup white wine**
**3 tomatoes, peeled, seeded, and chopped**
**¼ teaspoon ground cumin**

PREPARATION: Chop the onion, scallions, and celery. Tear the bread into small pieces.

In a large frying pan heat 3 tablespoons butter. Sauté the onion, scallions, celery, ham, and corn until onion is softened, about 4 minutes. Remove from heat and stir in salt, black pepper, cayenne, and red-pepper sauce. Toss with bread. Beat the egg and cream together with a whisk or fork and add to mixture. Check seasonings and stuff into the cavities of the trout. If necessary, use skewers or toothpicks to secure.

Combine the flour and cornmeal with salt and pepper. Coat both sides of the trout with the mixture.

**COOKING:** In the large frying pan heat the oil and remaining 2 tablespoons butter and sauté trout over medium heat until just cooked through and golden brown, 5 to 6 minutes per side. Remove trout from frying pan.

Add the wine to the frying pan and scrape bottom of pan with a wooden spoon to deglaze. Add tomatoes and cumin and stir over high heat for 1 minute. Season to taste.

**SERVING:** Spoon sauce over or around trout.

**YIELD:** 4 servings

variety of recipes including pesto. Real pesto-lovers sometimes make up batches just for freezing, but it's best not to add the cheese and butter until you have thawed the garlic-basil-oil mixture and are just about to use it.

## GRILLED CATFISH WITH SMOKED PEPPERS

Tasty catfish is increasingly available, but you can make this dish just as well with flounder, haddock, halibut, or snapper. The recipe is from Stephan Pyles' well-known Routh Street Café in Dallas, Texas.

**½ red pepper**
**½ yellow pepper**
**1 clove garlic**
**1 shallot**
**½ cup white-wine vinegar**
**½ cup dry white wine**
**4 catfish fillets (6 to 8 ounces each)**
**1 tablespoon oil *or* clarified butter**
**Salt**
**½ pound butter**
**1 tablespoon minced tarragon**

**PREPARATION:** Remove seeds and ribs from the peppers. Mince the garlic and shallot. Heat smoker or covered kettle grill with coals surrounding a drip pan for indirect heat. Add soaked hickory chips atop coals. Heat oven to 400°F. Smoke peppers for 25 minutes. Roast smoked peppers in preheated oven until soft, about 15 minutes. Peel and chop peppers and set aside. In a saucepan over high heat cook vinegar, wine, garlic, and shallot until reduced to 2 tablespoons, about 10 minutes.

**COOKING:** If fire is not hot enough to grill, add more hickory chips to smoker or grill. Rub both sides of catfish with oil or clarified butter and season with salt. Put catfish in a hinged rack or basket. Add butter to sauce mixture, 1 tablespoon at a time over the lowest possible heat, whisking so that it forms a creamy sauce but doesn't melt completely. Remove from heat and add chopped peppers and tarragon. Season to taste and keep warm. Grill catfish, uncovered, about 3 minutes per side.

**SERVING:** Spoon sauce on top of fish and serve.

**YIELD:** 4 servings

## MINT-MARINATED SALMON

This first course from Windows on the World chef Hermann Reiner can be made a week ahead. Wine director Kevin Zraly suggests an Alsatian Riesling to accompany it, ideally a good vintage with lots of body, such as an '85.

**2 tablespoons coarse salt**
**¼ cup sugar**
**1½ teaspoons cracked coriander seeds**
**1 tablespoon cracked peppercorns**
**1 small leek**
**½ small onion**
**1-pound salmon fillet**
**¼ cup chopped mint**
**2 tablespoons chopped parsley stems**
**2 tablespoons oil**

CUCUMBER SALAD

**1 cucumber**
**2 tablespoons chopped mint**

**⅓ cup crème fraîche *or* sour cream**
**Salt and pepper**
**1 lemon**
**1 head Boston lettuce**
**¼ cup mint leaves**

**PREPARATION:** Mix salt, sugar, coriander seeds, and peppercorns. Mince the leek, including green part, and the onion.

Put salmon, skin side down, in a shallow nonreactive pan and spread with spice mixture. Top with onion, leek, mint, and parsley. Cover with plastic wrap and marinate for 3 days, turning after 1 ½ days. Remove the seasoning from salmon and pat dry. Spread oil over the salmon. At this point, salmon can be wrapped in plastic wrap and refrigerated for up to 1 week.

FOR THE CUCUMBER SALAD: Peel the cucumber, halve lengthwise, and seed. Cut cucumber into small dice or shred with a coarse grater. Mix cucumber and mint with crème fraîche and season with salt and pepper. Refrigerate. Cut lemon into wedges.

**SERVING:** Put lettuce leaves on a plate and top with cucumber salad. Cut salmon into thin slices and arrange on the plate. Top with mint leaves and serve with lemon wedges.

YIELD: 4 servings

# SUMMER/FALL

## Smoked Fish Cakes with Green-Tomato and Red-Pepper Relish

Despite the elaborate sound of this recipe, the whole thing can be made, start to finish, in less than 45 minutes. It's an excellent use for green tomatoes but can be made with firm red ones as well and with either green or red peppers.

Fish Cakes

- **3 shallots**
- **1 egg**
- **½ pound smoked whitefish, trout, *or* other smoked fish**
- **¾ cup fresh bread crumbs**
- **Salt and pepper**
- **¼ cup heavy cream, approximately**

Green-Tomato and Red-Pepper Relish

- **2 red peppers**
- **2 green tomatoes**
- **1 small onion**
- **2 cloves garlic**
- **3 tablespoons olive oil**
- **Pinch red-pepper flakes**

**1 tablespoon balsamic vinegar**
**Salt and pepper**
**2½ tablespoons butter**
**¼ cup flour, approximately**
**1 tablespoon minced coriander**

**PREPARATION:** FOR THE FISH CAKES: Mince shallots. In a mixing bowl whisk egg lightly. Add shallots. Flake fish into bowl, discarding any skin and bones. Add bread crumbs, ¼ teaspoon pepper, and salt if needed. Stir together. Add enough cream to bind the mixture. Form into 8 patties.

FOR THE RELISH: Seed and chop the peppers and tomatoes. Chop the onion. Mince the garlic. Heat olive oil in a frying pan over medium heat. Cook peppers, tomatoes, and onion until soft, about 5 minutes. Add garlic and cook 1 minute. Add red-pepper flakes, vinegar, and salt and pepper to taste. Cook, stirring, 1 minute.

**COOKING:** Reheat relish if necessary. Heat butter in a large frying pan over medium heat. Dredge patties in flour and sauté until brown, about 4 minutes on each side. Stir coriander into relish.

**SERVING:** Serve smoked fish cakes with relish on the side.

YIELD: 4 servings

# FALL/WINTER

## Mushroom-Stuffed Trout

Mushroom expert James Moore, chef of the Mountain Home Inn in Mill Valley, California, likes to use dramatic *trumpet of death* mushrooms with trout. You'll find that other mushrooms work well, too.

**¼ teaspoon fennel seeds**
**1 large clove garlic**
**1 large onion**
**½ rib celery**
**1½ pounds *trumpet of death* or other mushrooms + ¼ pound for garnish, optional**
**6 tablespoons butter**
**1 cup uncooked rice**
**1½ cups Chicken Stock (page 49)**
**2 tablespoons chopped parsley + more for garnish**
**Salt**
**4 whole boned trout *or* Coho salmon (about 6 ounces each, boned weight)**
**Melted butter for brushing**
**Lemon slices for garnish**

**PREPARATION:** Toast fennel seeds in a frying pan over medium heat for 5 minutes, shaking pan constantly. Crush them in a mortar with a pestle or with a flat part of a knife. Crush the garlic. Mince the onion and celery. Slice 1½ pounds mushrooms. Melt 6 tablespoons butter in a frying pan. Sauté garlic just long enough to flavor the butter, about 30 seconds, and discard garlic. Cook onion and celery in butter over low heat, until tender, about 10 minutes. Add rice and stir to coat with butter. Heat stock and add ⅓ of it at a time to rice. Simmer until each addition of stock is almost absorbed. Add sliced mushrooms and fennel seeds with last addition of stock and simmer, stirring constantly, until liquid is almost absorbed. Add parsley and salt to taste.

**COOKING:** Heat oven to 375°F. Butter a baking pan. Lightly brush inside of fish with melted butter. Sprinkle cavities with salt. Fill with rice/mushroom mixture and press cavities closed. Put fish in buttered pan and bake in preheated oven, turning once, until fish just tests done, 7 to 10 minutes per side.

Slice remaining ¼ pound mushrooms and sauté for garnish if desired.

**SERVING:** Serve fish brushed with butter and garnished with lemon slices, parsley, and optional sautéed mushrooms.

**YIELD:** 4 servings

# SAUTÉED SOLE IN CREAM SAUCE

John Clancy's Restaurant in New York City specializes in fish, and this is one of chef Kenneth Pulomena's favorite recipes.

**½ pound shrimp**

SHRIMP STOCK

**1 onion**
**1 quart Chicken Stock (page 49)**
**1½ teaspoons thyme leaves**
**Shells from ½ pound shrimp (above)**
**1 cup white wine**

**½ cup flour**
**Salt and pepper**
**¼ cup sun-dried tomatoes**
**4 anchovy fillets**

**½ cup oil**
**1½ pounds Dover sole fillets *or* other lean white fish fillets**
**12 tablespoons butter**
**½ cup white wine**
**1 cup heavy cream**
**¼ cup minced chives *or* scallion tops**

**PREPARATION:** Peel and devein shrimp, reserving shells for stock.

FOR THE STOCK: Quarter the onion. Put the ingredients into a saucepan and bring to a boil. Reduce heat and simmer for 30 minutes. Strain. Refrigerate until ready to use.

Mix flour with salt and pepper. Mince sun-dried tomatoes. Mash anchovies.

**COOKING:** Heat oil in a large frying pan. Dust sole with seasoned flour. Sauté in batches over medium heat until just cooked through, about 2 minutes per side. Transfer to warm plates.

Drain the oil from pan and wipe clean. Add 4 tablespoons butter and sauté the shrimp until pink, 1 to 2 minutes. Remove. Add stock, sun-dried tomatoes, and anchovies to frying pan. Bring to a boil and reduce heat to a simmer. Add wine and cream and reduce by half, about 5 minutes. Return the shrimp to the pan. Whisk in the remaining 8 tablespoons butter, 1 tablespoon at a time, over the lowest possible heat. The butter should soften and form a creamy sauce but not melt completely. Remove from heat and season to taste.

**SERVING:** Divide shrimp among fillets and pour sauce over all. Sprinkle with chives.

YIELD: 4 servings

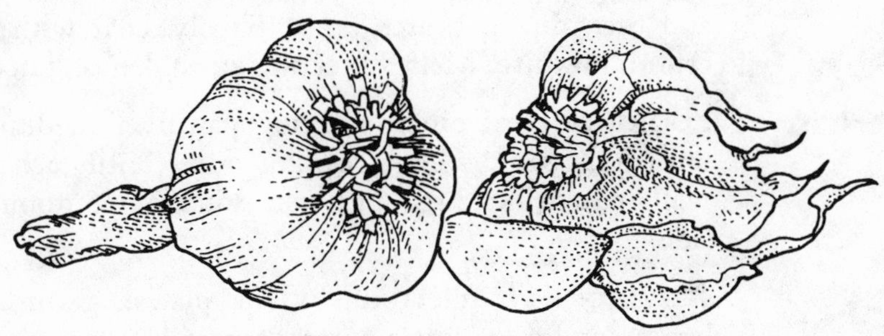

# SESAME-SAUTÉED CATFISH WITH LEMON BUTTER

In this example of the new Southern cuisine, plain fried catfish is updated with a sesame-seed coating and a lemon-butter sauce.

- **½ cup minced parsley**
- **1 cup dry bread crumbs**
- **½ cup sesame seeds**
- **Salt and pepper**
- **¼ cup flour**
- **2 eggs**
- **1 teaspoon water**
- **4 catfish fillets (6 to 8 ounces each)**
- **3 tablespoons butter**
- **1 tablespoon lemon juice**
- **3 tablespoons peanut oil**
- **4 lemon wedges**

**PREPARATION:** In a shallow bowl combine parsley, bread crumbs, sesame seeds, and salt and pepper. Put flour in another shallow bowl. In a third shallow bowl beat eggs with water. Dredge each catfish fillet in flour and then dip in beaten eggs. Finally, coat with bread-crumb mixture. Melt butter and stir in lemon juice.

**COOKING:** Heat oil in a frying pan over medium heat until hot. Sauté fillets, turning once, until each side is well browned and fish just tests done, 3 to 5 minutes per side.

**SERVING:** Put fillets on warm plates, garnish with lemon, and pass lemon butter separately.

**YIELD:** 4 servings

# Halibut Blackened in Soy and Lemon with American Caviar

Inventive Moncef Meddeb of L'Espalier in Boston developed this dish using ideas from the Orient, Russia, and our own Cajun country.

- **2½ tablespoons light soy sauce**
- **2½ tablespoons lemon juice + more for garnish, optional**
- **¼ cup heavy cream for garnish, optional**
- **¼ teaspoon white pepper**
- **4 ¾-inch-thick halibut fillets (about 6 ounces each)**
- **4 heaping tablespoons American caviar, optional**

**PREPARATION:** In a small bowl mix soy sauce and 2½ tablespoons lemon juice. Whip cream and season with a few drops of lemon juice. Refrigerate until ready to use.

**COOKING:** Heat a large well-seasoned cast-iron frying pan on high heat until bottom begins to turn whitish gray, 4 to 6 minutes. Sprinkle white pepper on fish. Cook 2 of the fish fillets until lightly charred and fish just tests done, 1 to 1½ minutes per side.

Pour ½ of soy/lemon mixture over fish to glaze and cook 15 seconds, turning fish once to coat with glaze. Transfer halibut to warm plates. Repeat with remaining fish.

**SERVING:** Garnish fish with caviar and a dollop of whipped cream.

**YIELD:** 4 servings

# BLACKENED FISH

Pan-blackened redfish, popularized by Paul Prudhomme, is made by cooking a spice-encrusted fish fillet in a super-hot ungreased frying pan. This forms a fragrant crust on the outside and leaves the inside moist and tender. Pan-blackening generates a great deal of smoke, so, if you do not have a strong exhaust fan nor a desire to activate your smoke alarm, you may wish to try the procedure outdoors, heating the frying pan on a barbecue grill. Lacking redfish, use bass, halibut, or snapper. The following recipe comes from John Silberman, a Prudhomme-trained chef who owns the popular Cajun Yankee restaurant in Cambridge, Massachusetts.

CAJUN SPICE MIXTURE

**4 teaspoons salt**
**1 tablespoon garlic powder**
**1 tablespoon onion powder**
**2 teaspoons black pepper**
**2 teaspoons white pepper**
**2 teaspoons cayenne pepper**
**2 teaspoons dried thyme**
**2 teaspoons dried oregano**
**1 teaspoon paprika**

**¼ pound clarified butter *or* ½ cup oil**
**4 ½-inch-thick fillets of redfish *or* other lean fish (about 6 ounces each)**
**Lemon wedges for garnish**

**PREPARATION:** Combine the ingredients for the spice mixture.

**COOKING:** Heat a dry cast-iron frying pan upside down over high heat until it turns a white/bluish-gray color, 10 to 15 minutes. Meanwhile, spoon a few tablespoons of clarified butter or oil on each fish fillet and spread it with your fingers. Sprinkle the fillets with spice mixture. They should be evenly coated, although not too thickly crusted. Coat the other sides with remaining butter and spice powder.

Very carefully turn pan right side up. Put the fish into the super-hot frying pan and cook, turning once, until it tests done, about 2½ minutes total. Don't be disconcerted by all the smoke. The fish should be singed on the exterior but not quite burned.

**SERVING:** Transfer the fish to warm plates and garnish with lemon wedges.

YIELD: 4 servings

# ALL SEASON

## Deep-Fried Smelt with Tartar Sauce

The delectable smelt is most available in the spring, but any small fish may be fried in this way—or use fillets that have been cut in small pieces. The rice-flour batter is the crispest we know.

Tartar Sauce

**1 egg yolk**
**1 teaspoon Dijon mustard**
**½ teaspoon lemon juice**
**½ teaspoon anchovy paste**
**Salt and pepper**
**1 cup olive oil**
**2 cornichons**
**2 teaspoons grated onion**
**2 teaspoons chopped capers**
**1 tablespoon chopped parsley, tarragon, *and/or* chives, optional**
**2 tablespoons cornichon liquid**

Rice-Flour Batter

**1 cup rice flour**
**1 cup water**
**Salt and pepper**

**Oil for frying**
**1 pound smelt *or* other small fish**
**Salt and pepper**
**Lemon wedges for garnish**

**PREPARATION:** FOR THE TARTAR SAUCE: Whisk together egg yolk, mustard, lemon juice, anchovy paste, ¼ teaspoon salt, and ⅛ teaspoon pepper. Whisk in oil very slowly at first and then, when the mayonnaise has thickened, in a thin stream. Chop cornichons. Add to mayonnaise the onion, capers, cornichons, herbs, cornichon liquid, and salt and pepper to taste.

FOR THE BATTER: Stir together rice flour, water, 2 teaspoons salt, and 1 teaspoon pepper. Consistency should be like that of yogurt or sour cream. Add more flour or water as necessary.

**COOKING:** Heat oil in a deep fryer or large frying pan to 375°F. to 400°F. Dip smelt, 1 at a time, into batter and gently lower into oil. Fry until golden, about 1½ minutes. Remove and drain on paper towels. Season to taste with salt and pepper.

**SERVING:** Serve with tartar sauce and lemon wedges.

YIELD: 4 servings

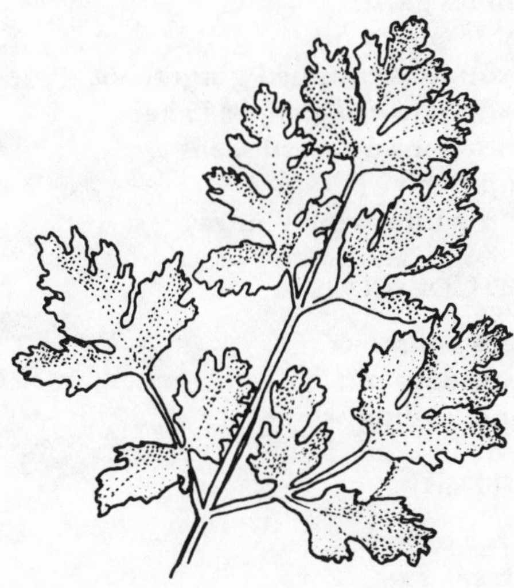

# COUSCOUS AND CURRIED FISH WITH HOT LIME AND CUCUMBER PICKLE

Ethnic dishes have long been popular in America, but only recently have we begun to combine ingredients and techniques from various cuisines on a single plate. It's a natural progression: the foods in the melting pot are finally beginning to blend. Indian curried fish with Moroccan couscous? Why not?—the combination is delicious. You won't be disappointed using this unusual recipe as a whole, but the various parts are useful separately, too. The fish is good with plain rice. The couscous is an interesting side dish for many entrées. Try the Hot Lime and Cucumber Pickle with other curries or as a counterpoint to simpler flavors such as grilled chicken or chops.

### HOT LIME AND CUCUMBER PICKLE

**6 limes**
**2 tablespoons coarse salt**
**2 cucumbers**
**2 onions**
**2 cloves garlic**
**2 tablespoons oil**
**1½ teaspoons chopped gingerroot**
**1½ teaspoons red-pepper flakes**
**2 teaspoons mustard seeds**
**½ cup sugar**
**¼ cup white-wine vinegar**

### STEAMED COUSCOUS

**1½ cups couscous**
**2 teaspoons salt**
**3 cups boiling water**

### CURRIED FISH

**2 large onions**
**1 rib celery**

## LEMONS AND LIMES

Lemons and limes are versatile, relatively inexpensive, and available year-round—what more could a cook ask? In addition to adding flavor to all sorts of dishes, lemons and limes have myriad other uses in the kitchen. Their juice keeps fruits such as apples and avocados from turning brown. (You should be aware that lemon juice can also "bleach" certain vegetables, like broccoli, turning them an unappetizing gray-green.) The acid in the juice can also break down the tough connective tissues in raw meat or fish, thereby "cooking" it. The same properties make the juice a tenderizing agent in many marinades. The zest of both fruits is also an important flavoring agent. When using zest, the colored outer part of the peel, avoid the bitter white pith underneath.

Room-temperature lemons or limes will yield more juice than those straight from the refrigerator. Before cutting into a lemon or lime, gently roll the fruit back and forth across a countertop for the maximum juice yield. When cutting these acidic fruits, use a stainless rather than carbon steel knife. They will discolor carbon steel and can discolor and pit aluminum utensils and containers. Aluminum has an

**2 cloves garlic**
**6 tablespoons butter**
**3 plum tomatoes**
**1 apple**
**1 teaspoon minced gingerroot**
**1 teaspoon cumin**
**1 teaspoon ground coriander**
**½ teaspoon turmeric**
**½ teaspoon cayenne**
**¼ teaspoon ground cloves**
**¼ teaspoon ground cinnamon**
**1½ teaspoons flour + more for dredging**
**⅓ cup golden raisins**
**Salt and pepper**
**1¾ pounds firm-fleshed boneless fish, such as scrod *or* monkfish**

**5 tablespoons butter**
**2 tablespoons oil**
**½ cup white wine**

**PREPARATION:** FOR THE HOT LIME AND CUCUMBER PICKLE: Wash and dry the limes. Remove zest from limes and chop into ½-inch pieces. Toss with 2 teaspoons salt and set aside for 3 to 4 hours. Peel white pith from limes and discard. Cut flesh into ¼-inch slices and put in a large bowl.

Peel ½-inch lengthwise strips from the cucumbers, leaving equally wide strips of green peel on for a striped effect. Halve lengthwise and remove seeds. Cut into ½-inch slices and add to bowl.

Cut the onions into thin slices and add to the lime and cucumber. Sprinkle with remaining 4 teaspoons coarse salt, toss, and set aside 3 to 4 hours.

Rinse zest and put in a small saucepan. Add water to cover and bring to a boil. Lower heat and simmer until tender, about 15 minutes. Drain.

Mince garlic. Rinse lime slices, cucumbers, and onions, drain and pat dry. In a large frying pan heat oil. Add garlic, gingerroot, pepper flakes, and mustard seeds and cook 10 seconds. Add lime/cucumber/onion mixture and toss 20 seconds. Stir in sugar and vinegar and

adverse effect on the taste of acidic ingredients, too.

When selecting either fruit, choose those with thin skins that feel heavy for their size. The fruit should feel firm but not overly hard. Thick, bumpy lemon skins mean little flesh and juice inside. Look for lemons with fine-grained skin and intensely dark green, rather than yellowish, limes.

Lemons and limes will keep for about a week at room temperature and up to a month or so in the refrigerator. But both will spoil or dry out after too long. Most cooks keep at least a lemon or two on hand, and there is certainly no need to resort to bottled lemon or lime juice. Get fresh, bright flavor from the real thing.

cook 2 minutes. Remove from heat and cool. Transfer to a covered container and refrigerate until ready to use.

FOR THE STEAMED COUSCOUS: Put couscous in a large bowl and sprinkle with salt. Pour in boiling water. Cover loosely and set aside for 10 minutes. Fluff with a fork.

FOR THE CURRIED FISH: Mince the onions, celery, and garlic. Melt 6 tablespoons butter in a large saucepan. Add onions and celery and cook over low heat, stirring occasionally, until onions are very soft but not browned, about 20 minutes. Peel, seed, and cut the tomatoes into thin strips. Peel, core, and chop the apple. Add garlic, gingerroot, and apple to the saucepan and cook 5 minutes. Stir in cumin, coriander, turmeric, cayenne, cloves, and cinnamon and cook, stirring, over medium-high heat 2 minutes. Sprinkle on 1½ teaspoons flour and cook, stirring, 2 minutes. Stir in 2½ cups water, tomato strips, raisins, and salt and pepper to taste. Simmer sauce, stirring occasionally, 10 minutes. Cut the fish into 2-inch chunks.

**COOKING:** Put a steamer rack in a large pot and fill pot with water to ½ inch below rack (water must not touch grains of couscous). Spread couscous on rack and cover pot. Bring water to a boil, lower heat, and steam, covered, for 30 minutes.

Meanwhile, sprinkle fish with salt and pepper, dredge lightly in flour, and shake off excess. In a large frying pan, melt 2 tablespoons butter with oil. Sauté fish over medium-high heat until golden and fish just tests done, 5 to 7 minutes. Remove fish.

Pour wine into pan, raise heat, and scrape bottom of pan with a wooden spoon to deglaze. Add wine to sauce with fish and any accumulated juices. Season to taste with salt and pepper and gently reheat. Toss couscous with remaining 3 tablespoons butter.

**SERVING:** Serve the fish with the couscous and pass hot lime and cucumber pickle separately.

YIELD: 4 servings

CHAPTER 6

# POULTRY

**SPRING:**

Chicken with Artichoke Sauce

Asparagus, Scallion, and Smoked Turkey Risotto

**SUMMER:**

Thai Basil Chicken

Picnic-Style Chicken

Roasted Duck and Sweet-Onion Salad

Chicken with Tomato Cream Sauce

Grilled Chicken with Aioli and Potatoes

**FALL/WINTER:**

Chicken Breasts Stuffed with Mushrooms

Curried Chicken and Apples with Brandy Cream Sauce

Roast Goose Stuffed with Cranberries, Apples, and Potatoes

Casserole-Roasted Pheasant with Celery Root and Mushrooms

Roast Turkey and Garbanzo-Chorizo Stuffing with Salsa Verde

**ALL SEASON:**

Chicken Quenelles with Shallot and Red-Pepper Sauce

Filbert Chicken Breasts

Sautéed Chicken with Roasted Garlic and Candied Lemon Zest

Chicken Mole

Roasted Chicken with Sausage and Grape Stuffing

Pennsylvania-Dutch Chicken with Dumplings

Roast Capon with Cornbread, Bacon, and Pecan Stuffing

Bulgur-Stuffed Quail

Roast Quail

SIDEBARS

Sweet Onions

Cranberries

Grapes

# SPRING

## Chicken with Artichoke Sauce

This delectable recipe combines chicken with artichokes and, optionally, tiny shrimp. It's surprising how fine a complement any shellfish is to chicken, so feel free to substitute for the shrimp if you like.

- **6 large artichokes**
- **2 lemons**
- **4-pound chicken**
- **½ cup white wine**
- **1 cup Chicken Stock (page 49)**
- **2 tablespoons heavy cream**
- **Salt and pepper**
- **¼ pound tiny shrimp, optional**

**PREPARATION:** Cut the stems off the artichokes. Rub the cut surfaces of artichokes with ½ lemon to prevent discoloration. Squeeze 1 teaspoon juice and set aside. Put artichokes in a pot of boiling salted water. Squeeze juice from remaining 1½ lemons into the pot. Weigh the artichokes down with a heatproof plate. Boil, covered, until bottoms are easily pierced with a knife and the leaves can be pulled out easily, about 30 minutes. Drain and cool. Remove outer leaves from artichokes; discard innermost leaves. Scrape out fuzzy chokes with a teaspoon and discard. Scrape the flesh from the bottom of each leaf, reserving a few of the leaves for garnish. Combine 4 of the artichoke bottoms and the scraped flesh in a food processor or mortar and pestle and purée until smooth. Cut remaining 2 artichoke bottoms into ⅛-inch slices and toss with reserved 1 teaspoon of lemon juice. Cut chicken into 8 pieces.

**COOKING:** Bring wine and stock to a boil in a deep frying pan and cook for 5 minutes. Add the chicken and cook, covered, over medium-low heat until just cooked through, about 15 minutes. Remove chicken from the pan. Bring liquid to a boil over high heat and reduce by ¼. Whisk in the cream and artichoke purée. Season to taste with salt and pepper. Add sliced artichokes and shrimp if desired and bring to a simmer. Return chicken to pan and heat through.

**SERVING:** Serve chicken garnished with reserved artichoke leaves.

**YIELD:** 4 servings

## Asparagus, Scallion, and Smoked Turkey Risotto

This twist on classic Italian risotto sports new flavors but should have the traditional consistency—tender but separate grains of rice suspended in a saucy liquid.

- **4 ounces smoked turkey**
- **6 scallions**
- **1 pound asparagus**
- **¾ cup white wine**
- **6 cups Chicken Stock (page 49)**
- **3 tablespoons butter**
- **1½ cups rice, preferably arborio**
- **3 tablespoons minced chervil *or* parsley**
- **Salt and pepper**

**PREPARATION:** Cut turkey into thin strips. Cut the scallions, including 2 inches of the green tops, into thin slices. Trim the asparagus and cut the stalks on the diagonal into 1-inch pieces.

**COOKING:** In a nonreactive saucepan heat the wine and stock. Add the asparagus and cook until tender, about 6 minutes. Remove with a slotted spoon and reserve. Keep liquid hot.

Heat the butter in a heavy nonreactive saucepan. Sauté the turkey over medium-high heat until golden, about 3 minutes. Remove turkey with a slotted spoon and reserve. Add the scallions to the pan and sauté over medium-low heat for 1 minute. Add the rice and cook, stirring, until it becomes opaque, about 1 minute.

Add enough simmering stock mixture to cover the rice, about ¾ cup. Cook over medium heat, stirring continually and keeping the mixture at a gentle simmer, until most of the liquid is absorbed, about 5 minutes. Add more stock mixture to cover rice again and cook in the same manner, adding more stock mixture as needed. When done, the rice should be tender and the remaining liquid should be thickened to a sauce. Stir in the chervil, turkey, and asparagus and heat through. Season to taste with salt and pepper if necessary.

**SERVING:** Serve immediately.

YIELD: 4 servings

# SUMMER

## Thai Basil Chicken

Plain white rice and cold beer are the best accompaniments to this spicy dish.

Thai Marinade

**4–5 hot chili peppers**
**1 tablespoon chopped gingerroot**
**¼ cup soy sauce**
**¼ cup dry sherry**
**½ cup oil**

**2 boned and skinned chicken breasts, about ¾ pound**
**¼ pound thin green beans**
**¼ pound yellow summer squash**
**1 large carrot**
**1 yellow bell pepper**
**4–5 hot chili peppers**
**3 tablespoons chopped basil**
**Salt**
**Chili oil, optional**

**PREPARATION:** FOR THE MARINADE: Chop hot peppers and combine in a nonreactive dish with the next 4 ingredients. Cut chicken into 1-inch cubes and put in marinade. Cover with plastic wrap and chill at least 4 hours.

Trim beans and cut into 1½-inch lengths. Cut squash

and carrot into ⅛-inch diagonal slices. Seed yellow pepper and slice into thin strips. Seed and chop hot peppers.

**COOKING:** Heat wok or frying pan over high heat until almost smoking. While heating, remove chicken cubes from marinade. Strain marinade and reserve. Add chicken to wok. Stir-fry over high heat until chicken is almost done, about 3 minutes. Remove from wok and set aside. Add beans, carrot, and strained marinade to wok. Cook about 2 minutes, stirring. Add squash and all peppers and cook 2 minutes. Turn off heat. Return chicken to wok and toss. Add basil, salt, and chili oil if desired.

YIELD: 4 servings

## PICNIC-STYLE CHICKEN

These grilled chicken breasts get extra flavor from pesto spread between the meat and the skin. Serve either hot or cold with the salad outlined here or all alone. This recipe is from Aliza Green, chef of Apropos in Philadelphia, Pennsylvania.

PESTO

**4 cloves garlic**
**½ cup pine nuts**
**2 cups basil leaves**
**½ cup virgin olive oil**
**⅔ cup grated Parmesan *or* aged Monterey Jack**
**Salt and pepper**

**8 chicken breasts with wings attached (about 2½ pounds total**

TOMATO, RED ONION, AND MINT SALAD

**3 large tomatoes**
**¼ red onion**
**1 tablespoon chopped mint**
**2 tablespoons olive oil**

**2 teaspoons red-wine vinegar**
**Salt and pepper**

PREPARATION: FOR THE PESTO: Chop the garlic in a food processor, add the pine nuts, and process 30 seconds. Add the basil and purée. While the machine is still running, slowly pour in the olive oil to make a smooth paste. Add the cheese and season with salt and pepper to taste.

Gently poke your fingers under the chicken skin and lift the skin slightly. Being careful not to tear the membrane that connects the skin to the chicken, gently stuff pesto between the membrane and the skin of each breast.

COOKING: Heat grill. FOR THE SALAD: Cut the tomatoes and onion into thin wedges and put in bowl. Stir in remaining ingredients. Grill the chicken breasts, turning once, until they just test done, about 12 minutes total.

SERVING: Serve chicken hot or cold with the salad.

YIELD: 4 servings

# ROASTED DUCK AND SWEET-ONION SALAD

This salad is great for a picnic or for a special summer lunch or supper. Just add sliced tomatoes, bread and a simple fruit dessert.

**4-pound duck**
**Salt and pepper**
**2 tablespoons oil**
**2 sweet onions, such as Vidalia, Maui, or Walla Walla**
**½ cup Chicken Stock (page 49)**
**½ cup white wine**
**2 tablespoons chopped parsley**
**½ cup sour cream**

**PREPARATION:** Heat oven to 450°F. Season the cavity and outside of duck with salt and pepper. Put the bird on a rack in a roasting pan. Roast in preheated oven for 1½ hours. Remove duck and let cool. Pour out all fat from pan and replace with the oil. Cut onions into large dice and add. Season with salt and pepper and cook over medium heat until the onions are tender, about 5 minutes. Pour in stock and cook until almost dry, about 10 minutes. Add wine, bring to a simmer, scraping bottom of pan with a wooden spoon to deglaze, and simmer over medium heat until reduced by half, about 5 minutes. Remove from heat and put in a large bowl.

When duck is cool enough to handle, remove meat from bones, cut into large dice, and add to bowl. Add parsley, stir in sour cream, and season to taste with salt and pepper.

**SERVING:** Serve at room temperature or slightly chilled.

**YIELD:** 4 servings

## SWEET ONIONS

Sweet onions? We're not talking about the large yellow Spanish onions or the mild red Bermudas that add a little verve to a salad. We're talking onions with as much natural sugar as you'd find in an orange; onions so sweet that many people enjoy eating them out of hand like an apple.

Sweet onions hail from three diverse locations in the United States—Vidalia, Georgia; Walla Walla, Washington; and Kula, Maui, Hawaii. Something about the soil and climate in those places makes the familiar-looking bulbs uncommonly sweet. You won't even cry when you cut them up.

The original sweet onion is the Walla Walla. The seeds were brought to Washington early in this century by Corsican immigrants. Grown in the Walla Walla soil, the onions were sweeter and milder than anything the Italians were used to. A little crossbreeding and experimentation later, and today's Walla Walla sweet was born. The northwestern onions are available only from late June through the middle of August.

Vidalia and Maui onions grow from ordinary Granex onion seeds. When planted in Texas, Southern California, or other onion-growing areas, Granex seeds grow into strong-tasting

# Chicken with Tomato Cream Sauce

The flavorings for the quick sauce in this recipe can be varied as you like. Keep the tomato, wine, and cream base, but substitute scallions or garlic for the shallot—or try basil in place of the parsley.

Tomato Cream Sauce

**1 shallot**
**2 regular *or* 4 plum tomatoes**
**1½ tablespoons butter**
**¼ cup dry white wine**
**½ cup heavy cream**
**Salt and pepper**
**1 tablespoon minced parsley**

**4 boned and skinned chicken breasts (about 1½ pounds total)**
**1 tablespoon olive oil**
**Salt and pepper**

**PREPARATION:** FOR THE SAUCE: Mince shallot. Peel, seed, and chop tomatoes. Melt butter in a frying pan over medium heat. Sauté shallot 1 minute. Add tomatoes and cook 1 minute. Add wine and cook until liquid is reduced by one-half, about five minutes. Add cream and simmer until thick enough to coat the back of a spoon, about 5 minutes. Season to taste with salt and pepper and stir in parsley.

Brush chicken with olive oil and season with salt and pepper.

**COOKING:** Heat grill. Grill chicken until it just tests done, about 8 minutes total. Reheat sauce if necessary. Put chicken on plates and surround with cream sauce.

**YIELD:** 4 servings

yellow or white onions. Planted in the rich Georgia red clay or the volcanic, loamy Hawaiian earth, however, and raised in the gentle climate of either area, they grow into mild, sweet onions with a high sugar content and a delicate flavor. Vidalias are on the market from early May through July; Mauis, from May until October.

As when selecting other onions, choose bulbs that are firm and dry and well covered by papery outer skin. Avoid onions that have begun to sprout; their cores will be soft. Four graded sizes of sweet onions are available. The biggest, jumbos from Maui, can weigh up to a pound apiece. The smallest, called pearls or peewees, are a mere inch or so in diameter.

Most growers recommend storing sweet onions for no longer than a month or two in a cool, dry area, preferably elevated on wire racks and not touching one another. Sweet onions do not last as well as regular onions, nor are they good travelers. Their perishability combined with limited production add up to prices that are almost always higher than those of regular onions.

# GRILLED CHICKEN WITH AIOLI AND POTATOES

You'll find a multitude of uses for the aioli in this recipe. It comes from Barry Wine, chef and owner of The Quilted Giraffe in New York City, who makes his version of the traditional garlic mayonnaise with three different oils. Give it a try on plain fish or cooked or raw vegetables. It makes a dynamite roast beef sandwich or potato salad, too.

**3 cloves garlic**
**¼ cup olive oil**
**¼ cup sesame oil**
**3 tablespoons minced gingerroot**
**1 large chicken (about 5 pounds)**
**Salt and pepper**

AIOLI

**2 cloves garlic**
**1 teaspoon lemon juice**
**1 egg yolk**
**2 tablespoons olive oil**
**2 tablespoons sesame oil**
**2 tablespoons peanut oil**
**2 tablespoons heavy cream**
**Salt and pepper**

**3 large baking potatoes**
**3 shallots**
**3 tablespoons butter**
**Salt and pepper**
**3 sprigs thyme**

**PREPARATION:** Mince the garlic. Combine oils, garlic, and gingerroot in a frying pan. Cook over very low heat for 10 minutes. Pour into a shallow dish.

Cut the chicken into 8 pieces and add to dish. Season with salt and pepper, turn to coat, and marinate, refrigerated, for at least 3 hours, turning several times.

*Roast Goose Stuffed with Cranberries, Apples, and Potatoes, page 132*

*Chicken Mole, page 143*

*Elote con Queso (Corn Custard), page 193*

*Bulgur-Stuffed Quail, page 150*

*Baked Sweet Dumpling Squash, page 194*

*Broccoli with Starfruit, page 197*

*The Very Best Angel Food Cake, page 222*

*Champagne-Poached Figs with Heavy Cream, page 228*

*Poached Peaches with Champagne Sabayon, page 229*

*Berry Tart, page 227*

*Apple and Cider Soup with Raisins, page 238*

*Apple Charlotte, page 231*

*Café à la Mousse, page 246*

FOR THE AIOLI: Bring all ingredients to room temperature. Mince garlic. In a bowl whisk together lemon juice and egg yolk. Whisk in oils slowly, drop by drop at first and then, when thickened, in a thin stream. Add cream, garlic, and salt and pepper to taste. Aioli can be made ahead and stored, covered, in refrigerator.

Heat oven to 450°F. Brush a baking sheet with oil. Cut unpeeled potatoes into ¼-inch rounds. Chop the shallots. Melt the butter.

Put potato slices on prepared baking sheet. Roast in preheated oven, flipping occasionally, until they are tender and lightly browned on both sides, about 10 minutes. Season with salt and pepper and toss with butter, shallots, and thyme sprigs. Wrap potato mixture in foil.

**COOKING:** Heat grill. Bring aioli to room temperature if chilled. Remove chicken from marinade and pat dry. Grill chicken and foil pouch on covered grill, 20 to 30 minutes.

**SERVING:** Spoon aioli over grilled chicken and serve with hot potatoes.

YIELD: 4 servings

# FALL/WINTER

## Chicken Breasts Stuffed with Mushrooms

James Moore of the Mountain Home Inn in Mill Valley, California, developed this recipe for trumpet of death mushrooms, the black, horn-shaped delicacies. But the dish is good with all sorts of mushrooms. In spring, you might try it with morels and sweet onions.

- **1 cup sour cream**
- **3 tablespoons buttermilk**
- **4 boned and skinned chicken breasts (about 1½ pounds total)**
- **Salt**
- **1 pound mushrooms**
- **4 onions**
- **4 tablespoons butter**
- **4 cups Chicken Stock (page 49)**
- **⅓ cup chopped parsley**

**PREPARATION:** In a small bowl mix sour cream with buttermilk. Carefully cut a pocket in each chicken breast. Sprinkle breasts with salt and rub with sour cream/buttermilk mixture. Refrigerate overnight or as long as possible.

Trim the mushrooms. Dice the onions. In a frying pan cook mushrooms in butter over medium heat for 3 minutes. Add onions.

Bring stock to a boil in a saucepan and add to mushrooms and onions. Simmer until mushrooms are tender, about 2 minutes. Strain and reserve liquid. Set mushrooms and onions aside. Slice a few mushrooms for garnish.

Reduce liquid over high heat to a syrupy consistency. Add parsley.

**COOKING:** Heat oven to 375°F. Wipe cream and milk mixture from chicken breasts. Brush breast pockets with some of the mushroom glaze, reserving some glaze for later, and sprinkle with salt. Fill pockets with mushrooms and onions and press closed. Bake in preheated oven until just done, about 15 minutes.

**SERVING:** Coat chicken breasts with remaining mushroom glaze and garnish with reserved mushroom slices.

**YIELD:** 4 servings

## Curried Chicken and Apples with Brandy Cream Sauce

This luxurious dish can be made in minutes. Chicken, cream, brandy, and apples are a time-honored combination, here given the exotic touch of curry powder.

**4 boned and skinned chicken breasts (about 1½ pounds total)**
**1 teaspoon curry powder**
**Salt and pepper**
**⅓ cup flour**
**1 small shallot**
**4 tablespoons butter**
**1 tart apple**
**3 tablespoons applejack *or* other brandy**
**½ cup heavy cream**

**PREPARATION:** Pound chicken breasts lightly and sprinkle with curry powder and salt and pepper. Dip chicken into flour to coat and shake off excess. Mince the shallot.

**COOKING:** Heat 2 tablespoons butter in a frying pan. Sauté chicken over medium heat until golden brown and springy to the touch, about 8 minutes total. Remove and cover to keep warm.

Peel, quarter, and core apple and cut it into ¼-inch slices. Add remaining 2 tablespoons butter to pan. Add apple slices and shallot and sauté over medium heat, stirring, until apples begin to soften, 3 to 4 minutes. Add applejack or brandy and turn heat to high. Cook, stirring, until glazed, about 1 minute. Remove apples with a slotted spoon and set aside.

Add cream to pan and reduce, stirring, over medium-high heat until sauce is lightly thickened, about 2 minutes. Add salt and pepper to taste.

**SERVING:** Spoon some sauce onto 4 warm plates. Top with chicken and garnish with apple slices.

YIELD: 4 servings

## Roast Goose Stuffed with Cranberries, Apples, and Potatoes

The traditional holiday goose with a kick. Tart cranberries are a perfect counterpoint to the rich meat, and here they're inside, rather than alongside, the bird.

STUFFING

**16 small boiling potatoes**
**4 apples**
**1 red onion**
**1 rib celery**
**½ cup minced parsley**
**2 teaspoons minced rosemary *or* ½ teaspoon dried**
**2 teaspoons minced chives *or* green onion tops**
**1 tablespoon oil**
**½ cup fresh cranberries**
**Salt and pepper**

**2 9- to 10-pound geese**
**Salt and pepper**

### CRANBERRIES

Good cranberries bounce. One of the earliest sorting methods used on small English cranberries was to pour the fruit down a flight of stairs; the ones that bounced to the bottom were the best. If you're reluctant to try this method in the market, just look for berries that are firm.

Early American settlers found larger cranberries growing wild in New England. Because harvesting runs from September and continues through December, fresh cranberries do not appear in the markets until fall and winter and, except for canned and frozen, are almost impossible to

**3 cups Chicken Stock (page 49)**
**¼ cup arrowroot**

**PREPARATION:** FOR THE STUFFING: Bring a pot of salted water to a boil. Peel the potatoes and cut into ½-inch dice. Core and peel the apples and cut them into eighths. Put potatoes and apples into boiling water, bring back to a boil, and cook 2 minutes. Drain.

Quarter the onion, cut crosswise into thin slices, and separate. You should have 2 cups. Mince the celery. You should have ½ cup. In a small bowl combine parsley, rosemary, and chives.

In a large heavy pan heat oil. Add onion, celery, and cranberries and sauté over medium heat until onion wilts, about 5 minutes. Add ½ the herbs. Mix in apples and potatoes, season with salt and pepper, and cool.

Remove necks and wing tips from geese and reserve. Clean cavities.

**COOKING:** Heat oven to 450°F. Season cavities of geese with salt. Stuff each bird, close openings with skewers, and truss with string. Put necks and wing tips of geese in a large roasting pan. Put geese on top of bones, being careful not to crowd. Roast for 20 minutes in preheated oven. Lower heat to 350°F. Add 1½ cups water to pan. Cover geese loosely with foil. Roast until juices run clear when inside of leg is pierced, about 20 minutes per pound. Meat thermometer should read 180°F. Remove from pan and let rest 30 minutes.

Remove as much fat as possible from the pan. Add chicken stock and simmer 5 minutes, scraping the bottom of the pan with a wooden spoon to deglaze. Remove bones from pan and strain stock into a saucepan. Bring stock to a simmer.

Dissolve arrowroot in ¼ cup cold water. Slowly pour ½ of mixture into stock, whisking constantly. Season to taste with salt and pepper. Add more arrowroot mixture until sauce has desired thickness.

**SERVING:** Remove stuffing from geese and toss with remaining herbs. Carve birds and pass the sauce separately.

**YIELD:** 12 servings

find other times of year. Raw cranberries do freeze well. If you like to use cranberries year round, just pop bags of them in the freezer when they're available.

Along with blueberries, cranberries are among the very few native American berries and began to shape up as a commercial crop in the early 1800s, when farmers in Massachusetts and New Jersey started transplanting wild shrubs to new bog areas. Today Massachusetts, New Jersey, Wisconsin, Oregon and Washington produce most of the crop. Of the more than one hundred varieties of cranberries, commercial growers concentrate on four—Early Blacks, Howes, Searles, and McFarlins—but processing plants usually sort and package them without regard to strain. A large rosy berry of one type is just as ripe and ready to use as another kind that is smaller and of a deep red hue.

Cranberries, a relative of blueberries, are longer lasting than most berries, thanks to a tough outer skin and firm flesh, but refrigeration is still recommended. Sort through the berries, picking off any stems and discarding any berries that are shriveled or soft (and therefore don't bounce).

# CASSEROLE-ROASTED PHEASANT WITH CELERY ROOT AND MUSHROOMS

The flavor of pheasant is delectable, but all too often the meat is dry. Cooking it covered, with butter and Madeira to further ensure moistness, solves the problem. The celery root garnish is excellent with pheasant, but you might want to try sweet potato slices instead.

- **2 onions**
- **4 cloves garlic**
- **2 small carrots**
- **2 small ribs celery**
- **¼ pound cooked ham**
- **½ pound shiitake *or* other mushrooms**
- **1½ pounds celery root**
- **2 2½- to 3-pound pheasants, including giblets**
- **Salt and pepper**
- **4 sprigs thyme**
- **12 tablespoons butter + more if necessary**
- **½ teaspoon chopped thyme *or* pinch dried**
- **4 tablespoons olive oil + more if necessary**
- **⅔ cup Madeira**
- **2 cups Chicken Stock (page 49)**
- **¼ teaspoon lemon juice**
- **¼ cup chopped parsley**

**PREPARATION:** Quarter 1 onion and chop the other. Crush the garlic. Chop the carrots, celery, and ham. Remove stems from mushrooms and chop stems. Cut mushroom caps into thick slices. Peel celery root and cut into thin wedges.

Pat pheasants dry and season with salt and pepper inside and out. Tuck onion quarters, thyme sprigs, and garlic cloves into cavities. Truss birds.

**COOKING:** Heat oven to 350°F. In a large heavy frying pan heat 2 tablespoons butter over medium heat. And chopped onion, carrots, celery, ham, chopped mushroom stems, and chopped thyme. Sauté for 10 minutes.

Transfer to a heavy covered roaster or another pot large enough to hold pheasants snugly. Reserve frying pan.

In the same frying pan heat 4 tablespoons butter with 2 tablespoons olive oil over medium-high heat. Put birds in frying pan on their sides and scatter giblets around them. Sauté, shaking pan occasionally to prevent sticking, until browned on 1 side. Carefully turn birds and sauté until browned on all sides, about 10 minutes in all. Arrange birds, breast-side up, on sautéed vegetables. Reserve liver for another use and scatter remaining giblets around birds. Pour any excess fat from frying pan over birds. In same frying pan melt 4 more tablespoons butter. Pour into a bowl and set aside for basting. Reserve frying pan. Cover roasting pan tightly and roast in preheated oven, basting occasionally with melted butter, for 30 minutes.

Meanwhile, add Madeira to frying pan, scraping bottom of pan with a wooden spoon to deglaze. Strain and set aside. In the same frying pan heat 2 tablespoons each of butter and olive oil over medium-high heat. Add celery root and salt and pepper, tossing until it begins to brown lightly, 5 to 7 minutes. With a slotted spoon scatter celery root around pheasants. Pour reserved Madeira over birds. Cover tightly and roast until juices run clear when thigh is pierced and celery root is tender, about 12 minutes more.

Sauté mushroom caps over medium-high heat in same frying pan, about 4 minutes. Season with salt and pepper. Add more butter and olive oil if needed. Transfer pheasants to a warm serving platter and remove strings. With a slotted spoon arrange celery root and sautéed mushroom caps around birds, leaving giblets and as much of chopped vegetables and ham as possible in roaster. Cover platter loosely with foil to keep warm.

Put pan with vegetables, giblets, and liquid over medium-high heat. Add stock and bring to a boil. Reduce by almost half. Degrease, add lemon juice, and strain. Adjust seasonings with salt and pepper as needed.

**SERVING:** Sprinkle chopped parsley over celery root and mushrooms. Pass sauce separately.

**YIELD:** 4 servings

# ROAST TURKEY AND GARBANZO-CHORIZO STUFFING WITH SALSA VERDE

The flavor combination in this stuffing—chorizo, garbanzos, and chicken livers—accents the mild taste of the roasted turkey. The fragrant coriander-laced sauce should be made at least 1 hour before serving.

GARBANZO-CHORIZO STUFFING

- **Garbanzos (see recipe below *or* use 15 ounces canned garbanzos)**
- **1½ pounds chorizo**
- **2 onions**
- **2 large cloves Mexican garlic *or* 3 cloves regular garlic**
- **1 pound chicken livers + liver from the turkey**
- **2 teaspoons salt**
- **¼ pound butter**
- **2 tablespoons minced parsley**

SALSA VERDE

- **1 pound tomatillos *or* 13 ounces canned tomatillos**
- **4 fresh mild green chilies *or* 8 ounces canned chilies**
- **½ onion**
- **1 clove Mexican garlic *or* 1 large clove regular garlic**
- **1 cup coriander leaves**

- **15- to 17-pound turkey**
- **1 tablespoon salt**
- **¼ pound butter + more if necessary**

**PREPARATION:** FOR THE STUFFING: Prepare garbanzos. Remove casings from the chorizo and cut sausage into thin slices. Chop the onions. Mince the garlic. Trim and quarter the livers.

Cook chorizo in a large frying pan over medium-high heat until lightly browned. Drain off all but 2 tablespoons fat and add garbanzos. Add salt and cook until browned, about 15 minutes. Remove from heat.

In another frying pan melt butter. Add onions and garlic and cook until onions are soft. Add livers and fry, stirring, until livers are crispy-brown on the outside. Break up livers by mashing with a fork or potato masher. Combine with garbanzos and chorizo. Add parsley and salt to taste. Chill stuffing.

FOR THE SALSA VERDE: Remove husks and stems from tomatillos if using fresh and steam them until soft, about 5 minutes. Peel and seed chilies if using fresh. Chop the onion. Combine all ingredients in a food processor or blender until smooth. Allow sauce to sit at least 1 hour before serving so that the flavors will meld.

**COOKING:** Heat oven to 400°F. Rub turkey inside and out with salt. Stuff neck and internal cavities of turkey with chilled stuffing. Truss. Put on a rack in a roasting pan and slide into preheated oven. Melt the butter. Brush the turkey with melted butter every 15 minutes until juices collect and then baste frequently with juices. Roast until turkey is golden brown and internal temperature is 185°F. at leg joint and stuffing is 170°F., 3½ to 4 hours. Remove from oven and let rest for 25 minutes before carving.

YIELD: 12 servings

## Garbanzos

**10 ounces dried garbanzos (1½ cups)**
**1 rib celery**
**1 onion**
**1 carrot**
**¼ pound ham end *or* a pork bone *or* 3 slices bacon**
**1 bay leaf**
**1 sprig thyme *or* ½ teaspoon dried**
**5 parsley stems**
**Salt**

**PREPARATION:** Pick through beans and rinse with cold water. Put in a pan and add water to cover by 2 inches. Either soak for 8 to 10 hours or bring to a boil, cover, and set aside off heat for 1 hour. Drain and rinse. Quarter the celery, onion, and carrot. Tie all ingredients except garbanzos and salt in a cheesecloth bag. In a large pot combine garbanzos, cheesecloth bag, and water to cover well. Bring to a boil, lower heat, and simmer, skimming occasionally, for 1 hour. Add salt and cook until beans are tender, about 30 minutes. Drain garbanzos and discard bag. Adjust seasoning.

**YIELD:** 4 cups

# ALL SEASON

## Chicken Quenelles with Shallot and Red-Pepper Sauce

To call these quenelles "chicken dumplings" might be accurate but would give no idea of their refined texture. They are so light they almost melt in your mouth. Quenelles rarely stand alone. They're floated in soup or served with a sauce. The shallot and red-pepper sauce given here is a contemporary variation of hollandaise, made in the food processor. To shape the traditional smooth oval quenelles with tapered ends, use two spoons dipped in hot water and scrape the quenelle mixture from spoon to spoon, rotating it slightly each time.

**1 pound chicken breast meat (about 3 breasts), chilled**
**Salt and white pepper**
**½ teaspoon grated nutmeg**
**2 egg whites**
**1 small green bell pepper**
**2 red bell peppers**
**3 large shallots**
**¼ cup white-wine vinegar**
**¼ cup dry white wine**
**2 cups heavy cream, chilled**
**3 egg yolks**
**½ teaspoon Dijon mustard**
**½ pound butter**

**PREPARATION:** Cut chicken breasts into pieces. In a food processor purée chicken, 1 teaspoon salt, pinch of white pepper, and nutmeg until smooth. Add egg whites, 1 at a time. Push mixture through a sieve. Chill well.

During chilling time, roast green and red peppers over a gas flame, under the broiler, or on a grill until skin is blackened. Peel, seed, and remove ribs from peppers. Cut green pepper into 2-inch by ⅛-inch julienne.

Mince the shallots. Put shallots, vinegar, and wine in a saucepan. Reduce over medium-high heat to 2 tablespoons. Set aside.

Return quenelle mixture to processor and, with machine running, slowly add cold cream. Chill. Using 2 tablespoons, form the mixture into smooth ovals.

**COOKING:** Bring a saucepan of salted water to a simmer. Slide the quenelles into liquid and cook until they are slightly firm to the touch, 5 to 8 minutes.

Purée red peppers in a food processor. Add reduced shallot mixture, egg yolks, and mustard and process until completely smooth. Melt butter and, while still very hot, pour it into the running machine in a slow, steady stream.

**SERVING:** Transfer quenelles to a warm platter, spoon sauce over them, and garnish with green pepper.

**YIELD:** 4 servings

# Filbert Chicken Breasts

Wine and food expert Shirley Sarvis developed this carefully balanced recipe especially to go with Fiano di Avellino, an Italian wine with filbert nuances. It's a lovely, easy recipe whose use shouldn't be restricted by availability of a particular wine. Sarvis suggests substituting a Riesling from either California or Alsace if you can't find Fiano di Avellino. In that case use almonds rather than filberts and 3 tablespoons chopped watercress in place of the parsley.

- **½ cup chopped toasted filberts (hazelnuts)**
- **4 boned and skinned chicken breasts (about 1½ pounds total)**
- **Salt and pepper**
- **3 tablespoons butter**
- **½ cup Fiano di Avellino**
- **1 cup heavy cream**
- **1 teaspoon lemon juice**
- **1½ tablespoons minced parsley**

**PREPARATION:** Toast the filberts in a 325°F. oven until golden and fragrant, 10 to 15 minutes. Cool, rub off loose skin, and chop.

Put each chicken breast between 2 sheets of waxed paper and pound lightly until ⅝-inch thick. Season with salt and pepper.

**COOKING:** In a large heavy frying pan heat butter over medium heat until it bubbles. Add chicken breasts and sauté until golden on both sides, about 8 minutes in all. Transfer to warm plates.

Add wine to pan drippings and cook over high heat, stirring, until reduced to 2 tablespoons. Add cream and cook, stirring, until slightly thickened. Stir in lemon juice and season with salt and pepper.

**SERVING:** Pour sauce over chicken and sprinkle with nuts and parsley.

YIELD: 4 servings

# SAUTÉED CHICKEN WITH ROASTED GARLIC AND CANDIED LEMON ZEST

This recipe was developed by innovative Michael Roberts, chef/owner of Trumps in West Hollywood, California. We've suggested simply quartering the chickens, but for a slightly fancier presentation you might like to bone the quartered chickens as they do at Trumps: Remove the breastbones, leaving the unboned wing attached, and bone each thigh, leaving the meat attached to the unboned drumstick.

CANDIED LEMON ZEST

**1 large lemon**
**½ cup sugar**

**1 large head garlic**
**2 small chickens**
**3 tablespoons olive oil**
**1⅓ cups Chicken Stock (page 49)**
**3 tablespoons lemon juice**

**PREPARATION:** FOR THE CANDIED LEMON ZEST: Remove zest from lemon in very thin strips with a citrus zester or remove zest in wider strips with a sharp paring knife and then cut crosswise into thin shreds. Put zest in a small saucepan with 1 cup water and sugar. Simmer over medium heat, stirring until sugar dissolves and zest is translucent, about 5 minutes. Remove zest from syrup with a slotted spoon and reserve.

Separate the garlic into cloves but don't peel. Quarter the chickens.

**COOKING:** Heat oven to 450°F. In a large ovenproof frying pan or flameproof casserole heat olive oil. Add garlic and chickens. Use 2 pans if necessary so that the chicken isn't crowded. Brown chicken and garlic over medium heat, 10 to 12 minutes.

Add stock and lemon juice and bring to a boil. Transfer to preheated oven and bake, uncovered, for 5 minutes. Remove breast pieces. Bake leg pieces until just done, 7 to 10 minutes. Remove leg pieces.

Reduce liquid over high heat until it is thick enough to coat the back of a spoon, 3 to 5 minutes.

**SERVING:** Arrange chicken on serving plate, pour sauce and garlic cloves over it, and top with candied lemon zest.

**YIELD:** 4 servings

## CHICKEN MOLE

This Mexican favorite is best made at least 1 day ahead to give it time to mellow before serving.

- **1 onion**
- **2 tomatoes *or* ½ cup canned tomatoes**
- **2 jalapeños *or* other hot chili peppers**
- **1 tablespoon cornstarch**
- **2 tablespoons red wine**
- **¼–½ ounce unsweetened chocolate**
- **½ teaspoon coriander seeds**
- **2 cloves garlic**
- **¼ teaspoon aniseed**
- **Pinch ground cinnamon**
- **Pinch ground cloves**
- **Salt and pepper**
- **1–2 tablespoons oil**
- **8 boned chicken thighs (about 1½ pounds total)**
- **1½ cups Chicken Stock (page 49)**

**PREPARATION:** Chop the onion. Peel, seed, and chop the tomatoes or seed and chop the canned tomatoes. Cut the chilies in half lengthwise, remove membranes and seeds, and keep the seeds. Dissolve the cornstarch in the red wine. Grate the chocolate.

In a dry heavy frying pan toast seeds from chilies with

coriander seeds and unpeeled garlic over medium heat, shaking pan frequently, for 3 minutes. Add aniseed and cook 2 minutes. Remove garlic, peel, and crush it with the side of a knife. Crush the toasted spices, garlic, cinnamon, cloves, ¼ teaspoon salt, and ¼ teaspoon pepper to a paste.

Add 2 teaspoons oil to the pan and fry chilies over medium heat, stirring constantly, until they begin to brown, 2 to 3 minutes. Leave the oil in the pan and put chilies in a small bowl and cover with warm water.

Cook onion in chili-flavored oil over low heat until it is soft and begins to brown, 8 to 10 minutes. Add spice paste. Drain and chop chilies and add them to the pan with tomatoes. Cook over medium-low heat until almost all moisture evaporates, 5 to 10 minutes. Remove mixture from pan and set aside.

Raise heat and add enough oil to coat the bottom of the pan. Add chicken pieces in a single, uncrowded layer. Brown well on both sides in 2 batches if necessary. Pour off fat, add tomato mixture and stock, and stir to mix. Cover and simmer until chicken is tender, about 30 minutes. Degrease and stir in cornstarch mixture and chocolate to taste. Simmer over medium heat, stirring, until slightly thickened, about 2 minutes. Refrigerate 8 hours or longer to develop flavor.

**SERVING:** Reheat and serve.

YIELD: 4 servings

# Roasted Chicken with Sausage and Grape Stuffing

This recipe uses our favorite method for ensuring a moist roasted chicken: Spread butter between the skin and the meat before cooking. The delicious and unusual stuffing is excellent with Cornish game hens, too.

Sausage and Grape Stuffing

**3 slices firm white bread**
**1 small bunch seedless green *or* red grapes**
**6 ounces pork sausage**
**½ teaspoon dried thyme**
**¼ cup heavy cream**
**Salt and pepper**

**4-pound chicken**
**6 tablespoons softened butter**

**PREPARATION:** FOR THE STUFFING: Toast the bread and cut into ½-inch cubes. Halve the grapes. You should have 1½ cups. Remove the sausage from its casing and sauté meat in a frying pan over medium heat until it just loses its pink color and is cooked through, about 10 minutes. Drain and add the thyme. Cool slightly. Add bread cubes and grapes. Mix in cream. Season to taste with salt and pepper.

**COOKING:** Heat oven to 350°F. Loosen the skin of the chicken breast beginning at the neck end and being careful not to tear the skin. Spread the butter over the breast with your hand or a small spatula. Replace skin over breast, stuff cavity, and truss. Roast in preheated oven until thermometer reads 180°F., about 1 hour and 10 minutes. To test without a thermometer, poke the inner thigh with a fork. The first juices should run clear, and the last drops should be slightly pink.

**YIELD:** 4 servings

## GRAPES

Thompson seedless grapes remain the favorite U.S. grape by far, but there are at least a dozen or so major varieties appearing in the marketplace. The three main grape categories are green (or white), red, and blue/black. The *Perlette Seedless* are the first to appear. In season from May through July, they are round, fairly small, and greenish-white, with a very sweet taste and inviting crunchiness. The familiar *Thompson Seedless* grapes, larger and light green in color, come onto the market slightly later, in June, and their season extends through November. A notable green grape with seeds is the green-gold *Italia*, a type of Muscatel grape available from August through October; it is especially full-flavored. *Calamerias* have become a common choice in the winter months, from October through February. These large, elongated greenish-gold berries have a mild, sweet taste.

Most of the red grapes available do have seeds, but a few new seedless varieties have recently appeared and are becoming very popular. Most flavorful is the *Flame Seedless*, with light red, round berries and a crisp, tart taste. They are in season from mid-June through mid-September. *Ruby*

*Seedless* grapes are available from August through January, but their dark red berries tend to be less flavorful than the Flames. The *Tokay, Queen* and *Emperor* are the most commonly available red grapes. The Emperor is the best known; available from August through the winter months, it often turns up in a holiday centerpiece—and since it has less flavor than the other red grapes that may be the best place for it. Better choices are the large, crunchy, sweet Tokays, available from August through November, or the Queens, large, pretty berries, that have a mild, sweet flavor but that are in season only during August and September.

Just about all the blue/black grapes have seeds. The two types most likely to show up at the produce stand are the early *Exotic* and the ever-popular *Ribier.* The Exotic, in season from June into August, has impressive, large, almost black berries but less flavor than the Ribier. Ribier grapes are available from August through February, and their blue-black berries are delicious.

No matter what the type, look for grapes that still have their bloom, that hazy film that rubs off easily. It's an indication of freshness. Store grapes in the refrigerator, and rinse them in cold water just before using.

# PENNSYLVANIA-DUTCH CHICKEN WITH DUMPLINGS

This version of old-fashioned chicken and dumplings comes from food historian Joan Nathan, courtesy of the Boyerstown, Pennsylvania Historical Society.

**2 4-pound chickens**
**1 onion**
**6 carrots**
**Salt**
**6 peppercorns *or* ground black pepper**
**6 potatoes**

DUMPLINGS

**1 egg**
**½ cup milk**
**2 cups flour**
**4 teaspoons baking powder**
**½ teaspoon salt**
**3 tablespoons butter**

**PREPARATION:** Cut each chicken into 8 pieces. Chop the onion. Cut the carrots in half.

**COOKING:** Put chicken in water to cover in a large saucepan, bring to a boil, and skim the froth. Add 1 tablespoon salt, peppercorns or black pepper, and onion. Cover, reduce heat, and simmer 30 minutes. Peel and halve potatoes.

FOR THE DUMPLINGS: Combine egg and milk in a bowl. In another bowl combine flour, baking powder, and salt. Cut in butter until it resembles coarse meal. Stir in egg/milk mixture.

Add carrots and potatoes to chicken. Add water to cover if needed and adjust seasoning. Drop dumpling mixture by tablespoons into the pot, replace lid, and simmer 30 minutes. Do not remove lid until done. If possible, use a glass lid so that you can observe simmering process without uncovering. Do not boil or dumplings will fall apart.

**SERVING:** Serve chicken, vegetables, and dumplings in large bowls with some of the broth poured over each serving.

**YIELD:** 6 to 8 servings

## ROAST CAPON WITH CORNBREAD, BACON, AND PECAN STUFFING

We guarantee you won't go wrong using this Southern-accented recipe for a holiday dinner.

### CORNBREAD, BACON, AND PECAN STUFFING

**⅓ cup Chicken Stock (page 49) *or* Capon Stock (recipe follows)**
**2 cups cornbread (recipe follows)**
**1 rib celery**
**1 onion**
**¼ pound bacon**
**1 capon liver, optional**
**⅓ cup chopped pecans**
**2 tablespoons butter**
**½ teaspoon dried thyme**
**½ teaspoon dried sage**
**Salt and pepper**
**¼ cup heavy cream**
**2 tablespoons dry sherry**

**1 tablespoon butter**
**7- to 8-pound capon**
**Salt and pepper**

### SHERRY CREAM SAUCE

**¾ cup dry sherry *or* white wine**
**1½ cups Chicken Stock (page 49) *or* Capon Stock (recipe follows)**
**1½ cups heavy cream**
**Salt and pepper**

**PREPARATION:** Make the stock. You'll need 2 cups in all. Make the cornbread and crumble 2 cups for the stuffing. Chop the celery and onion. Dice the bacon. Mince the liver if using.

Heat oven to 325°F. On a baking sheet toast cornbread and pecans in preheated oven until golden, about 10 minutes. In a heavy frying pan cook bacon over medium-low heat until crisp, about 5 minutes. Transfer bacon with a slotted spoon to a large bowl and pour off all but 2 tablespoons drippings. Add cornbread and pecans to bacon.

Melt butter in the frying pan with bacon drippings. Add celery and onion and cook over medium heat, stirring frequently, until vegetables are tender, about 2 minutes. Stir in optional liver, thyme, sage, and salt and pepper. Add to bowl.

Add cream, ⅓ cup stock, and the sherry to frying pan, stirring with a wooden spoon to deglaze the pan. Add to bowl and season the mixture to taste. Chill until ready to use.

**COOKING:** Heat oven to 400°F. Melt butter for brushing capon. Season cavity of capon with salt and pepper. Stuff and truss. Brush with butter and sprinkle with salt and pepper. Roast capon in preheated oven for 15 minutes and then reduce heat to 350°F. Roast until juices run clear when the inner thigh is pierced and internal temperature of the meaty part of thigh reads 175°F., a total of 2½ to 3 hours. Transfer capon to a warm platter and let rest.

FOR THE SAUCE: Add sherry or wine to roasting pan and bring to a boil, stirring with a wooden spoon to deglaze the pan. Add 1½ cups stock and any juices from capon and boil, stirring often. Add cream and boil until sauce is reduced to about 1¾ cups. Adjust seasonings with salt and pepper and strain sauce.

**SERVING:** Remove stuffing, carve the capon, and pass sherry cream sauce separately.

YIELD: 8 servings

### Cornbread

**1 egg**
**3 tablespoons butter**
**1 cup cornmeal**
**½ cup flour**
**1 cup milk**
**1 tablespoon baking powder**
**½ teaspoon salt**

**PREPARATION:** Heat oven to 400°F. Beat the egg. Melt the butter. Put an 8-inch frying pan or baking pan in the oven. In a large mixing bowl combine cornmeal, flour, milk, egg, 1 tablespoon butter, baking powder, and salt. Beat until smooth.

Put remaining 2 tablespoons butter in heated pan and brush over sides. Pour in batter. Bake on center rack in preheated oven until set and lightly browned, 25 to 30 minutes. Turn cornbread out onto a rack.

### Capon Stock

**1 carrot**
**1 rib celery**
**1 small onion**
**1 clove**
**Neck and giblets (except liver) from capon, above**
**1 quart water**
**½ teaspoon salt**
**⅛ teaspoon black peppercorns**

**PREPARATION:** Cut carrot and celery into 2-inch lengths. Halve onion and stick with clove.

Put all ingredients in a saucepan. Bring to a boil, skim froth, and reduce heat. Simmer, uncovered, until liquid is reduced to 2 cups. Strain stock, cool, and refrigerate until ready to use.

**YIELD:** 2 cups

# BULGUR-STUFFED QUAIL

This is a beautiful and special dish for a small dinner party. The earthiness of bulgur (cracked wheat) complements the dark-meated quail perfectly.

STUFFING

**1 shallot**
**½ clove garlic**
**Salt and coarse pepper**
**3 tablespoons butter**
**¼ cup chopped pecans**
**1 tablespoon chopped rosemary *or* 1 teaspoon dried**
**½ cup bulgur (cracked wheat)**
**1 cup Chicken Stock (page 49)**

**8 quail**
**Salt and pepper**
**2 teaspoons oil**
**Fried rosemary sprigs for garnish, optional**
**1 cup Chicken Stock (page 49)**
**4 tablespoons butter**
**Radicchio and curly endive for serving, optional**

**PREPARATION:** FOR THE STUFFING: Mince the shallot. Mash the garlic with a pinch of salt to a paste. In a saucepan melt the butter. Sauté the shallot, garlic, and pecans until shallot is soft but not colored. Add the rosemary and bulgur. Add the stock and bring to a simmer. Season to taste with salt and pepper, cover, and simmer over medium-low heat for 15 minutes. Remove from heat and let sit, covered, for at least 15 minutes.

**COOKING:** Heat oven to 450°F. Rub the quail inside and out with salt and pepper. Cut off wing tips and reserve with necks. Lightly stuff birds with cool stuffing, about ¼ cup per quail. Truss if desired. Heat oil in a roasting pan over medium-high heat. Put birds into preheated pan. Brown on all sides, about 5 minutes. Remove from heat, move birds to the side, and put wing tips and necks on bottom of the pan to act as a rack. Put the birds on top.

Roast quail until just done, about 10 minutes. If you want to garnish the birds with fried rosemary, heat 1 inch oil in a frying pan to 350°F. Carefully add a few rosemary sprigs with long tongs (oil will splatter). Fry until crisp, about 15 seconds. Drain and season with salt. Remove birds from pan when done and let rest.

Put the roasting pan with necks and wing bones over medium-high heat. Add stock and bring to a simmer. Remove from heat and whisk in butter, a little at a time. The butter should soften and thicken the sauce but not melt completely. Season to taste with salt and pepper. Strain.

**SERVING:** Put birds on a bed of radicchio and curly endive if desired. Pour sauce over quail. Garnish birds with sprigs of fried rosemary if desired.

**YIELD:** 4 servings

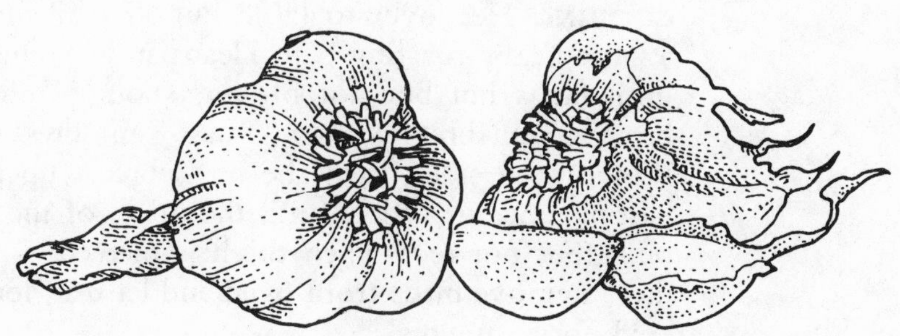

# ROAST QUAIL

A basic recipe for roasting quail successfully that can be varied at will. If you don't like the taste of juniper, leave the berries out. Or replace the lemon wedge and watercress garnish with arugula and cherry tomatoes.

**24 juniper berries**
**1 small onion**
**1 small lemon**
**8 fresh quail**
**Salt and pepper**
**¼ cup olive oil**
**2 tablespoons butter**
**Lemon wedges for garnish**
**Watercress sprigs for garnish**

**PREPARATION:** Toast juniper berries in a dry frying pan over medium heat until crisp, about 3 minutes. Crush berries. Cut onion and lemon into 8 wedges each.

Pat quail dry. Season birds inside and out with salt and pepper. Tuck 3 juniper berries and a wedge of onion and lemon inside each bird. Tuck wing tips underneath; truss securely.

**COOKING:** Heat oven to 450°F. Put olive oil and butter in a large heavy roasting pan. Heat pan in preheated oven until fat is hot but not brown, about 5 minutes. Put birds in pan, breasts down. Roast 8 minutes, turning to brown each side. Turn the birds breast up and roast, basting once or twice, until the juices of the thigh run pink (but not red) when thigh is pierced, 5 to 7 minutes. Remove birds from oven and let rest, loosely covered, for 5 minutes.

**SERVING:** Remove lemon wedges, juniper berries, and onion wedges from the cavity of each bird. Arrange birds on a heated serving plate. Garnish with fresh lemon wedges and sprigs of watercress and serve immediately.

**YIELD:** 4 servings

CHAPTER 7

# MEAT

**SPRING:**

Lamb Loin with Artichoke-Tarragon Sauce and Mushroom-Leek Compote

Sautéed Veal Chops and Fiddlehead Ferns

**SUMMER:**

Grilled Salad of Pork Chops and Vegetables

Grilled Pork Chops with Clams

Grilled Steak with Pepper and Garlic Butter

Lamb with Rosemary Sauce

Grilled Lamb Sausage with Watercress and Warm Potato Salad

Individual Meat Loaves with Blue-Cheese Butter Sauce

Grilled Steak and Potato Salad

**FALL/WINTER:**

Veal Rib Roast

Roast Beef and Winter Squash with Fried Thyme

Lamb Steaks with Pomegranate Pinot Noir Sauce

**ALL SEASON:**

Pork and Carrots Vinaigrette

Cajun Ham and Sausage Jambalaya

Roast Tenderloin of Beef with Shiitake-Mushroom Cream Sauce

Stuffed Loin of Lamb au Jus

SIDEBARS

Garlic

Watercress

Carrots

# SPRING

## Lamb Loin with Artichoke-Tarragon Sauce and Mushroom-Leek Compote

A delicious knock-'em-dead dish from chef Dean Fearing of Mansion on Turtle Creek in Dallas, this recipe is also practical for a dinner party because nearly all the elements can be made ahead of time. At the last moment, just reheat the compote and sauce and cook the boned lamb loin for 10 minutes. If you have the butcher bone the lamb, be sure to get the bones for the stock.

Mushroom-Leek Compote

**1 large leek**
**1 pound mushrooms, such as pleurotte, morel, chanterelle, oyster, *and/or* shiitake**
**1 small bunch chives**
**1 tablespoon peanut oil**
**2 tablespoons Marsala**
**2 tablespoons butter**
**Salt**
**Few drops lemon juice**

Artichoke-Tarragon Sauce

**4 artichokes**
**3 small shallots**
**3 mushrooms**

**2 tablespoons peanut oil**
**1 sprig thyme *or* 1/4 teaspoon dried**
**1 teaspoon cracked black peppercorns**
**3 cups lamb stock, approximately (recipe follows)**
**1 large sprig tarragon *or* 1/4 teaspoon dried**
**1½ cups heavy cream**
**5 spinach leaves**
**Few drops lemon juice**
**Salt**

**2 boneless, trimmed lamb loins (about 1¾ pounds total)**
**Salt and black pepper**
**White pepper, optional**
**Cayenne**
**2 tablespoons peanut oil**

**PREPARATION:** FOR THE COMPOTE: Trim away root and all but 2 inches of green part of leek. Cut the remainder lengthwise into 1/4-inch slices and then at an angle into diamond shapes. Chop the mushrooms into bite-size pieces. Cut the chives into 1½-inch lengths.

In a frying pan heat the oil over medium-low heat. Cook the leek, covered, for 4 minutes. Add mushrooms and cook, uncovered, for 4 minutes, stirring frequently. Add Marsala and scrape bottom of pan with a wooden spoon to deglaze. Add the butter and chives. Season with salt and lemon juice to taste and set aside.

FOR THE SAUCE: Cook the artichokes in boiling salted water until tender, about 30 minutes. Drain, cool, and pull leaves off, saving 8 of the better-looking ones for garnish. Reserve remaining leaves for another use. Use a small spoon to remove fuzzy chokes from artichoke bottoms. Chop the shallots. Slice the mushrooms.

In a saucepan heat the oil over medium heat. Sauté the shallots, mushrooms, thyme and peppercorns for 3 minutes. Add the lamb stock and tarragon and simmer, stirring occasionally, until reduced to 1 cup, 20 to 30 minutes.

Add cream and bring to a boil. Strain into a food processor or blender. Add artichoke bottoms and spinach leaves and blend until smooth. If the sauce is too thick, thin with a little more stock or water. Strain again. Season with lemon juice and salt to taste.

**COOKING:** Heat the oven to 400°F. Season lamb with salt, black pepper, white pepper if desired, and cayenne. In a roasting pan heat the oil over medium-high heat. Sear the lamb loins on all sides for 4 minutes in all. Cook in preheated oven, turning once, until done, about 5 minutes for medium-rare. Transfer lamb to a warm platter to rest. Gently reheat sauce and compote.

**SERVING:** Pour sauce onto 4 warm plates. Slice lamb and overlap pieces in a semicircle in center of each plate. Arrange 2 artichoke leaves behind each semicircle of lamb. Put a small mound of compote in the center of the lamb and serve.

YIELD: 4 servings

## LAMB STOCK

- **1½ pounds lamb bones**
- **1 carrot**
- **1 rib celery**
- **1 onion**
- **2 cloves garlic**
- **¼ cup white wine**
- **2 tablespoons tomato paste**
- **¼ teaspoon dried rosemary**
- **¼ teaspoon dried thyme**
- **2 sprigs parsley**
- **1 bay leaf**
- **¾ teaspoon crushed black peppercorns**

**PREPARATION:** Heat oven to 425°F. Roast bones, stirring and turning occasionally, until they begin to brown, 20 to 30 minutes.

Chop carrot, celery, onion, and garlic. Add to roasting pan and cook, stirring, until browned, 20 to 30 minutes.

Put bones and vegetables into a stockpot. Add wine to roasting pan, scrape bottom with a wooden spoon to deglaze, and add to stockpot along with remaining ingredients. Fill pot with enough water to cover ingredients by 2 inches.

Bring to a boil and reduce heat. Simmer 3 to 4 hours, skimming any froth and fat that rises to the surface. Strain through a sieve lined with cheesecloth.

YIELD: about 1 quart

## Sautéed Veal Chops and Fiddlehead Ferns

Fiddleheads are not really a variety of fern but rather a stage that all ferns go through in the spring. When the stems poke up out of the ground, the leafy tops are tightly furled, resembling a fiddlehead. Not every variety of fern is edible, however; unless you know what you're doing, it's better to get your fiddleheads from the produce market than from the woods. The veal chops and brown butter in this recipe are also delicious with asparagus.

**2 shallots**
**½ pound fiddlehead ferns**
**4 tablespoons butter**
**2 tablespoons oil**
**8 1-inch-thick veal chops**
**Salt and coarse black pepper**

PREPARATION: Cut the shallots in thin slices. Trim fiddleheads.

COOKING: Cook fiddleheads in boiling salted water until tender, about 5 minutes. Drain.

Melt the butter in the same pan over medium-high heat until it smells nutty and begins to turn brown, about 2 minutes. Set aside.

Heat oil in a frying pan over medium heat. Add the shallots and sauté lightly, about 1 minute. Add veal chops and sauté over medium-high heat, turning once, about 4 minutes total.

Put the brown butter over medium-high heat, add the fiddleheads, and toss. Season to taste with salt and coarse pepper and heat through, about 1 minute.

**SERVING:** Serve veal chops with fiddleheads alongside. Pour remaining butter over all.

YIELD: 4 servings

# SUMMER

## GRILLED SALAD OF PORK CHOPS AND VEGETABLES

Perfect for hot weather, this is a complete meal cooked on the grill. It's as delicious as it is colorful.

- **3 tablespoons lime juice**
- **2 teaspoons chopped thyme *or* 1 teaspoon dried**
- **¼ cup peanut oil**
- **2 tablespoons olive oil**
- **Salt and pepper**
- **4 thin pork chops**
- **1 green pepper**
- **1 yellow pepper**
- **2 tomatoes**
- **2 baking potatoes**
- **8 scallions**

**PREPARATION:** In a shallow dish combine lime juice, thyme, oils, and salt and pepper to taste. Add pork chops and turn to coat completely. Let stand at room temperature for about 15 minutes, turning 2 to 3 times. Quarter and seed peppers. Halve tomatoes horizontally and seed. Cut unpeeled potatoes lengthwise into ¼-inch slices.

**COOKING:** Heat grill. Drain chops, reserving marinade, and put on hottest part of grill to sear. Cook meat until it just loses its pink color, turning once and basting frequently, about 8 minutes total.

Brush both sides of potato slices and peppers with reserved marinade and put them on the grill rack. Grill until tender and slightly charred, turning once and basting frequently, about 6 minutes total.

Brush tomato halves and scallions with marinade and grill until tender and slightly charred, turning once and basting frequently, about 3 minutes in all. Season meat and vegetables to taste with salt and pepper.

**SERVING:** Arrange pork chops and vegetables on warm plates. Serve immediately.

**YIELD:** 4 servings

## GRILLED PORK CHOPS WITH CLAMS

This variation on the wonderful Portuguese combination of pork and clams was developed by Jasper White, chef/owner of the highly respected Restaurant Jasper in Boston. He recommends that the pork chops be grilled only to medium-rare or at most medium, and we agree that this is when pork is at its juicy best. Experts now know that an internal temperature of 137°F. kills trichinae. If you prefer well-done pork by all means cook it longer.

- **½ pound pork bones and scraps, approximately, optional**
- **2 onions**
- **2 cups Chicken Stock (page 49)**
- **6 whole allspice berries**
- **5 cloves garlic**
- **4 1-inch-thick pork rib chops (about 2½ pounds total)**
- **¼ cup olive oil, approximately**

**Salt and pepper**
**4 bay leaves**
**24 littleneck clams**
**Pinch red-pepper flakes, optional**
**2 tablespoons chopped flat-leaf parsley**

**PREPARATION:** Heat oven to 425°F. Brown bones and scraps, if using, in a roasting pan in preheated oven, turning occasionally, about 25 minutes. Quarter 1 onion and add it to the bones. Cook until bones and onion are browned, about 15 minutes. Transfer to a pot. Add ½ cup water to roasting pan, stirring with a wooden spoon to deglaze. Pour over bones and add stock. Bring to a boil and skim the froth. Reduce heat to a very slow simmer. Add allspice and cook until reduced to 1 cup, about 25 minutes. Add 1 cup water and reduce again to 1 cup, about 15 minutes. Strain and discard solids. If you're not using the bones, simply simmer the stock with the onion and allspice until reduced to 1 cup.

Cut garlic into thin slices. Chop remaining onion.

**COOKING:** Heat grill. Rub the pork chops with a little olive oil and season with salt and pepper. Grill until medium-rare to medium, about 13 minutes total.

In a large pot brown bay leaves in remaining olive oil over medium heat. Discard bay leaves and turn the heat to high. Add garlic and chopped onion and cook, stirring, until lightly browned, about 1 minute. Add stock and clams, cover, and boil until clams open, about 4 minutes.

**SERVING:** Arrange clams around each pork chop on warm plates. Season the stock with salt and pepper to taste and red-pepper flakes if desired. Add parsley to stock and spoon over clams and pork.

**YIELD:** 4 servings

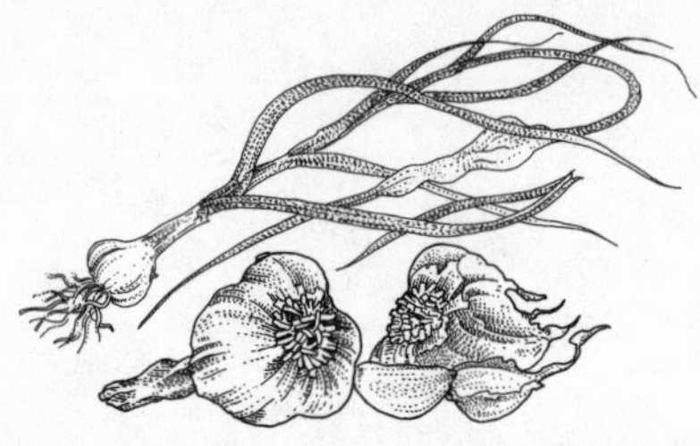

## GARLIC

"El ajo es lo que nos deja vivir," a Spanish woman we know avers. "Garlic is what lets us live." In the Mediterranean and anywhere in the world where Mediterraneans have settled, garlic is a staple, not an occasional condiment. This pungent member of the lily family varies considerably in flavor and quality depending on where it is grown, how it is cured, how long it is kept after harvest, and how it is cooked.

Garlic falls into a couple of general types—white and red. White-skinned garlic can be used interchangeably with the slightly more pungent red- or purple-skinned type. Elephant garlic, so-named because its heads are four to five inches in diameter, has a mild garlic flavor but is actually a different species.

Right after it is picked in early summer and for a short time afterwards, garlic's flavor is at its most delicate. The traditional raw-garlic mayonnaise sauces, aioli and rouille, or pesto make the most of young cloves; they are also good sautéed or gently stewed and eaten as a vegetable. As garlic ages, the flavor becomes

# GRILLED STEAK WITH PEPPER AND GARLIC BUTTER

Developed by Ken Schloss, chef of Main Street Bar & Grill and Washington Street Restaurant & Bar in Yountville, California, this recipe is simplicity itself. The red-pepper and garlic butter can be made well ahead of time. Use whatever cut of steak you like best.

PEPPER AND GARLIC BUTTER

- **¼ pound butter**
- **1 red pepper**
- **2 cloves garlic**
- **1 tablespoon chopped parsley**
- **Salt and pepper**

- **4 ¾-pound steaks**
- **Salt and pepper**

**PREPARATION:** FOR THE PEPPER AND GARLIC BUTTER: Bring butter to room temperature or soften in a microwave. Grill or broil red pepper until skin is charred. Peel, seed, and chop pepper. Mince garlic. Combine all butter ingredients.

**COOKING:** Heat grill. Season both sides of steaks with salt and pepper. Grill 4 inches from heat source, turning once, about 8 minutes total for medium-rare.

**SERVING:** Put steak on plates and top with a dollop of pepper and garlic butter.

**YIELD:** 4 servings

# Lamb with Rosemary Sauce

Rosemary is the traditional lamb herb, but if you particularly like another herb, such as thyme or tarragon, feel free to substitute. The lamb loin in this recipe is boned, trimmed, cut into medallions, and then gently pounded. The butcher can do all of this, but do request the bones so that you can make the stock for the sauce. This dish is delicious with pasta tossed with butter and the same herb used in the sauce or with roasted potatoes seasoned with the same herb and coarse salt.

**2 cups Lamb Stock (page 156)**
**3 tablespoons chopped rosemary *or* 1 tablespoon dried**
**2 boneless, trimmed lamb loins (about 1¾ pounds total)**
**1 to 2 tablespoons olive oil**
**Salt and pepper**
**5 tablespoons butter**

**PREPARATION:** Make the stock. Add 2 tablespoons fresh or 1 tablespoon dried rosemary to stock and cook over medium heat until reduced to ½ cup. Strain. Cut the lamb into ¼-inch-thick medallions and pound to flatten slightly.

**COOKING:** In a frying pan heat 1 tablespoon of oil over medium-high heat. Season lamb medallions with salt and pepper and sear them in batches for 1 minute on each side. Add more oil if needed. Transfer to warm serving plates.

Pour off any fat, add stock to pan, and scrape bottom with a wooden spoon to deglaze. Stir in remaining 1 tablespoon fresh rosemary leaves if using. Turn off heat and whisk in butter, bit by bit, until mixture thickens slightly. Butter should not melt completely but just soften to form a creamy sauce. Season sauce with salt and pepper to taste.

**SERVING:** Pour sauce around lamb and serve immediately.

**YIELD:** 4 servings

sharper and more lingering, and many cooks feel the garlic is better slowly and thoroughly cooked. Immature garlic is delicious, too, harvested when the bulb just begins to swell—bigger than a scallion but before the cloves begin to form.

Whatever the season, mashing, pounding, or puréeing will release the maximum amount of garlic's potent juices. To purée a clove, first peel it—easily accomplished by smashing the clove with the flat side of a knife so that the skin will slip off. Or, to peel many cloves quickly, drop them briefly into boiling water to loosen the skins. Chop the garlic, sprinkle with a little coarse salt, and mash with the flat side of the knife. Used raw, the purée will have the strong flavor that popular culture credits with scaring away vampires (or possibly your date). Minced it is still strong but not so potent.

Roasted whole cloves, on the other hand, are quite another thing—the cloves become mellow and nutty. Roast the cloves unpeeled and then squeeze the softened garlic out of its skin to use as a spread or to stir into a soup.

Choose heads that are firm and dry and show no green sprouts. If you do discover green sprouts in the center of the cloves, cut them out; they will be bitter. Store garlic in a dark, cool, well-ventilated place if possible. If not, the refrigerator will do.

# GRILLED LAMB SAUSAGE WITH WATERCRESS AND WARM POTATO SALAD

Sausage is so simple—just a matter of grinding meat and seasoning it—that it's a shame home cooks don't make it more often. Try this recipe from Alfred Portale of The Gotham Bar & Grill in New York City, and you'll be convinced sausage making is worthwhile. Though grilled meat and potato salad are summer treats, the ingredients for this dish are available year-round, and you can always sauté the sausages rather than grilling them. In the winter, this would make an interesting first course. Just cut all quantities in half.

LAMB SAUSAGE

**1¼ pounds boneless lamb shoulder, well chilled**
**1 pound fatty pork shoulder, well chilled**
**¼ teaspoon chopped rosemary *or* pinch dried**
**¼ teaspoon chopped thyme *or* pinch dried**
**1¼ teaspoons chopped sage *or* pinch dried**
**2 tablespoons chopped flat-leaf parsley**
**½ small clove garlic**
**Salt and white pepper**
**¼ teaspoon sugar**
**Pork casings, optional**

**3 shallots**
**3 tablespoons chopped flat-leaf parsley**
**1 red pepper**
**1 yellow pepper**
**1 bunch watercress**
**8 small red potatoes**
**2 tablespoons red-wine vinegar**
**Salt and pepper**
**½ cup virgin olive oil**

**PREPARATION:** FOR THE SAUSAGE: Grind the meats together once using the medium plate on a grinder. Or hand chop with a heavy knife. Mince herbs and garlic

## WATERCRESS

Appropriately named, watercress requires a lot of water to thrive. The wild plant is found along streams or in marshy wetlands, where you can help yourself if you are certain that the water is unpolluted.

The watercress sold in most markets is cultivated, with leaves slightly larger than those of the wild variety. It is available all year, though perhaps a bit easier to find from late spring through the fall.

Watercress's spicy bite makes it the perfect accompaniment to lamb and other meats or poultry, whether as a garnish or instead of lettuce in a sandwich. Of course, more delicate sandwiches of watercress, butter, and crustless white bread epitomize English tea. Watercress also is delicious in salads by itself, tossed with milder greens, or as a refreshing contrast to the sweetness of fruits such as oranges and pears.

Watercress is extremely perishable; it's usually not even worth looking at if your greengrocer hasn't kept it standing in water. It's best to use watercress almost immediately. If it's in very good condition, it can be wrapped in damp paper towels, slipped into a plastic bag, and refrigerated for a day or two.

and add to meat with 2½ teaspoons salt, ½ teaspoon white pepper, and sugar.

To taste for seasoning, form a small patty and cook until it just loses its pink color. Taste and adjust seasoning. Stuff sausage meat into rinsed pork casings using a sausage stuffer and tie into links. Or form by hand into patties.

Cut the shallots into very thin slices. Cut peppers into fine dice. Cut large stems from the watercress.

**COOKING:** Heat the grill. In a saucepan of boiling salted water cook the potatoes until tender, 20 to 25 minutes. Drain and set aside until cool enough to handle. In a small bowl whisk together the vinegar and salt. Whisk in oil. While potatoes are still warm, slice and put into a large bowl. Sprinkle potatoes with shallots, parsley, and peppers. Pour enough vinaigrette over to moisten well, reserving some to dress the watercress. Adjust seasoning with salt and pepper if necessary. Cover to keep warm.

Cook patties or sausages on the grill until they just lose their pink color, about 8 minutes.

**SERVING:** Toss watercress with reserved vinaigrette. On individual plates, arrange sausages on either side of the potato salad and garnish with the watercress.

**YIELD:** 4 servings

# INDIVIDUAL MEAT LOAVES WITH BLUE-CHEESE BUTTER SAUCE

Transform these individual meat loaves into a year-round dish by sautéing rather than grilling. Served on toast, these patties are a cross between meat loaf and cheeseburgers. They take less than half an hour to make and are a great family supper.

MEAT LOAVES

**1 egg**
**¾ pound ground chuck**
**½ pound ground pork**
**½ pound ground veal**
**Salt and coarse black pepper**
**¼ cup fine fresh bread crumbs**
**½ teaspoon minced chives**

BLUE-CHEESE BUTTER SAUCE

**3 tablespoons butter**
**2 tablespoons soft blue cheese**
**¼ teaspoon minced chives**

**4 ½-inch slices Italian *or* French bread**

**PREPARATION:** Beat egg lightly. In a mixing bowl lightly but thoroughly combine chuck, pork, veal, 1 teaspoon salt, ½ teaspoon pepper, bread crumbs, egg, and chives. Gently form into four 1-inch-thick patties.

FOR THE SAUCE: In a small saucepan combine butter, cheese, and chives.

**COOKING:** Heat grill. Cook patties on preheated grill until brown and crisp but still slightly pink inside, about 7 minutes per side.

Near end of grilling, set saucepan with sauce ingredients at edge of grill so butter and cheese will melt. Toast bread at the edge of the grill.

**SERVING:** Brush toasted bread with a small amount of sauce, top with a patty, and pour remaining sauce over all.

**YIELD:** 4 servings

## Grilled Steak and Potato Salad

At Michael Stuart's in Chicago, chef Jon Lindsay serves this salad as a first course. Double the quantities to serve four as a main-dish summer salad. Since it's served at room temperature, it can be made in advance.

Steak Marinade

**1½ teaspoons dry mustard**
**1 tablespoon Worcestershire sauce**
**1 tablespoon soy sauce**
**¼ cup olive oil**

**¾ pound flank steak**
**1 pound baking potatoes**
**1 head Bibb lettuce**
**1 large scallion**
**1 small red pepper**
**1 small green pepper**
**1 small red onion**
**1 large rib celery**
**1 tomato**
**Salt and pepper**

**PREPARATION:** FOR THE MARINADE: Whisk mustard into Worcestershire sauce and add soy sauce and oil.

Pour marinade over steak in a nonreactive container, turn to coat, and marinate at least 1 hour. Meanwhile, peel potatoes, cut in quarters, and put in a pot with cold salted water to cover. Cover and bring to a boil. Uncover, lower heat, and simmer until done, about 25 minutes. Drain and cool.

Heat grill. Drain steak, reserving marinade, and grill to medium-rare, turning once, about 10 minutes total. Remove steak from grill and cool to room temperature.

Wash and dry the lettuce. Cut scallion into thin slices. Cut peppers, onion, and celery into ¼-inch pieces and put in a mixing bowl. Peel and seed tomato, cut into ¼-inch dice, and add to bowl.

Cut potatoes and steak into ½-inch cubes and add to bowl with reserved marinade. Season with salt and pepper to taste and toss.

**SERVING:** Arrange a bed of lettuce on each plate and mound salad on top. Garnish with sliced scallion.

**YIELD:** 4 servings

# FALL / WINTER

## VEAL RIB ROAST

For a special dinner, nothing is easier than a roast with a vegetable garnish browned in the same pan. Although expensive, veal rib roast is a delectable treat. To make it easier to slice, have your butcher cut just through the chine bone (the bone to which the ribs connect) or remove the chine bone entirely. We're willing to bet you'll love rutabaga cooked in this way, but if you'd rather, try sweet or baking potatoes, celery, or onions.

**1 rutabaga (about 1 pound)**
**1 3½-pound veal rib roast**
**Salt and pepper**

PREPARATION: Peel rutabaga and cut into ½-inch dice.

COOKING: Season the roast generously with salt and pepper. Heat oven to 500°F. Put roast in a large roasting pan, add the rutabaga, and sear in preheated oven for 15 minutes. Lower heat to 350°F. and roast until internal temperature is 130°F. for a pink roast, about 40 minutes (about 16 minutes per pound). Let roast rest for 20 minutes.

SERVING: Cut the roast into chops. Serve roasted rutabaga on the side.

YIELD: 4 servings

# ROAST BEEF AND WINTER SQUASH WITH FRIED THYME

Here mouth-watering prime rib is roasted with potatoes and sweet squash, drizzled with browned butter, and garnished with fried thyme sprigs. We think roasts are generally tastier and juicier cooked on the bone, but a beef rib roast is such a nuisance to carve that we recommend cutting it free from the bones and then tying it back on. The convenience is worth the slight compromise, and it can be done by the butcher.

**1 4½-pound beef rib roast**
**½ pound butter**
**Coarse salt and pepper**
**2 pounds sweet dumpling squash**
**3 cloves garlic**
**2 pounds boiling potatoes**
**5 teaspoons chopped thyme *or* 2 teaspoons dried**
**Oil for frying thyme sprigs**
**8 large thyme sprigs**

**PREPARATION:** Bone and trim rib roast and tie bones back on. Or have your butcher prepare the roast in this way.

Melt butter over medium heat until it sizzles, turns brown, and smells nutty. Season to taste and set aside. Cut squash in half and remove seeds. Peel and cut into ½-inch dice. Mince the garlic.

**COOKING:** Heat oven to 500°F. Season beef well with salt and pepper. Put in a large roasting pan and sear in preheated oven for 20 minutes. Without opening oven, lower heat to 350°F. and roast 12 minutes per pound.

Cut unpeeled potatoes into ¼-inch slices. Season with salt and pepper. Thirty minutes before roast is done, remove and pour off fat. Arrange potatoes and squash around beef, return to oven, and roast until internal temperature of beef is 125°F., stirring potatoes and squash occasionally.

Remove roast from oven and transfer to a warm platter. Set aside to rest for 15 minutes. Raise oven temperature to 500°F.

Degrease potatoes and squash and add garlic and chopped thyme. Check seasoning. Return pan to oven until potatoes are golden and squash is soft, stirring periodically with a wooden spoon, 5 to 10 minutes.

In a frying pan heat 1 inch oil to 350°F. Carefully add a few thyme sprigs with long tongs (fat will spatter). Do not crowd. Fry until crisp, about 15 seconds. Drain.

Reheat browned butter.

**SERVING:** Cut strings from roast, pull away bones, and carve meat into thin slices. Arrange potatoes and squash around beef and garnish with herb sprigs. Drizzle browned butter over meat and serve immediately.

**YIELD:** 8 servings

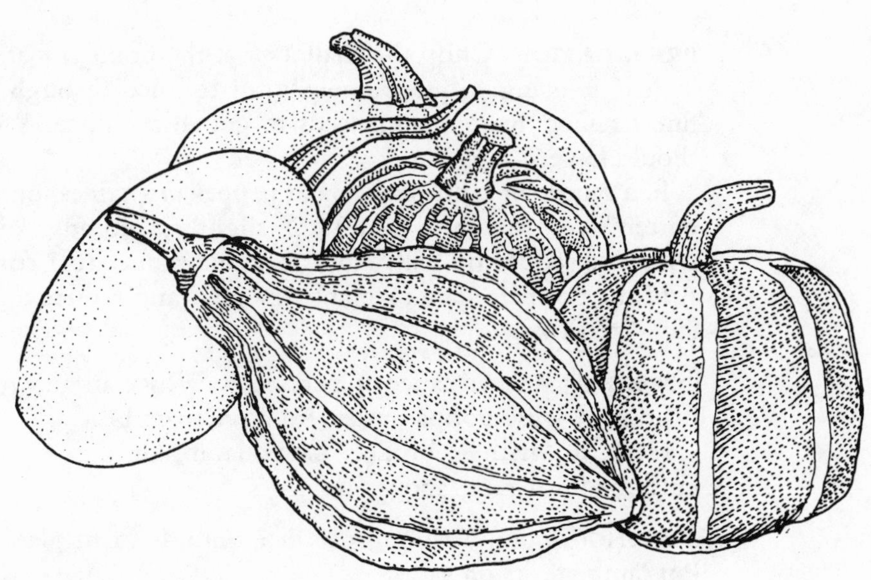

# LAMB STEAKS WITH POMEGRANATE PINOT NOIR SAUCE

The deep-red sauce in this dish, developed by Alan Kantor and Josh Latkin of Salmon Point Restaurant in Albion, California, is a wonderful use for pomegranates. We find, however, that you can get a very similar sauce with the tart flavor and brilliant color of cranberry juice. If you want to make the stock for the sauce, be sure to ask the butcher for bones.

- **1 small shallot**
- **3 pomegranates *or* 2 cups cranberry juice**
- **1 teaspoon cracked black pepper**
- **8 tablespoons butter**
- **1 cup Pinot Noir *or* other red wine**
- **1 quart Lamb Stock (page 156) *or* Chicken Stock (page 49)**
- **4 8-ounce boneless lamb steaks**

**PREPARATION:** Chop the shallot. Cut the pomegranates in half if using. Squeeze pomegranate juice through a fine strainer, pressing the seeds to get all the juice. You should have 2 cups.

In a saucepan sauté shallot and pepper in 4 tablespoons butter over medium heat until slightly colored. Add wine and reduce by half. Add stock and reduce to 1 cup. Add the pomegranate or cranberry juice and reduce to 1 cup. Strain sauce.

**COOKING:** Reheat sauce if necessary. Whisk in the remaining 4 tablespoons butter. Remove from heat.

Heat the grill or broiler. Cook lamb, turning once, until medium-rare, about 6 minutes.

**SERVING:** Spoon a ribbon of sauce onto 4 warm plates. Put lamb steaks on sauce.

**YIELD:** 4 servings

# ALL SEASON

## Pork and Carrots Vinaigrette

Pork is seldom used in salads but is delicious that way. Rather than starting with fresh pork chops, you could use leftover pork roast, beef, lamb, or veal.

- **2½ pounds pork chops**
- **Salt and pepper**
- **6 tablespoons corn oil**
- **2 carrots**
- **4 large shallots**
- **2 tablespoons red-wine vinegar**
- **⅓ cup minced parsley**

**PREPARATION:** Season pork with salt and pepper. Heat 2 tablespoons oil in a large frying pan over high heat until very hot. Add pork chops and cook, turning once, until just done, about 10 minutes total, depending on thickness. Remove the pork chops and set the pan aside.

Slice the carrots and cook in boiling salted water until tender, about 10 minutes. Drain and put in a large bowl.

Cut the shallots into thin slices. Add ½ of the shallots to the reserved frying pan and cooked over medium heat until soft, about 5 minutes. Add the vinegar, stirring with a wooden spoon to deglaze pan. Put cooked shallots and pan juices in the large bowl.

Remove the pork meat from the bones, trim, and cut

### CARROTS

Carrots are so inexpensive and so abundant that they lack glamour. Many cooks relegate them to the stockpot and other supporting roles. Good carrots are, however, both aromatic and naturally sweet. Bad ones are bitter and uninteresting. To get the best, choose the thinnest you can find and bend one to make sure that it is crisp rather than rubbery. Exceptionally large or tough carrots may require removing the woody core.

You may have wondered if carrots sold with greens attached, like the ones Bugs Bunny always munched, are better than their topless counterparts. The greens do indicate the state of the carrots. If the foliage is crisp and deep green, the carrots are fresh. The greens, however, draw moisture from the roots, and carrots with tops begin to wilt (and lose nutrients, too) after a week or so even under the best conditions. Topless ones remain fresh much longer. So buy carrots with fresh-looking greens attached if possible and cut the tops off as soon as you get home.

into bite-size cubes. Add the meat and its juices to the large bowl. Add parsley and raw shallots. Toss salad with remaining 4 tablespoons oil. Season to taste with salt and pepper. Refrigerate if making ahead.

**SERVING:** Serve at room temperature or slightly chilled.

**YIELD:** 4 servings

## CAJUN HAM AND SAUSAGE JAMBALAYA

This spicy jambalaya includes not only ham and sausage but chicken and beef as well. It is equally delicious reheated the second day.

- **2 onions**
- **1 rib celery**
- **3 cloves garlic**
- **1 tomato, fresh *or* canned**
- **½ pound boned chicken breasts**
- **½ pound top-round steak**
- **Salt and pepper**
- **½ teaspoon cayenne**
- **½ teaspoon paprika**
- **¾ pound cooked ham**
- **½ pound smoked sausage, such as kielbasa**
- **3 tablespoons vegetable shortening *or* lard**
- **1 cup uncooked long-grain rice**
- **1½ cups Chicken Stock (page 49), approximately**
- **6 scallions**
- **¼ cup minced parsley**

**PREPARATION:** Chop onions and celery. Mince garlic. Peel and dice tomato. Cut chicken breasts into ¾-inch chunks. Trim steak and cut into ¾-inch chunks.

In a bowl combine ½ teaspoon salt, ½ teaspoon black pepper, cayenne, and paprika. Coat chicken and beef with this mixture. Dice ham. Cut sausage into thin slices.

**COOKING:** In a large heavy pot with a tight-fitting lid heat shortening until it begins to smoke. Add chicken and beef and sear on medium heat until all sides are golden, about 3 minutes. Remove chicken and beef and set aside, reserving fat. Lower heat to medium. Add onions, celery, and garlic and sauté until vegetables are soft, about 2 minutes. Add tomato and stir to blend. Add rice and cook until it is light golden, about 2 minutes. Add stock, chicken and beef, sausage, and ham. Bring to a full boil, stirring. Lower heat, cover, and cook over low heat for 30 minutes.

Meanwhile, chop scallions. Check rice for tenderness. If mixture seems too dry but rice is not yet tender, add more stock or water, cover, and continue to cook.

**SERVING:** When rice is done, season to taste with salt and pepper. Add scallions and parsley, toss lightly to combine, and serve.

**YIELD:** 4 servings

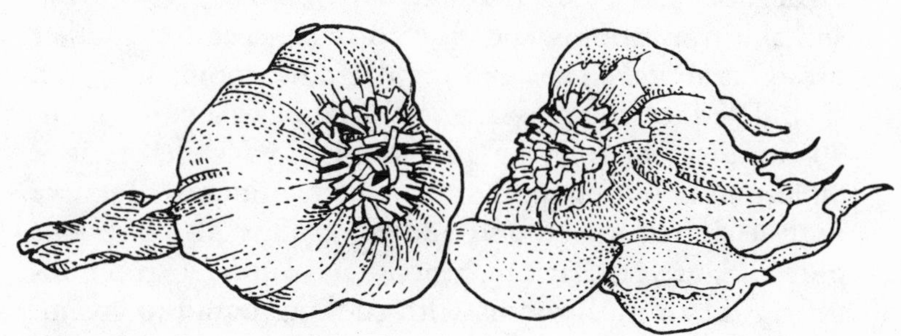

# ROAST TENDERLOIN OF BEEF WITH SHIITAKE-MUSHROOM CREAM SAUCE

A simple roast with a special do-ahead sauce—this is an ideal dinner party dish. The sauce can be varied with other mushrooms if you like.

SHIITAKE-MUSHROOM CREAM SAUCE

- **½ pound shiitake mushrooms**
- **½ pound regular mushrooms**
- **4 cups heavy cream**
- **4 tablespoons butter**
- **3 tablespoons oyster sauce**
- **2 teaspoons balsamic vinegar**
- **Salt and pepper**

- **1 clove garlic**
- **1 tenderloin of beef (about 3½ pounds)**
- **1 tablespoon sesame oil**
- **2 tablespoons soy sauce**

**PREPARATION:** FOR THE SAUCE: Remove stems from shiitake mushrooms and discard or reserve for another use. Cut shiitake caps and regular mushrooms into thin slices. Reduce cream over medium heat to 2 cups, about 30 minutes. In a frying pan sauté sliced shiitakes in 2 tablespoons butter until soft, 5 to 6 minutes. Remove with a slotted spoon and add remaining 2 tablespoons butter. Sauté regular mushrooms until soft, 4 to 5 minutes. Add all mushrooms with cooking liquid to cream. Add oyster sauce and vinegar and season to taste with salt and pepper.

Mash garlic. Trim and tie tenderloin and put in a shallow roasting pan. In a small bowl mix sesame oil, soy sauce, and garlic. Rub mixture over meat.

**COOKING:** Heat oven to 375°F. Roast meat in preheated oven until meat thermometer reads 130°F., about 30 minutes. Allow roast to sit undisturbed for 15 minutes before slicing. Reheat sauce.

**SERVING:** Coat roast with some of the sauce. Pass remaining sauce separately.

**YIELD:** 6 servings

## STUFFED LOIN OF LAMB AU JUS

The pièce de résistance for a luxurious dinner party. All the preparation can be done ahead of time, so the roast can cook unattended while you join your guests for drinks. A whole loin (often called the saddle) is used here. The lamb and pork for the stuffing are ground and so can be less desirable cuts. This recipe is from chef Hermann Reiner of Windows on the World in New York City.

### RED-WINE SAUCE

- **1 quart Lamb Stock (page 156)**
- **¼ pound shiitake mushrooms**
- **Salt and pepper**

### LAMB STUFFING

- **½ pound boneless lamb**
- **6 ounces lean boneless pork**
- **2 ounces calf's *or* chicken liver**
- **Shiitake mushroom caps (from sauce, above)**
- **1 shallot**
- **12 tablespoons butter**
- **Salt and pepper**
- **1½ tablespoons brandy**
- **1½ teaspoons chopped rosemary *or* ½ teaspoon dried**
- **1 egg**

- **1 whole boneless, trimmed loin of lamb (about 4¼ pounds)**
- **Salt and pepper**

**PREPARATION:** FOR THE SAUCE: Make the stock. Separate mushroom stems from caps and reserve caps for stuffing. Put stock in a saucepan, add mushroom stems, and simmer until reduced to 1 cup, about 40 minutes. Strain and skim fat. Adjust seasoning with salt and pepper.

Meanwhile, FOR THE STUFFING: Dice lamb, pork, and liver. Cut mushroom caps into thin slices. Chop shallot. In a large frying pan melt 6 tablespoons butter over medium-high heat. Sauté the pork and lamb until partially cooked but still pink, about 3 minutes, and remove. Sauté liver very briefly until browned but still very rare inside. Remove. Season meats with salt and pepper. Add brandy to pan and scrape bottom with a wooden spoon to deglaze. Pour pan juices over meats. Cool. Grind meats in a grinder fitted with a fine blade or mince by hand.

In the same frying pan sauté the sliced mushroom caps in remaining 6 tablespoons butter over low heat until soft, about 7 minutes. Remove from heat and add rosemary and shallot. Add to the ground meat and combine. Mix in egg. Season with salt and pepper.

Season lamb loin with salt and pepper. Spread stuffing over lamb, roll up and tie with string. Season outside with salt and pepper.

**COOKING:** Heat oven to 375°F. Cook lamb in preheated oven until medium-rare (125°F. to 130°F.), about 1 hour. Let rest 15 minutes before slicing. Reheat sauce.

**SERVING:** Cut lamb into ½-inch slices. Arrange on plates and pour sauce over lamb.

YIELD: 8 servings

CHAPTER 8

# VEGETABLES

**SPRING:**

Turnip Greens with Salt Pork
Sugar Snap Peas with Scallions
Quelites con Tomates (Spinach with Chili Powder and Cherry Tomatoes)
Asparagus with Lemon and Walnut Oil

**SUMMER:**

Zucchini Beer Chips
Tomatoes Stuffed with Zucchini Soufflé
Plain and Simple Boiled Beans
Beans in Curry Cream Sauce with Curried Almonds
Bean Bundles
Sautéed Oriental Eggplant with Black Vinegar
Eggplant Gâteau
Curried Eggplant
Elote con Queso (Corn Custard)

**FALL/WINTER:**

Baked Sweet-Dumpling Squash
Quick Creamed Kale
Winter Vegetable Purée
Broccoli with Starfruit
Celeriac Chips

**ALL SEASON:**

Shredded Vegetable Pancakes
Swiss Chard Gratin

SIDEBARS

Fresh Beans
Eggplant
Kale

# SPRING

## Turnip Greens with Salt Pork

Hot peppers lend piquancy to this combination of greens and salt pork. The traditional long cooking of a "mess of greens" is here shortened to just 15 to 20 minutes, resulting in a fresher, brighter dish.

**4 ounces salt pork**
**¾ pound young turnip greens**
**1½ fresh hot peppers, such as jalapeños**
**¾ teaspoon sugar**
**Salt and pepper**

PREPARATION: Cut salt pork into large dice. Remove stems from turnip greens and discard. Chop hot peppers. In a saucepan blanch salt pork in boiling water to cover for 5 minutes. Drain and pat dry.

COOKING: In a large frying pan cook salt pork over medium heat until golden, 3 to 5 minutes. Add 1½ cups water, turnip greens, sugar, 1 teaspoon salt, and hot peppers. Reduce heat to medium and cook, covered, until greens are tender, 15 to 20 minutes. Season to taste with salt and pepper.

YIELD: 4 servings

# Sugar Snap Peas with Scallions

Deliciously sweet and tender Sugar Snap peas are now available at specialty produce markets and increasingly in supermarkets as well.

- **2 scallions**
- **½ pound Sugar Snap peas**
- **1 tablespoon peanut oil**
- **1 tablespoon soy sauce**
- **Few drops sesame oil**

**PREPARATION:** Chop the scallions. String the peas. Cook peas in a pot of boiling salted water until tender, about 5 minutes. Drain, plunge into cold water, and drain again.

**COOKING:** Heat the peanut oil in a frying pan or wok, add the peas, and stir-fry over medium-high heat for 3 minutes. Stir in the soy sauce, sesame oil, and chopped scallions and remove from heat.

**YIELD:** 4 servings

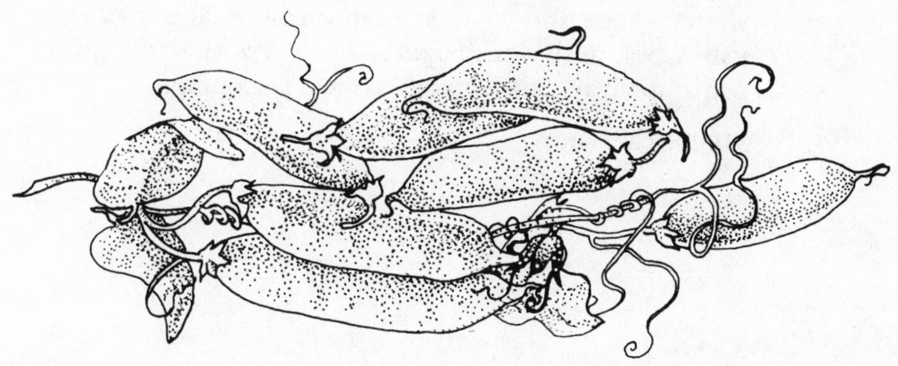

# QUELITES CON TOMATES (SPINACH WITH CHILI POWDER AND CHERRY TOMATOES)

*Quelites* is traditionally made with native greens, such as lamb's quarters, but it is excellent with spinach. The recipe generally includes bacon fat or lard, onion, garlic, and a mild chili. Lacking poblano or Anaheim chili powder, good-quality paprika will do. The not-quite-traditional cherry tomatoes add a cheery note.

**¼ onion**
**1 clove garlic**
**1 pound spinach**
**1 tablespoon bacon fat**
**Salt**
**½ pint cherry tomatoes**
**½ teaspoon ground mild chili powder, such as poblano or Anaheim**

PREPARATION: Chop onion. Mince garlic. Remove stems from spinach.

COOKING: In a large frying pan heat bacon fat. Add onion and garlic and stir-fry until just golden, about 5 minutes. Add spinach and cook, stirring, until it just becomes limp. Add salt to taste. Remove spinach with a slotted spoon and cover to keep warm. Add tomatoes to pan. Cook until skins begin to burst. Put spinach back in pan and stir in chili powder. Adjust seasonings.

YIELD: 4 servings

# Asparagus with Lemon and Walnut Oil

The earthy taste of walnut oil is an inspired complement to asparagus. If you don't have any on hand, use any light oil and sprinkle chopped walnuts over the asparagus.

**1 pound asparagus**
**1 teaspoon dry mustard**
**1 clove garlic**
**1½ tablespoons lemon juice**
**Salt and pepper**
**¼ cup walnut oil**

**PREPARATION:** Trim and peel asparagus. Mix the mustard with 1 teaspoon cold water in a small bowl and allow to sit for 10 minutes. Mince the garlic.

Whisk mustard mixture with the garlic, lemon juice, and salt and pepper to taste. Whisk in walnut oil.

**COOKING:** Cook asparagus in plenty of boiling salted water until tender, about 7 minutes. Drain well and toss with the walnut oil sauce.

**SERVING:** Serve warm, room temperature, or chilled.

**YIELD:** 4 servings

# SUMMER

## Zucchini Beer Chips

We guarantee that these fried zucchini slices will be savory and crisp every time.

- **12 ounces beer**
- **1 clove garlic**
- **2 zucchini**
- **Oil for deep frying**
- **1 egg**
- **1 cup flour**
- **Salt and pepper**
- **1 teaspoon cayenne, optional**

**PREPARATION:** Pour beer into a large bowl. Mince the garlic and add to the beer. Cut the zucchini into ⅛-inch slices. Soak the zucchini slices in the beer mixture for 15 minutes.

**COOKING:** Heat 2 inches oil to 375°F. in a large frying pan or deep fryer. Drain the zucchini, reserving 1 cup of the beer mixture. Pat the zucchini dry. Lightly whisk the egg and mix in flour and reserved beer mixture. Dip the zucchini in the batter and fry in batches, taking care not to crowd the pan, until crisp and golden, about 5 minutes. Drain on paper towels and sprinkle with salt, black pepper, and cayenne if desired.

**YIELD:** 4 servings

# Tomatoes Stuffed with Zucchini Soufflé

This pairing of summer favorites makes a special and very attractive side dish or first course.

- **8 ripe, firm tomatoes**
- **Salt and pepper**
- **4 zucchini (about 1¼ pounds total)**
- **2 shallots**
- **6 tablespoons butter**
- **3 tablespoons flour**
- **1 cup milk**
- **3 eggs**
- **½ cup + 2 teaspoons grated Parmesan cheese**

**PREPARATION:** Slice top quarter from tomatoes. Scoop out pulp, leaving walls of tomatoes intact. Cut a very thin slice from the bottom of each tomato, if necessary, so it will stand upright. Season insides with salt and pepper. Set aside, upside down, to drain.

Shred zucchini into a bowl, salt generously, and stir well. Set aside for 30 minutes. Drain zucchini, rinse with cold water, and squeeze by handfuls to remove as much liquid as possible.

Mince the shallots. In a frying pan melt 3 tablespoons butter and sauté shallots for 2 minutes. Add zucchini and sauté until it is tender and just begins to brown slightly, about 3 minutes.

Melt remaining 3 tablespoons butter in a heavy saucepan over low heat. Add flour and cook, stirring constantly, for 3 minutes. Add milk and cook, whisking constantly, until mixture is smooth, about 5 minutes. Separate eggs. Beat in egg yolks, 1 at a time. Add ½ cup Parmesan and salt and pepper to taste. Stir in zucchini mixture.

In a large bowl beat egg whites to firm peaks. Stir ¼ of whites into the zucchini mixture to lighten it. Gently fold in remainder of whites.

Pat tomato shells dry and fill them with zucchini mixture, mounding slightly. Sprinkle with remaining 2 teaspoons Parmesan.

**COOKING:** Heat oven to 350°F. Lightly butter a large casserole. Put tomatoes in prepared pan and bake in preheated oven until soufflés are puffed and golden, about 20 minutes. Serve immediately.

**YIELD:** 4 servings

## PLAIN AND SIMPLE BOILED BEANS

When beans are at their summer peak, there's no better way to serve them than boiled and buttered.

**1 pound beans (any kind)**
**2 to 3 tablespoons butter**
**Salt and pepper**

**PREPARATION:** Trim and wash the beans. Add the beans to a pot of boiling salted water and stir. Cook until tender, 5 to 7 minutes, depending on thickness. Drain and refresh under cold running water.

**COOKING:** Heat butter over medium heat. Toss beans with butter and salt and pepper to taste until heated through.

**YIELD:** 4 servings

### FRESH BEANS

We all grew up calling them string beans and never knowing why. Up until the late 1800s, all beans had stringy fibers along the seam connecting the two pod sections. This was convenient for those beans grown specifically for their seeds—just pull the string and out pop the edible beans. But for green beans and wax beans it was a nuisance.

After years of research, American horticulturists developed a stringless bean. Today, most fresh beans are stringless, although some varieties that are stringless when young and tender develop strings as the pods mature and toughen. Fresh beans, also called snap beans for the sharp sound that very fresh pods make when broken, are at their peak from June through August, with the exception of Chinese long beans, which peak in late summer and early autumn.

# Beans in Curry Cream Sauce with Curried Almonds

These full-flavored beans taste almost like a main dish. Serve with simple meats such as sautéed pork chops or broiled chicken.

**1 large onion**
**1 pound wax *or* green beans**
**2 tablespoons butter**
**½ cup slivered almonds**
**1 tablespoon curry powder**
**1 tablespoon oil**
**2 teaspoons ground cumin**
**2 cups Chicken Stock (page 49)**
**¼ cup heavy cream**
**Salt and pepper**

**PREPARATION:** Slice onion. Trim and wash beans.

In a small frying pan melt 1 tablespoon butter over medium heat. Add the almonds and 1 teaspoon curry powder and sauté 4 minutes, stirring constantly to avoid burning. Drain almonds on paper towels.

**COOKING:** In a saucepan heat remaining 1 tablespoon butter and the oil over medium heat. Add the onion and sauté until soft but not brown, about 4 minutes. Stir in remaining 2 teaspoons curry powder and the cumin and sauté 1 minute. Add the beans and sauté 1 minute. Pour in the stock and let the mixture come to a boil. Reduce the heat, cover, and simmer until beans are tender, about 8 minutes. Remove the beans with a slotted spoon, transfer to a warm serving plate, and cover to keep warm.

Add the cream to the stock, raise the heat, and boil until thickened and reduced to 1 cup, about 5 minutes. Taste for seasoning.

**SERVING:** Pour sauce over the beans and sprinkle with almonds.

**YIELD:** 4 servings

There are dozens of regional varieties of beans available to American cooks. The most popular include green beans, purple beans, wax beans, haricots verts, Kentucky wonder beans, Italian snap beans, and Chinese long beans.

*Green beans* are the most basic type. They are slender and crisp and should be picked when fairly young—about three to five inches in length and one-quarter inch in diameter. As the beans mature, the seeds enlarge and the meaty part of the bean becomes more fibrous and starts to shrivel. *Purple beans* look dramatic raw, but they taste like regular green beans and in fact turn green when cooked. *Wax beans* are an American favorite. They are nearly identical in taste to green beans with a slightly sweeter flavor and a distinctive chartreuse color.

*Haricots verts, Kenya beans,* or *French beans* are slender and very delicate. This French variety has recently become popular in the United States. *Kentucky Wonder beans* grow prolifically and are also known as *Texas Pole, Old Homestead,* and *Egg Harbour beans.* They are prized for their meaty bean flavor. *Italian snap beans,* also known as *Romanos,* have slightly flattened pods and can be yellow or greenish. They are an exception to the stringless rule.

*Chinese long beans,* also called *long beans, yard-long beans,* and *asparagus beans* look just like they sound—very (12 to 30 inches) long. The dark green beans, which are actually related more closely to black-eyed peas than to beans, are best when almost pencil-thin (less than ⅜ inch in diameter). They are sold fresh in Asian markets and have a slightly chewy texture. Choose long beans that are all green, smooth-skinned, and pliable but firm. Avoid beans that look yellow or wrinkled. Long beans are susceptible to bacteria and rust and should be used as soon as possible.

## BEAN BUNDLES

This easy, do-ahead recipe has the Italian flavors of prosciutto, garlic, olive oil, and Parmesan.

**¾ pound haricots verts *or* young, tender green beans**
**½ pound thin-sliced prosciutto**
**3 cloves garlic**
**3 tablespoons butter**
**1 tablespoon olive oil**
**Pepper**
**⅓ cup grated Parmesan cheese**

PREPARATION: Trim the beans and blanch in a large pot of boiling salted water until almost tender, about 4 minutes. Drain beans and refresh under cold running water. Drain thoroughly.

Gather beans into small bundles of 8 to 10 beans each. Trim the ends of the bundles to an even length.

Cut prosciutto slices in half lengthwise. Put 1 bean bundle at 1 end of each piece of prosciutto. Roll the prosciutto around the bundles. Put in a baking pan.

Mince the garlic. In a small saucepan heat the butter, olive oil, and garlic over low heat. Simmer 2 to 3 minutes. Pour the garlic butter over the beans and sprinkle with pepper to taste.

COOKING: Heat the oven to 350°F. Bake beans in preheated oven for 10 minutes. Remove beans from oven and heat the broiler. Sprinkle the cheese evenly over the beans. Broil until the cheese is bubbling and golden brown, about 1 minute.

YIELD: 4 servings

# Sautéed Oriental Eggplant with Black Vinegar

Asian eggplants, either the long purple "Chinese" or the smaller, almost black "Japanese," are so sweet that they needn't be salted to remove bitterness. If you can't find China's famous black Chinkiang vinegar, another mild vinegar, such as balsamic, will do. Or you can substitute Worcestershire sauce.

- **3 tablespoons black Chinkiang vinegar *or* balsamic vinegar**
- **2 teaspoons sugar**
- **Salt**
- **1¼ pounds Oriental eggplant**
- **⅓ cup olive oil**
- **½ teaspoon crushed dried red pepper *or* to taste**
- **2 tablespoons minced parsley**

**PREPARATION:** Mix the vinegar, sugar, and ¾ teaspoon salt and set aside. Cut the eggplant into 3-inch by ½-inch strips.

**COOKING:** Heat the oil in a wok or large frying pan over medium-high heat. Add the eggplant and cook, stirring constantly, until lightly browned, about 5 minutes. Cook in 2 batches if necessary. Add the pepper and stir briefly. Remove pan from heat and add the vinegar mixture. Stir until the liquid is thoroughly absorbed, 1 to 2 more minutes. Stir in the parsley.

**SERVING:** Serve warm or at room temperature.

**YIELD:** 4 servings

## EGGPLANT

There is nothing egglike about the color, size, or taste of most eggplants—although the eggplants introduced to England in the sixteenth century were the small white species that indeed does resemble a goose egg. Eggplants are available throughout the year, though they are at their peak and cheapest during the summer. The varieties most commonly available to American cooks include purple eggplant, Italian or Neapolitan eggplant, Oriental eggplant, and white eggplant.

*Purple eggplant,* the basic supermarket variety, can be used for most dishes that call for eggplant. *Italian or Neapolitan eggplant* is smaller and more slender, ranging in length from three to six inches. This type is ideal for stuffing, as a half makes a good single portion. *Oriental eggplant,* one of the most delectable members of the family, is distinguished by bright purple skin, a long slender shape, and tiny seeds. The skin is edible, and the flesh lacks the bitter juices found in western varieties. *White eggplant* has delicate flesh and white skin. It can be large or close to egg size.

Most eggplants, with the exception of the Oriental variety, taste best after disgorging—salting the pulp to leach out the bitterness and get rid of excess moisture. To disgorge eggplant, cut it into slices, strips, cubes, or cut it in half and make deep slashes in the pulp. Sprinkle with coarse salt and let stand in a colander for 20 minutes. Weighting the salted slices with a heavy plate will speed up the exit of the juices. Rinse under cold water and blot dry. Eggplant is notorious for soaking up oil, but disgorging will lessen its spongelike qualities and reduce the amount of oil needed for frying. Do not serve eggplant *al dente:* this is one vegetable that tastes best when cooked until soft.

To peel or not to peel, that is the question. Many cooks prefer the uniformly smooth texture of the peeled vegetable. Others like the flavor imparted by the skin, as well as the color it gives. Stuffed eggplant will hold its shape better unpeeled.

## EGGPLANT GÂTEAU

This rather elaborate dish might be the main attraction of an otherwise simple meal, perhaps chicken or lamb steaks cooked on the grill and accompanied by good bread. The gâteau can be assembled well ahead of time and baked just before serving.

**4 Italian *or* purple eggplants**
**Coarse salt**
**1 onion**
**2 cloves garlic**
**1 large red pepper**
**1 large yellow *or* green pepper**
**1 cubanelle pepper *or* other sweet pepper**
**2 small zucchini**
**3 tomatoes**
**¼ cup olive oil**
**3 tablespoons chopped herbs, including basil, oregano, rosemary, *and/or* parsley + sprigs for garnish**
**¼ cup fresh bread crumbs**
**1 egg**
**Salt and pepper**
**Cayenne**
**½ cup vegetable oil**
**Tomato Sauce (recipe below)**

PREPARATION: Peel 2 eggplants and cut them into ½-inch cubes. Sprinkle eggplant cubes with coarse salt and let stand in colander for 20 minutes. Rinse under cold water and blot dry.

Meanwhile, dice onion. Mince garlic. Core, seed, and cut peppers into ½-inch pieces. Halve zucchini lengthwise and cut into ¼-inch slices. Peel, seed, and chop tomatoes.

Heat olive oil in a large frying pan. Cook onion and garlic over medium heat for 2 minutes. Add eggplant cubes, peppers, and zucchini. Cook until peppers are soft, about 3 minutes. Add tomatoes and herbs and increase heat to high. Cook until liquid has evaporated, about 3 minutes. Stir in bread crumbs. Cool 10 minutes. Beat egg lightly and stir in. Season filling well with salt, black pepper, and cayenne.

Halve remaining 2 eggplants lengthwise and cut lengthwise into ⅛-inch-thick slices. Heat vegetable oil in a frying pan. Fry eggplant slices for 1 minute per side, being careful not to overcrowd. Drain.

Butter an 8-inch cake pan and line with an 8-inch circle of parchment paper or foil. Brush with butter again. Arrange eggplant slices in prepared pan, narrow end at center, wide end hanging over edge of pan. Overlap slices so that when gâteau is inverted, eggplant slices will look like petals of a flower. Spoon filling over eggplant slices. Fold eggplant slices over filling and cover pan with buttered foil.

**COOKING:** Heat oven to 350°F. Bake gâteau in preheated oven until filling is set, 40 to 50 minutes. Cool for 5 minutes. Heat tomato sauce.

**SERVING:** Invert gâteau onto a round platter and pour tomato sauce around it. Garnish with herb sprigs.

YIELD: 8 servings

## Tomato Sauce

**1 small onion**
**1 pound tomatoes**
**2 tablespoons butter**
**2 tablespoons red *or* white wine**
**4 teaspoons minced basil *or* 1 teaspoon dried**
**Salt and pepper**

**PREPARATION:** Chop the onion. Peel, seed, and chop the tomatoes.

In a frying pan heat butter. Add onion and sauté over medium heat until softened, about 4 minutes. Add wine and dried basil if using and cook 1 minute. Add tomatoes and salt and pepper to taste. Simmer over medium-low heat for 2 minutes. Add minced basil if using and simmer until slightly thickened, about 3 minutes.

YIELD: about 1½ cups

## CURRIED EGGPLANT

If you don't know Indian cooking well, it's hard to judge just by reading a recipe how an Indian-style dish will taste. Trust us—this one is fabulous. Serve it to round out an Indian meal or to add interest to plain meat, poultry, or fish.

**1 pound white eggplant *or* Oriental eggplant**
**Coarse salt**
**¼ teaspoon saffron, optional**
**1 teaspoon ground coriander**
**¼ teaspoon ground cumin**
**¼ teaspoon ground cardamom**
**¼ teaspoon cinnamon**
**Pinch ground cloves**
**Pinch ground cayenne**
**1 onion**
**1 hot chili pepper *or* to taste**
**Oil for frying**
**1 teaspoon fenugreek, optional**
**Juice of ½ lemon *or* to taste**
**½ cup coconut milk, see Note**
**Salt**
**2 tablespoons chopped coriander**

**PREPARATION:** Cut eggplant into 3-inch by ½-inch strips. If using white eggplant, sprinkle strips with coarse salt and let stand in colander for 20 minutes. Rinse under cold water and blot dry. (Oriental eggplants do not have to be disgorged.)

In a small bowl combine saffron if using, ground coriander, cumin, cardamom, cinnamon, cloves, and cayenne. Toss eggplant with spice mixture, reserving any extra mixture for sauce. Mince onion. Split and seed chili pepper.

**COOKING:** Heat ¼ inch oil in a frying pan. Brown eggplant strips in 2 to 3 batches, turning, for 3 minutes. Drain. Discard all but 2 tablespoons oil. Sauté onion, chili pepper, optional fenugreek, and any remaining spice mixture over medium heat until onion is soft, about 3 minutes. Add eggplant, lemon juice, coconut milk, and salt to taste. Simmer until sauce is thick and well reduced, about 10 minutes. Garnish with chopped coriander.

YIELD: 4 servings

NOTE: For the coconut milk, bring ⅔ cup water and 1 cup grated fresh coconut to a boil. Turn down heat and simmer 5 minutes. Strain through cheesecloth, squeezing out all liquid. You should have ½ cup.

## ELOTE CON QUESO (CORN CUSTARD)

This luscious Mexican corn pudding is rich with cheese and cream, yet light and delicate in texture. The green chilies add interest not heat.

- **1 fresh mild green chili pepper *or* ¼ cup canned chilies**
- **1 cup fresh *or* frozen corn kernels (from 2 ears)**
- **1 teaspoon baking powder**
- **¾ cup shredded Monterey Jack cheese**
- **¾ cup shredded Cheddar cheese**
- **1 tablespoon sugar**
- **3 eggs**
- **1 cup heavy cream**
- **1 teaspoon salt**

**PREPARATION:** Butter an ovenproof 1½-quart baking dish. Peel and seed fresh chili pepper or, if using canned chilies, drain them. In a food processor blend corn, baking powder, cheeses, chili pepper, and sugar until corn kernels are just broken up but not smooth.

In a bowl whisk together eggs and cream. Add to corn mixture, stir to combine, and add salt. Pour into prepared baking dish.

**COOKING:** Heat oven to 350°F. Bake in preheated oven until just set and a knife inserted into center comes out clean, about 45 minutes.

YIELD: 4 servings

# FALL/WINTER

## Baked Sweet-Dumpling Squash

Though we're partial to the aptly named sweet-dumpling squash, this is a fine recipe for any small squash. Try it for a holiday party.

- **2 carrots**
- **2 sweet-dumpling squash *or* acorn squash**
- **2 tablespoons golden raisins**
- **3 tablespoons maple syrup**
- **2 tablespoons butter**
- **Salt and pepper**

**PREPARATION:** Cut carrots into ⅛-inch dice. In a pot of boiling salted water blanch carrots for 4 minutes. Drain.

Halve and seed the squash. Slice a sliver off bottom of each squash half to prevent tipping. Put carrots and raisins in squash halves. Pour maple syrup over them and dot with butter. Season with salt and pepper. Put squash halves back together and wrap tightly with foil.

**COOKING:** Heat oven to 350°F. Put squash in a baking dish and bake in preheated oven until flesh is soft, 35 to 45 minutes. Halfway through baking, turn squash over. Unwrap and serve.

**YIELD:** 4 servings

# Quick Creamed Kale

If you've never tried kale, this recipe will make you a convert. It's especially good with fresh or cured pork.

- **1 pound kale**
- **1 shallot**
- **1 egg yolk**
- **¼ cup heavy cream**
- **1 lemon**
- **1 tablespoon oil**
- **2 tablespoons thyme leaves *or* 2 teaspoons dried**
- **Salt and pepper**

**PREPARATION:** Remove ribs from the kale and blanch leaves in plenty of boiling salted water until tender, about 10 minutes. Drain and squeeze out the excess water.

Mince the shallot. Whisk together the egg yolk and cream. Squeeze lemon to make 2 tablespoons juice.

**COOKING:** Heat the oil in a large frying pan over medium heat. Add the shallot and cook, stirring, until soft but not colored. Add the kale, thyme, and salt and pepper to taste, and cook, stirring, until the kale is heated through.

Remove from the heat and add egg yolk mixture, stirring constantly. Return to the stove and cook over very low heat until the mixture starts to thicken, about 2 minutes, being careful not to let it boil or the yolk will curdle. Add the lemon juice and adjust seasoning with salt and pepper if needed.

**YIELD:** 4 servings

## KALE

Kale is another of those once-scorned vegetables that has recently become popular. A member of the cabbage family, it has a milder flavor than other cabbages; some people compare it to collard greens. Kale has distinctive curly, "inside-out" leaves. Some varieties are pink or purple and are so attractive that they're sold in flower shops as ornamental plants. But the type usually found in the marketplace is dark green or bluish-green.

Kale is available year-round, but it is really at its best in the winter months. This very hardy plant can stand up to extreme cold, and in fact it tastes better after it has been through a frost. New spring kale, however, can be sweet and tender, and, although kale is generally cooked, the baby leaves can be eaten raw in a salad.

# WINTER VEGETABLE PURÉE

For textural contrast the creamy purée is punctuated by crunchy diced carrots and turnips.

**½ onion**
**1 small clove garlic**
**3 small carrots**
**3 small turnips**
**2 parsnips**
**3 tablespoons butter**
**2 thin slices gingerroot**
**2 small potatoes**
**Salt and pepper**
**2 tablespoons fresh bread crumbs**
**3 tablespoons heavy cream**
**2 eggs**
**1 egg yolk**

**PREPARATION:** Chop the onion. Halve the garlic. Cut 2 carrots, 2 turnips, and parsnips into thin slices. Cut remaining carrot and turnip into ¼-inch dice.

In a saucepan heat 2 tablespoons butter. Add onion, garlic, and gingerroot. Cover and cook over low heat until soft, about 10 minutes.

Peel potatoes and cut them into thin slices. Add remaining 1 tablespoon butter to pan with potatoes, sliced carrots and turnips, parsnips, and ¾ teaspoon salt. Cover and cook over very low heat, stirring occasionally, for 20 minutes. Add ⅓ cup water, cover, and cook until vegetables are tender enough to mash with the back of a wooden spoon, about 20 minutes. Remove from heat.

Butter four 5-ounce ramekins or custard cups. Coat ramekins with bread crumbs. Put a piece of brown paper or a dish towel on the bottom of a baking pan large enough to hold ramekins.

Purée cooked vegetables in a food processor or food mill. Let cool. When purée is cool, whisk in cream, eggs, and egg yolk. Stir in diced carrots and turnips.

Season to taste with salt and pepper. Divide mixture among prepared ramekins.

**COOKING:** Heat oven to 375°F. Pour boiling water into lined baking pan to come halfway up sides of ramekins. Bake in preheated oven until mixture is set and feels firm to the touch, 35 to 40 minutes. Allow to rest for 5 minutes in a warm place.

**SERVING:** Invert molds onto serving dishes and serve immediately.

**YIELD:** 4 servings

## Broccoli with Starfruit

The tartness of starfruit makes it an ideal complement to broccoli, and the star-shaped slices look charming. For this dish, the starfruit should still be slightly green.

- **1¾ pounds broccoli**
- **1 starfruit**
- **4 tablespoons butter**
- **Salt and pepper**

**PREPARATION:** Cut florets from stems of broccoli, saving stems for another use. In a large pot of rapidly boiling salted water cook florets, uncovered, until just tender, about 3 minutes. Drain, plunge into ice water, and drain thoroughly. Cut starfruit into thin slices.

**COOKING:** In a large frying pan or 2 smaller pans melt butter. Add broccoli, season to taste with salt and pepper, and gently sauté, being careful not to break florets, about 2 minutes. When broccoli is just heated through, add starfruit, and toss gently.

**YIELD:** 4 servings

# CELERIAC CHIPS

This recipe for crisp celeriac (or celery root) chips is from Hermann Reiner of Windows on the World in New York City. He likes to serve it with his Stuffed Loin of Lamb au Jus, page 177.

**1 celeriac (¾ pound)**
**¼ lemon**
**Oil for frying**
**Coarse salt**

**PREPARATION:** Peel the celeriac and cut into paper-thin slices. Squeeze lemon juice over slices and toss.

**COOKING:** In a large frying pan or deep fryer heat 1 inch oil to 300°F. Fry celeriac slices until crisp and light golden, turning if necessary, about 2 minutes. Remove chips with a slotted spoon and drain.

**SERVING:** Sprinkle chips with coarse salt and serve at once.

YIELD: 4 servings

# ALL SEASON

## Shredded Vegetable Pancakes

Quick, colorful, and crisp, these pancakes have a lot going for them. The potatoes and onions should remain constant, but you can substitute for the other vegetables as you please. Try Sugar Snap peas in the spring, green beans or yellow squash in the summer, or shredded kale in the fall.

**1 egg**
**¼ cup snow peas**
**1 onion**
**1 small carrot**
**½ small zucchini**
**1 baking potato (about 6 ounces)**
**1 tablespoon flour**
**Salt and pepper**
**1 tablespoon butter**
**1 tablespoon oil**

**PREPARATION:** Lightly beat egg in a bowl. Trim snow peas, cut crosswise into thin strips, and put in bowl. Grate onion into bowl. Shred ¼ cup each of carrot and zucchini. Peel and shred potato. Dry carrot, zucchini, and potato thoroughly with paper towels and add to bowl. Mix in flour and salt and pepper to taste.

**COOKING:** In a large frying pan heat butter and oil. Make 4 mounds of pancake mixture in the pan and flatten into 3½-inch pancakes with the back of a spoon. Cook over medium heat until bottom is golden brown and crisp, about 2 minutes. Turn with a spatula and cook 2 minutes more. Season with salt and pepper.

YIELD: 4 servings

## SWISS CHARD GRATIN

Making it into a creamy, golden-topped gratin is an excellent way to treat Swiss chard. This recipe was developed by Arthur Mangie of The Wooden Angel Restaurant in West Bridgewater, Pennsylvania.

**1 bunch Swiss chard (1 pound)**
**1 small onion**
**2 teaspoons butter**
**2 teaspoons flour**
**¾ cup milk**
**½ cup heavy cream**
**Salt and pepper**
**½ cup grated Swiss cheese**

PREPARATION: If Swiss chard is big and tough, pull off stringy fibers (as with celery). Trim ribs from the chard and chop into bite-size pieces. Tear leaves into pieces. Blanch ribs in a large pot of boiling salted water for 3 minutes. Add leaves and cook for 1 minute. Strain. Rinse under cold water and press out excess moisture.

Chop onion. Melt butter in a saucepan and sauté onion over medium heat until lightly browned, about 10 minutes. Add flour, whisk, and cook 1 minute. Whisk in milk and cream. Bring to a boil for 30 seconds, remove from heat, and stir in salt and pepper to taste.

COOKING: Heat oven to 375°F. Butter an 8-cup gratin dish and arrange chard stems and leaves in dish. Sprinkle with cheese and pour cream sauce on top. Put gratin dish on a baking sheet and bake in preheated oven until the gratin browns, about 45 minutes. Let rest 15 minutes before serving.

YIELD: 4 servings

CHAPTER 9

# POTATOES AND GRAINS

# SPRING

## WHITE RICE WITH HONEY MUSHROOMS

Small-capped tan and white honey mushrooms have a meaty texture and a mild, slightly sweet flavor. They should not be eaten raw but can be cooked any way that you would ordinary mushrooms.

**¼ pound honey mushrooms**
**6 tablespoons butter**
**4 scallions**
**1 cup white rice**
**2 cups Chicken Stock (page 49)**
**Salt and pepper**

**PREPARATION:** Trim the bunch of honey mushrooms, which will be joined together at the bottom. Divide into individual mushrooms and chop the base into pieces. Melt 4 tablespoons butter in a frying pan, add the mushrooms, and sauté over medium heat until just tender, about 5 minutes. Chop scallions.

**COOKING:** In a saucepan melt remaining 2 tablespoons butter. Add the rice and stir for 1 minute. Add stock, season to taste with salt and pepper, and bring to a boil. Reduce heat to a simmer, cover, and cook until rice absorbs nearly all the liquid, about 15 minutes.

Add the mushrooms and scallions, cover, and cook over low heat until rice is soft, about 5 minutes. Season to taste with salt and pepper.

**YIELD:** 4 servings

# SPRING / SUMMER

## Mashed New Potatoes with Garlic and Parsley

We promise you'll never have better mashed potatoes than these from Nicola Zanghi of Restaurant Zanghi in Glen Cove, New York.

**½ cup flat-leaf parsley**
**1 pound new potatoes (about 8)**
**12 cloves garlic**
**½ cup heavy cream**
**¼ pound butter**
**Salt and pepper**

**PREPARATION:** Cut parsley into thin strips.

**COOKING:** Put potatoes in a pot with cold salted water to cover. Cover pot and bring to a boil. Add garlic, reduce heat to a simmer, and cook, uncovered, until potatoes test done, about 12 minutes. Drain. Push the potatoes and garlic through a ricer, food mill, or sieve into a heavy pot. Add cream and stir over medium heat. Stir in butter, bit by bit. Stir in parsley and season with salt and pepper.

**YIELD:** 4 servings

## STEAMED POTATOES

Steamed new potatoes are sometimes an ideal simple accompaniment to a richly sauced dish. They look especially attractive when a band of skin is removed from the middle of each potato. If you don't have a steamer, you can rig one up with a rack set in a pot.

**2 pounds red new potatoes (about 16)**
**Salt and pepper**

**COOKING:** Bring 1 to 2 inches water to a boil in a steamer. Peel a band of skin from the middle of each potato. Put potatoes in the basket over the water. Cover and steam potatoes until just tender, 12 to 16 minutes.

**SERVING:** Put the potatoes in a warm serving dish and season with salt and pepper to taste. Serve immediately.

**YIELD:** 4 servings

## ROASTED POTATOES

Chef Stephan Pyles of Routh Street Café in Dallas, Texas, offers this recipe for crusty brown potatoes. He likes to use chicken or duck fat, but you could also use lard or vegetable oil.

**2 pounds new potatoes (about 16)**
**1 cup chicken *or* duck fat**
**Salt**

**COOKING:** Heat oven to 400°F. Put potatoes in a saucepan of rapidly boiling salted water and blanch until just tender when pierced with a knife, 4 to 5 minutes. Remove from water. Put potatoes in a heavy baking pan, melt fat, and pour over potatoes.

Put pan in preheated oven and roast until light brown, 20 to 25 minutes. Shake pan occasionally to brown potatoes evenly.

**SERVING:** Sprinkle with salt to taste and serve.

**YIELD:** 4 servings

## ROASTED NEW POTATOES WITH GARLIC

Here whole unpeeled garlic cloves are roasted along with the potatoes and at the end of cooking become soft and mellow. Squeeze them out of their skins over the hot potatoes. The recipe is from COOK'S columnist Alice Waters of Chez Panisse in Berkeley, California.

- **2 pounds new potatoes (about 16)**
- **8 cloves garlic**
- **¼ cup olive oil**
- **Several thyme branches**
- **Salt and pepper**

**PREPARATION:** Scrub and dry the potatoes but do not peel them. In a roasting pan toss potatoes with unpeeled garlic, oil, thyme, and salt and pepper.

**COOKING:** Heat the oven to 400°F. Roast in preheated oven until tender, 20 to 40 minutes, depending on size.

**SERVING:** Squeeze roasted garlic from skins over potatoes, toss, and serve.

**YIELD:** 4 servings

# RED POTATOES WITH SALT COD

Carol Brendlinger of Bay Wolf Restaurant sent us this recipe, which will delight salt cod fanciers and perhaps make a few converts. Allow plenty of time to soak the cod.

**3 ounces salt cod**
**1 clove garlic**
**¼ small red onion**
**2 tablespoons minced parsley**
**1½ tablespoons lemon juice**
**3 tablespoons olive oil**
**Salt and pepper**
**1 hard-cooked egg**
**1 pound red new potatoes (about 8)**
**4 teaspoons minced chives**

**PREPARATION:** Soak the cod for 3 days in cold water in the refrigerator. Change water twice daily. Poach cod in simmering water until tender, about 8 minutes. Drain and cool. Mince cod and garlic. Cut red onion into fine dice. Mix together cod, garlic, onion, parsley, lemon juice, olive oil, and salt and pepper to taste. Chill.

Grate the egg or push it through a sieve.

**COOKING:** Cut potatoes in half and put in a pot of cold salted water to cover. Cover and bring to a boil. Uncover, reduce heat to a simmer, and cook until tender, about 12 minutes. Drain.

**SERVING:** Serve warm potatoes with the cold salt cod. Scatter chives and egg over all.

YIELD: 4 servings

# Potato Salad with Dill and Thyme Dressing

Here's an herb-flavored potato salad that's perfect for spring and summer meals. Change the herbs to suit your taste.

**2 pounds new potatoes (about 16)**

Dill and Thyme Dressing

**1 shallot**
**2 egg yolks**
**1 tablespoon balsamic vinegar**
**2 tablespoons white-wine vinegar**
**½ cup chopped dill**
**2 tablespoons chopped thyme *or* 2 teaspoons dried**
**Salt and pepper**
**1 cup olive oil**

**PREPARATION:** Cut potatoes into bite-size pieces and put in a large pot with cold salted water to cover. Cover pot and bring to a boil. Uncover, reduce heat to a simmer, and cook until tender, about 10 minutes.

Meanwhile, FOR THE DRESSING: Mince shallot. Whisk together egg yolks, vinegars, herbs, shallot, and salt and pepper to taste. Still whisking, drizzle in olive oil. Adjust seasoning to taste.

Drain potatoes and toss with dressing while still hot. Season to taste with salt and pepper.

**SERVING:** Serve at room temperature.

YIELD: 4 servings

# SUMMER

## BROWN RICE MINT PILAF

This unusual pilaf, made with brown rice, has Middle Eastern accents. It's particularly good with grilled chicken.

- **2 tablespoons pine nuts**
- **2 onions**
- **2 cloves garlic**
- **2 tablespoons olive oil**
- **1 cup brown rice**
- **Salt and pepper**
- **2 tablespoons chopped mint *or* 2 teaspoons dried**
- **¼ cup minced flat-leaf parsley**
- **¼ cup dried currants *or* raisins**
- **2 cups Chicken Stock (page 49)**
- **1 tablespoon lemon juice**

**PREPARATION:** Toast pine nuts in a 325°F. oven until brown, 5 to 10 minutes. Chop onions. Mince garlic.

**COOKING:** In a heavy 12-inch frying pan heat olive oil over medium heat, add onions and garlic, and sauté until soft, about 8 minutes. Add rice and sauté for 5 minutes. Add 1 teaspoon salt, ¼ teaspoon pepper, mint, parsley, and currants. Pour in stock and lemon juice. Bring to a boil, lower heat, and cook, covered, over low heat until rice is tender and all liquid has been absorbed, about 1 hour.

**SERVING:** Toss pine nuts with pilaf and serve immediately.

YIELD: 4 servings

# FALL / WINTER

## Risotto with White Truffles

> **TRUFFLES**
>
> The Italians and French will probably forever debate the superiority of white versus black truffles. While there are black truffles to be found in Umbria, Italian truffles are primarily the white variety, harvested in the Piedmont, Romagna, and Tuscany regions. Regardless of variety, truffles do not take well to cultivation, making them scarce and, consequently, expensive. Some French firms, however, have been able to cultivate black truffles successfully, and in fact one is attempting to grow black truffles in Texas! The first U.S. crop is expected in 1988; the results should be interesting. Like European truffles, they will require truffle hounds for harvesting. Both specially trained pigs and dogs are used to find the truffle crop, but pigs are more likely to devour their precious find.

You'll be surprised how much luxury just half an ounce of truffle can add. Grate it over the risotto at the last minute.

**1 shallot**
**¼ cup white wine**
**4¼ cups Chicken Stock (page 49)**
**2 tablespoons butter**
**1 cup rice, preferably arborio**
**¼ cup grated Parmesan cheese**
**Salt and pepper**
**½ ounce white truffles**

**PREPARATION:** Mince the shallot.

**COOKING:** In a nonreactive saucepan heat the wine and stock.

Heat the butter in a heavy nonreactive saucepan. Cook the shallot over medium heat until soft, about 4 minutes. Add the rice and cook, stirring, until it becomes opaque, about 1 minute. Add enough simmering stock mixture to just cover the rice, about ½ cup. Simmer, stirring constantly, until most of the liquid is absorbed, about 5 minutes. Add stock mixture to cover rice again and cook in the same manner, adding more stock mixture as needed. When done, the rice should be tender and the remaining liquid should be thickened to a sauce. Stir in the cheese. Season to taste with salt and pepper if necessary.

**SERVING:** Grate some truffle over each serving.

**YIELD:** 4 servings

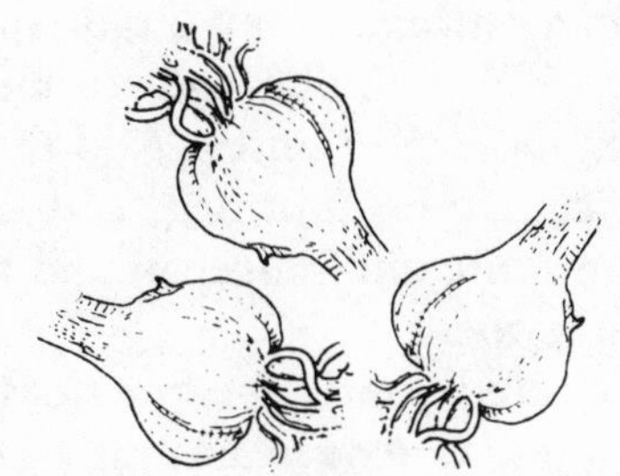

The season for both white and black varieties is rather brief, from late autumn through the winter. Look for truffles that are firm not spongy. Fresh truffles are quite perishable, but they will keep in the refrigerator for a week or two if protected from moisture. Keep them in a jar of raw rice, which absorbs moisture (and the truffle-flavored rice is a bonus). They also will hold for a day or two loosely wrapped in paper towels and refrigerated in a jar. A glass container is a necessity. The pungent smell will permeate plastic and make everything in the refrigerator smell of truffles.

To prepare truffles, flick off the dirt with a brush and wipe with a damp cloth. White truffles should never be cooked. They can be gently warmed through, but any more heat is ruinous to their flavor. Black truffles, on the other hand, are nearly always cooked.

Canned black truffles are available year-round, of course, but in our book they're not worth much. Frozen truffles are better, and newly available products such as truffle paste and truffle juice are worth a try.

## SWEET POTATOES

Sweet potatoes are not true potatoes. What's more, they aren't yams either, although one type is often called a yam in this country. (Real yams are a larger root vegetable, weighing up to ten pounds, with a woody outer skin. The pulp has a flavor and a texture similar to some sweet potatoes. True yams grow only in tropical regions—rarely in the United States.)

One of the two general types of sweet potato has light, yellow skin and pale flesh; the other has darker orange skin and sweeter, moister reddish-orange flesh. The pale, dry type—variously known as the Jersey sweet or the white sweet—thrives as far north as New Jersey, while the darker sweet potatoes (the ones that are sometimes called yams) grow best in warmer, moist climates. Both are widely marketed and available fresh for many months. The darker variety of sweet potato is more popular and is the foundation for traditional Southern dishes such as sweet potato pie and candied "yams."

Sweet-potato harvest begins in August, and until mid-November you can find uncured sweet potatoes in local markets. For the curing process, the tubers are put in storage for four to seven days at 85°F. with 85 to 90 percent humidity. Cured sweet potatoes keep well, though many people feel the uncured fresh sweets of fall are the most flavorful

# SWEET POTATO AND BANANA PURÉE

This unique recipe comes from chef Hermann Reiner of Windows on the World in New York City. The purée can be made several hours ahead and reheated when ready to serve.

- **2 pounds sweet potatoes**
- **8 tablespoons butter**
- **½ cup sugar**
- **½ cup orange juice**
- **½ cinnamon stick**
- **Pinch of nutmeg**
- **Salt and pepper**
- **½ lemon**
- **1 banana**

**PREPARATION:** Peel the sweet potatoes and cut into ½-inch pieces. In a saucepan melt 6 tablespoons butter over medium heat. Add the sugar and stir until mixture starts to caramelize, about 5 minutes. Add the sweet potatoes, orange juice, cinnamon, nutmeg, and salt. Squeeze juice from the lemon into the saucepan and add 3 cups water to cover the potatoes.

Simmer, covered, until the potatoes start to soften, about 15 minutes. Uncover and raise heat to high. Boil until liquid is reduced to 1 cup, about 30 minutes. Cut up the banana and add. Remove cinnamon stick. Put mixture through a ricer or purée in a food processor until smooth. Season with salt and pepper to taste.

**SERVING:** Reheat and top with remaining 2 tablespoons butter.

**YIELD:** 8 servings

# ALL SEASON

## Pommes Boulangère

Similar to scalloped potatoes made with stock instead of milk, this homey French dish comes from Bobby Vasquez of Tony's in Houston, Texas.

**2 onions**
**2 pounds potatoes**
**1 cup Chicken Stock (page 49)**
**1 tablespoon chopped parsley**
**Salt and pepper**
**3 tablespoons butter**

**PREPARATION:** Butter a shallow baking dish. Cut the onions into thin slices.

**COOKING:** Heat oven to 400°F. Peel the potatoes and cut into thin slices. Put the stock in a small pot and bring to a boil. Toss the potatoes and onions with the parsley and salt and pepper and put in prepared dish.

Pour hot stock over all, dot with butter, and bake in preheated oven until browned and cooked through and liquid is absorbed, about 40 minutes.

**YIELD:** 4 servings

### POTATOES

Pommes de terre, "apples of the earth" to the French, are truly worthy of that poetic description. Dozens of varieties are available in the United States, including some that are blue and others that are spotted. Most, however, fall into one of four categories: russets, round whites, round reds, and long whites.

Brown-skinned oval *russets* or Idahos are the classic baking potatoes thanks to their dry, mealy texture; they also make good French fries or mashed potatoes. *Round whites* have a dry, firm texture suitable for roasting, boiling, and mashing. Most are grown east of the Mississippi, primarily in Maine. Thin-skinned and waxy-textured, *round reds* are great for boiling or for salads. Remember to assemble salads while the spuds are still warm—they'll absorb the dressing better. Versatile *long whites,* sometimes called California potatoes after their state of origin, have thin yellowish skin and tiny eyes and are good almost any way—fried, roasted, boiled, baked, or mashed.

Some less common varieties are starting to show up in markets, too. *Yellow Finnish potatoes* are among the best and most flavorful, with a firm, buttery texture that makes them ideal for potato salads. The rather small potatoes look normal from the outside but have a butter-yellow interior. They are especially good boiled and served with salt and pepper or in other simple preparations that show off their flavor.

*New potatoes* or early potatoes appear in markets from early spring throughout the summer. Because new potatoes are harvested while the plant is still growing, they contain more sugar and a lot of flavor. Golf-ball size (or smaller) new potatoes are often served unpeeled, buttered, and garnished with parsley. "Old" or "maincrop" potatoes are dug after maturity. Naturally, they are larger and tougher-skinned, as well as somewhat dryer and softer.

Maincrop potatoes will keep for months if stored properly; new potatoes are best used within a week or so. New or old, potatoes should be stored in a cool, dry, dark place. Darkness is important because light causes toxic greenish alkaloids to develop and shortens shelf life. You should

# MILLET CAKES WITH TOMATOES AND MOZZARELLA

This delectable combination is the invention of Michael McLaughlin, chef/owner of The Manhattan Chili Company in New York City. The flavorful fried cakes topped with melting cheese could be a meal in themselves. Just double the recipe and serve with a salad.

**2 cloves garlic**
**8 sun-dried tomatoes**
**6 tablespoons olive oil**
**3 tablespoons minced rosemary *or* 1 tablespoon dried**
**1½ cups Chicken Stock (page 49)**
**Salt and pepper**
**⅔ cup millet (see Note)**
**2 eggs**
**½ pound mozzarella**

**PREPARATION:** Mince garlic. If not using oil-packed tomatoes, reconstitute dried tomatoes in warm water to cover. Drain and chop.

In a small saucepan warm 3 tablespoons olive oil over low heat. Add the garlic and cook, stirring, 3 minutes. Do not allow garlic to brown. Stir in the rosemary and cook, stirring, 1 minute. Add the stock, stir in 1½ teaspoons salt, and bring the mixture to a boil. Stir in the millet, cover, and reduce heat to very low. Cook undisturbed until the millet has absorbed all the liquid and is tender, about 25 minutes. Remove from heat and let stand, covered, 5 minutes. Cool to room temperature.

In a food processor combine ½ the millet and the eggs and process until smooth and creamy. Stir the purée into the remaining millet. Fold in the tomatoes and adjust the seasoning, adding pepper generously. Form the mixture into 8 small cakes 3 inches in diameter and ½-inch thick.

**COOKING:** In a large frying pan heat the remaining 3 tablespoons oil until very hot. Put the cakes in the hot frying pan. Lower the heat slightly and cook, turning once, until crisp and golden brown on both sides, about 10 minutes total.

Cut the mozzarella into 8 slices about the same size as the millet cakes. Put a slice of cheese on each cake. Cover the frying pan, remove from heat, and let stand until cheese has just melted, about 1 minute.

YIELD: 4 servings

NOTE: If your grocer doesn't stock millet, you can find it in a health-food store.

avoid potatoes that look greenish, but you can use them if you pare them deeply before cooking.

## Yogurt Whipped Potatoes

Sour cream or buttermilk are fine replacements for the yogurt. Or substitute milk or cream.

- **2 pounds boiling potatoes**
- **⅓ cup yogurt**
- **2 tablespoons butter**
- **2 tablespoons minced chives *or* scallion tops**
- **1 tablespoon minced parsley**
- **Salt and pepper**

**PREPARATION:** Peel potatoes and cut into 2-inch pieces. In a large saucepan cover potatoes with well-salted water and bring to a boil. Cook until tender, about 20 minutes. Drain potatoes, reserving a small amount of the cooking liquid.

Push potatoes through a food mill, ricer, or strainer back into the hot pan. Add yogurt and butter and enough of the reserved cooking liquid to make potatoes light and fluffy yet stiff enough to hold soft peaks. Stir in chives and parsley. Season with salt and pepper to taste and serve at once.

YIELD: 4 servings

## POLENTA

Italian polenta is a great favorite of ours, especially when it's enriched with chicken stock and butter. You can serve it warm as is or let it cool, cut it into squares, and fry until the edges are crisp. William Della Ventura of The 95th in Chicago, Illinois, developed this version.

**2¼ cups Chicken Stock (page 49), approximately**
**½ cup cornmeal**
**2 tablespoons butter**
**Salt and pepper**

**COOKING:** Heat stock over medium heat and slowly stir in cornmeal. Cook, stirring constantly, until very thick, about 20 minutes. Remove from heat. Stir in butter and season to taste with salt and pepper.

**SERVING:** Cool for 10 to 15 minutes before serving.

YIELD: 4 servings

CHAPTER 10

# DESSERTS

**SPRING:**
Sweet Cherry Gratin
Angel Shortcakes with Strawberries in Raspberry Sauce

**SUMMER:**
The Very Best Angel Food Cake
Berry Gelato
Brown-Sugar Angel Cake with Sliced Peaches and Rum Custard
Plum Ice Cream with Strawberries
Berry Tart
Champagne-Poached Figs with Heavy Cream
Poached Peaches with Champagne Sabayon

**FALL/WINTER:**
Apple Charlotte
Cranberry Bread Pudding with Whiskey Crème Anglaise
Pear Mincemeat Tart
Spiced Pumpkin Cream Roll
Apple and Cider Soup with Raisins
Walnut Crêpes with Caramelized Apples
Maple-Rum Squash Soufflé

**ALL SEASON:**
Orange Sherbet
Sugar Syrup
Lemon Granité
Chocolate Charlotte
Café à la Mousse

SIDEBARS
Sweet Cherries
Plums
Figs

# SPRING

## Sweet Cherry Gratin

### SWEET CHERRIES

Consider the cherry tree. It's the stuff of poetry, fodder for national legends, and the spur for countless springtime visits to the capital. Best of all is the wonderful, sweet fruit available from spring into summer.

The fresh cherries you purchase will most likely be *Bing* or *Lambert*, the two most common varieties of those clustered under the umbrella name sweet cherries. Sour cherries, used almost exclusively in processed cherry products such as pie fillings, rarely reach the fresh market. Bings arrive first each season, and a little later come the more perishable Lamberts. The nearly heart-shaped Lamberts have slightly lighter-colored skins than Bings, and some people consider them sweeter and more flavorful.

In parts of the West even the pollenizing cherries—those grown between the rows of Bing and

This delicious springtime dessert can be assembled up to 3 hours ahead and broiled just before serving. The pastry-cream topping can be made 1 day ahead.

Pastry Cream

- **2 egg yolks**
- **⅓ cup sugar**
- **3 tablespoons flour**
- **1 cup milk**
- **¼ teaspoon vanilla extract**

- **3 cups sweet cherries such as Bing or Lambert**
- **2 tablespoons sliced almonds**
- **1 tablespoon sugar**

**PREPARATION:** FOR THE PASTRY CREAM: Whisk yolks and sugar in a bowl until pale yellow. Whisk in flour.

In a saucepan bring milk to a boil. Slowly whisk hot milk into yolk mixture. Transfer mixture to a heavy pan and bring to a boil over medium heat, stirring constantly. Cook, stirring, for 1 minute. Remove from heat and add vanilla. If not using at once, transfer to a bowl and press plastic wrap directly on the surface to prevent formation of a skin. Cool to room temperature, and then refrigerate.

Pit cherries and arrange in a gratin dish. Pour pastry cream over cherries. Refrigerate if not using immediately.

**COOKING:** Heat broiler. Sprinkle almonds around edge of the dish. Broil 3 inches from heat source until browned, about 1 minute, watching closely so that gratin does not burn. Sprinkle with sugar and serve immediately.

**YIELD:** 4 servings

Lambert trees—turn up in the market. Some of the more frequently seen types include *Van, Chinook,* and *Republican.* They may be smaller, but they have the familiar sweet flavor and can substitute for each other.

Golden skin tinged with a red blush distinguishes *Royal Anne* and *Rainier* cherries. If you live in the Northwest, you'll already know that Rainier cherries are to be sought at any price. While Royal Annes are the most widely grown of all sweet cherries, few find their way to the market—they are used almost exclusively in the preparation of maraschino cherries.

When you shop for sweet cherries, look for shiny, firm fruit. Since cherries wither when left where their moisture can evaporate, refrigerate them in plastic bags and use them as soon as possible.

Buying and eating cherries fresh is best, but the season is so short that you may want to freeze some. For most uses, it's best to freeze cherries unsugared and individually. Wash the cherries in very cold water and then drain, stem, and pit them. (An inexpensive, hand-held cherry pitter simplifies this last task.) Next, put the dry cherries in a single layer on a cookie sheet and freeze. When the cherries are completely frozen, pack them into plastic bags or containers. As you fill the containers, gently shake the fruit to pack it closely. Since the cherries are frozen before they are put into containers or bags, they don't stick together and are easier to measure out as needed.

# ANGEL SHORTCAKES WITH STRAWBERRIES IN RASPBERRY SAUCE

Individual angel food cakes make lovely light "shortcakes." Strawberries are given extra interest with a raspberry sauce. You could use raspberries, or any seasonal berry, in place of the strawberries.

CAKE

- **6 tablespoons sugar**
- **6 tablespoons egg whites (about 3 large egg whites)**
- **¼ teaspoon cream of tartar**
- **Pinch salt**
- **¼ cup sifted cake flour**
- **½ teaspoon lemon juice**
- **½ teaspoon Grand Marnier *or* Cointreau**
- **¼ teaspoon almond extract**

STRAWBERRIES IN RASPBERRY SAUCE

- **1 cup strawberries**
- **2 tablespoons sugar, approximately**
- **1½ teaspoons Grand Marnier *or* Cointreau**
- **1 cup raspberries**

**PREPARATION:** Heat oven to 300°F. Lightly butter 8 individual ring molds or 6-ounce soufflé dishes. Put enough sugar into each mold to coat well. Tap out excess.

FOR THE CAKE: Sift 6 tablespoons sugar into a small bowl and set aside. Put egg whites in a large bowl. Sift cream of tartar over egg whites. Add salt and beat egg whites to very soft peaks. When bowl is tilted, whites should just flow and not run or slide out of bowl in a cohesive mass. Sprinkle 1 tablespoon of sugar over egg whites and fold in gently. Repeat until all sugar is thoroughly folded in, using as light a touch as possible. Sift 1 tablespoon flour over egg whites and fold in just as you did the sugar, using a light touch. Repeat until all flour is incorporated. Sprinkle lemon juice, Grand Marnier, and almond extract over batter and fold in gently.

Pour batter into prepared molds, filling each ⅔ full. Rap molds sharply against countertop once or twice to release air bubbles. Put molds on a baking sheet; they should not touch. Bake in preheated oven until cakes are pale tan and springy to the touch, about 35 minutes. Invert cakes at once. Cool upside-down in molds for 5 minutes. Using a knife, gently loosen cakes and remove from pans. Cool on a wire rack to room temperature.

FOR THE STRAWBERRIES IN RASPBERRY SAUCE: Set aside 4 of the best-looking strawberries for garnish. Hull and slice the rest of the strawberries and put in a bowl with sugar and Grand Marnier. Toss to mix. Purée raspberries in a food processor for 30 seconds. Put purée through a sieve and combine with sliced strawberries. Taste and add more sugar if necessary. Cover and refrigerate.

**SERVING:** Spoon berry mixture over and around cakes and garnish with reserved whole strawberries.

YIELD: 4 servings

# SUMMER

## The Very Best Angel Food Cake

We weren't exaggerating when we named this recipe. A slightly crisp exterior sets off the light sweetness of the cake to perfection. Whipped cream and berries are the suggested garnish. Try raspberries, blueberries, blackberries, or a combination.

**1¾ cups sugar**
**1¾ cups egg whites (from about 12 extra-large eggs)**
**1 teaspoon cream of tartar**
**¼ teaspoon salt**
**1¼ cups sifted cake flour**
**1½ teaspoons vanilla extract**
**¾ teaspoon almond extract**
**¾ teaspoon lemon juice**

**1 cup heavy cream**
**1 cup berries**

**PREPARATION:** Heat oven to 300°F. Sift sugar into a small mixing bowl and set aside. Put egg whites in a large bowl.

Sift cream of tartar over whites, add salt, and beat egg whites to very soft peaks. When bowl is tilted, whites should just flow and not run or slide out of bowl in a cohesive mass. Sprinkle 2 tablespoons sugar over whites and fold in very gently. Repeat until all sugar is thoroughly folded in, using as light a touch as possible. Sift 2 tablespoons flour over whites and fold in very gently. Repeat until all flour is incorporated, again using as light a touch as possible. Sprinkle vanilla, almond extract, and lemon juice over batter and fold in gently.

Pour batter into an ungreased 10-inch tube pan with a removable bottom and smooth the top. Rap pan sharply against counter once or twice to remove air bubbles.

Bake in preheated oven until pale brown and springy to the touch, about 1 hour and 10 minutes. Remove from oven, turn pan upside down and cool in pan 1 hour. If pan has no feet, invert over neck of a bottle. Meanwhile, whip the cream.

**SERVING:** Turn cake right side up and loosen around edges and central tube with a thin metal spatula. Remove cake gently from pan. Serve with whipped cream and berries.

**YIELD:** One 10-inch tube cake

## Berry Gelato

If red currants aren't available, you can make this gelato with all raspberries, or a combination of berries.

- **3 pints red raspberries**
- **1½ pints red currants**
- **1 pint heavy cream**
- **1 pint half and half**
- **1 cup sugar**

**PREPARATION:** Purée raspberries and currants and strain to remove seeds. Mix together purée, cream, half and half, and sugar. Freeze in an ice-cream machine according to manufacturer's instructions.

**YIELD:** about ½ gallon

# BROWN SUGAR ANGEL CAKE WITH SLICED PEACHES AND RUM CUSTARD

If you like angel food cake, do try this variation—brown sugar cake with a smooth custard sauce and the tart touch of peaches.

RUM CUSTARD

- **2½ cups half-and-half**
- **½ cup firmly packed light-brown sugar**
- **8 extra-large egg yolks**
- **2 tablespoons dark rum**
- **1 teaspoon vanilla extract**

PEACHES

- **5 large peaches *or* 1¼ pounds frozen unsweetened sliced peaches**
- **3 tablespoons sugar, approximately**
- **1 tablespoon lemon juice**
- **1 tablespoon dark rum**

CAKE

- **1 cup raw sugar *or* regular sugar**
- **½ cup firmly packed light-brown sugar**
- **1¾ cups egg whites (from about 12 extra-large eggs)**
- **1 teaspoon cream of tartar**
- **¼ teaspoon salt**
- **1¼ cups sifted cake flour**
- **2 teaspoons dark rum**
- **½ teaspoon vanilla extract**

**PREPARATION:** FOR THE CUSTARD: Bring half-and-half and sugar to a simmer in a heavy saucepan over medium heat. Beat egg yolks until frothy. Whisk 1 cup of the hot mixture into the yolks and stir back into pan. Cook over very low heat, stirring constantly, until custard thickens enough to coat the back of a spoon lightly (170°F.),

# PLUM ICE CREAM WITH STRAWBERRIES

Plum ice cream? Why not? It tastes wonderful, and it looks gorgeous topped with red strawberries. It's another gift to dessert lovers from Chez Panisse's Lindsey Shere.

PLUM ICE CREAM

**5 soft, ripe plums (¾ to 1 pound)**
**2 egg yolks**
**1⅛ cups heavy cream**
**¾ cup sugar**
**½ teaspoon vanilla extract, approximately**
**½ teaspoon kirsch, approximately**

**1 pint strawberries**
**2 tablespoons sugar, approximately**

**PREPARATION:** FOR THE ICE CREAM: Halve and pit plums. Put them in a nonreactive saucepan with ¼ cup water. Cover and bring to a simmer. Cook gently over medium-low heat, stirring occasionally to keep the plums from sticking, until they are tender, 10 to 15 minutes. Purée plums, including skins and cooking liquid, until almost smooth and let cool.

Lightly beat the egg yolks. Heat the cream with ¾ cup sugar over low heat until sugar melts, about 5 minutes. Gradually beat cream mixture into egg yolks to temper them. Return cream mixture to the pan and cook over very low heat, stirring constantly, until slightly thickened (170°F.), about 10 minutes. Immediately strain into a container and add plum purée. Flavor with vanilla and kirsch to taste and freeze in an ice-cream machine according to manufacturer's instructions.

Hull and slice the strawberries and add sugar to taste.

**SERVING:** Serve plum ice cream with the strawberries and their juices.

YIELD: 4 servings

## PLUMS

While many summer fruits now appear on greengrocers' shelves in the dead of winter, you still have to wait until May or June to bite into that first juicy plum. Occasionally you may see plums that have been imported from South America in February or March, but almost all of our plums come from California, where the season runs from late May until late October, peaking during July and August.

Because plums can be crossbred easily, there are now more than 150 varieties grown in the United States, from the *Red Beaut,* the first to appear, to the *Rovsum,* sometimes available as late as November. The colorful Red Beaut, the bright reddish-purple *Santa Rosa,* and the deep black *Friar* are the most common California plums, making up more than one-third of the crop, but you are likely to come across a dozen or so varieties in the marketplace. They range in color from yellow or green to crimson or purple to almost black. Their flesh is most likely to be yellow, but some hybrids have red flesh. And, when perfectly ripe, their tastes vary from a delicious tartness to an incredible sweetness.

Among the varieties to look out for is the *Santa Rosa,* the most popular and widely available. It

about 10 minutes. Do not boil. Strain and mix in rum and vanilla. Chill.

FOR THE PEACHES: Peel, pit, and slice peaches and combine with sugar, lemon juice, and rum. Add more sugar to taste if necessary.

FOR THE CAKE: Heat oven to 300°F. With your fingers, rub sugars together, pressing out all lumps. Set aside.

Put egg whites in a large bowl, sift cream of tartar over them, and add salt. Beat to very soft peaks. When bowl is tilted, whites should just flow and not run or slide out of bowl in a cohesive mass. Sprinkle 2 tablespoons sugar mixture over whites and fold in gently. Repeat until all sugar mixture is added, using as light a touch as possible. Sift 2 tablespoons flour over whites and fold in just as you did the sugar. Repeat until all flour is incorporated. Sprinkle rum and vanilla over batter and fold in. Pour batter into an ungreased 10-inch tube pan with a removable bottom and smooth the top. Rap pan sharply on counter once or twice to remove air bubbles.

Bake in preheated oven until pale brown and springy, about 1 hour and 10 minutes. Turn pan upside down immediately. Cool upside-down in pan 1 hour. If pan has no feet, invert over neck of bottle.

Turn cake right side up and loosen around edges and central tube with a thin spatula. Remove cake gently, turn right side up, and center on a plate. Using a serrated knife, enlarge the center hole by cutting a circle into top of cake about midway between outer edge and center. Cut only halfway through cake and, working from cut circle to center hole, lift out wedges of cake and use them to plug center so that the cake forms a container. The floor of the scooped-out area should be relatively level.

**SERVING:** Put 1 cup of custard in hollowed-out cake. Arrange peaches on top, mounding them in center. Drizzle remaining custard over peaches.

YIELD: 10 servings

# Berry Tart

The filling for this berry-topped tart is creamy Italian mascarpone. If you start a day or two ahead, you can make your own and allow time for it to thicken. (Or you can simply buy it.) Instead of berries you can also use other summer fruits such as sliced peaches, nectarines, or apricots. The recipe is from Lindsey Shere, long-time pastry chef at Berkeley, California's Chez Panisse.

MASCARPONE

- **1 cup heavy cream**
- **1⁄16 teaspoon tartaric acid (see Note)**

PASTRY

- **1 cup flour**
- **Pinch of salt**
- **1 teaspoon sugar**
- **1 lemon**
- **¼ pound unsalted butter**
- **1 tablespoon cold water, approximately**
- **½ teaspoon vanilla extract**
- **1 teaspoon + a few drops kirsch**
- **Sugar for mascarpone**
- **1½ pints strawberries, raspberries *or* blackberries**
- **4 teaspoons raspberry jelly, approximately**

**PREPARATION:** FOR THE MASCARPONE: Warm the cream to 180°F. in a double boiler. Add tartaric acid and stir 30 seconds. Remove pan from hot water and stir for 2 minutes. Pour into a refrigerator container and chill for 1 or 2 days.

FOR THE PASTRY: Mix flour, salt, and sugar. Grate zest from ½ the lemon into the flour and combine. Cut in the butter or work it with your hands until it is incorporated and mixture begins to hold together when pressed. Mix water and vanilla and stir into flour mix-

has a bright purple-crimson skin and yellow flesh and an appealing, slightly tart flavor. Others in this family include the *Queen Rosa* and the *Simka Rosa,* in season during late June and early July. The *Laroda* and the *El Dorado* are among the best of the darker-red plums, while the early *Black Beaut* and the late *Angeleno* are two of the almost black-skinned plums you may see.

There also are several types of green-skinned California plums, including the *Wickson,* available in late June, and the *Kelsey,* at its peak from mid-July through late August. The darker-green Kelsey is by far the better choice, with excellent taste and texture. The *Greengage* plum is a smaller, and usually more expensive, European specialty. Choose plums still touched with their protective bloom if possible. In general, look for those that are just about ripe—slightly firm rather than mushy but with some "give" to them. Plums will ripen at room temperature. When they are ripe, they feel soft at the tip end. Plums spoil rapidly. Eat them within a few days, or put them in the refrigerator once ripe. Even chilled they won't keep for more than two or three days longer.

In addition to the California plums, you will also find *prune plums* late in the season. These smaller, oval-shaped fruits with deep-purple skins and yellow flesh are usually called Italian prune plums. They have a delicious taste of their own but are perhaps at their best cooked. The *Damson* is another excellent prune plum, often used in preserves and jellies. Unfortunately, Damsons are no longer as popular as they once were and are difficult to find except in specialty stores.

ture. Add a little more water, 1 teaspoon at a time, if needed so that the dough holds together. Press dough into a ball, wrap, and chill at least 30 minutes. Press into a 9-inch fluted tart pan and chill for 1 hour or freeze for 20 minutes.

Heat oven to 375°F. Bake tart shell in preheated oven until golden brown, 20 to 25 minutes. Cool.

Beat the mascarpone with 1 teaspoon kirsch until it just mounds and holds a shape. Sweeten lightly with sugar to taste. Spread in the cooled tart shell. If using strawberries, hull them. Arrange the fruit on top of the mascarpone. Warm the jelly, add kirsch to taste, and brush the fruit with the glaze. A few drops of water can be added to the glaze if needed to thin.

YIELD: One 9-inch tart

NOTE: Tartaric acid is available at wine-making supply stores.

## CHAMPAGNE-POACHED FIGS WITH HEAVY CREAM

A simple yet luxurious dish from caterer and author Martha Stewart. You lose very little by substituting a less expensive still wine.

**½ bottle dry Champagne *or* sparkling white wine**
**Zest of ½ lemon**
**½ cup sugar**
**¼ vanilla bean**
**2 3-inch cinnamon sticks**
**12 fresh figs, preferably purple**
**Fig leaves for garnish, optional**
**1 cup heavy cream**

COOKING: In a saucepan combine wine, lemon zest, sugar, vanilla bean, and cinnamon sticks. Bring to a boil and cook for 5 minutes. Reduce heat. Add figs and poach over low heat until they are tender but still retain

### FIGS

Like the persimmon, quince, and other "old-fashioned" fruits, fresh figs are making a comeback in this country. Improved transport for this delicate, highly perishable commodity has helped. Fig varieties number in the hundreds; in addition to white, brown, and black varieties, they span the spectrum from red to yellow-green to purple. The most popular domestic types include the succulent *Calimyrna* (descended from the esteemed Turkish Smyrna fig) and the purple-skinned, crimson-fleshed *Black* or *Mission fig.*

their shape, 20 to 30 minutes. Transfer the figs to a serving dish. Reduce poaching liquid to ¾ cup. Strain liquid over figs.

**SERVING:** Serve at room temperature, garnished with fig leaves if desired, and pass heavy cream separately.

YIELD: 8 servings

## Poached Peaches with Champagne Sabayon

A lovely, flexible summer dessert from Lindsey Shere of Chez Panisse. Almost any berry or pitted fruit is delicious with the airy sabayon. And the sabayon itself can be made with a still white wine, either dry or sweet.

### Poached Peaches

- **½ vanilla bean**
- **1⅓ cups sugar**
- **1 quart water**
- **1 or 2 strips lemon zest**
- **8 small firm but ripe peaches (or 4 large)**

### Raspberry Sauce

- **½ cup raspberries**
- **¼ teaspoon kirsch, approximately**
- **1½ teaspoons sugar, approximately**

### Champagne Sabayon

- **3 egg yolks**
- **2 tablespoons sugar**
- **⅓ cup Champagne**
- **⅓ cup heavy cream**
- **1 unsprayed, untreated rose *or* candied rose petals *or* violets, optional**

**PREPARATION:** FOR THE POACHED PEACHES: Split the vanilla bean and scrape seeds into a nonreactive sauce-

You'll find fresh figs in the market for a short time in June and then again from late summer through early November. Their fragile skin makes shipping expensive, so you should expect to pay a stiff price. Choose figs that are plump, soft, and fresh-smelling. They will last, covered and refrigerated, for a day or two but are best used as soon as possible. Avoid hard, underripe figs. They won't continue to ripen off the tree.

Unless you have your own fig trees, you'll probably want to serve the fruit simply so that it shines as the main attraction rather than being lost in a complicated dish. Take a leaf from the Italians' book and make an appetizer of prosciutto and fresh figs. Or you can pair the luxurious fruit with a mild cheese; buffalo-milk mozzarella and figs served with Sauternes make a sublime dessert. Figs look especially pretty halved to show their juicy, seedy flesh. They're delectable on their own, either raw or poached, with nothing more than a topping of heavy cream.

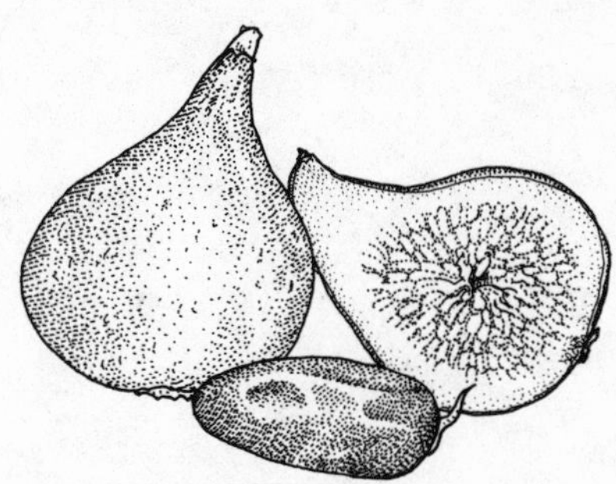

pan. Add the pod, sugar, water, and zest and bring to a boil. Add the peaches and simmer slowly until peaches are just cooked through but still hold together, 15 to 30 minutes. Cool in the syrup.

FOR THE RASPBERRY SAUCE: Purée the raspberries in a food processor and strain out the seeds. Add kirsch and sweeten to taste with a little sugar. If the purée is too thick, add a little water.

FOR THE CHAMPAGNE SABAYON: Beat egg yolks and sugar together in a double boiler. Beat in the Champagne and set over simmering water. Beat until the mixture thickens, about 10 minutes. Chill, whisking occasionally. Beat the cream to very soft peaks and fold it into the chilled sabayon.

**SERVING:** Gently pull the petals off the roses. Divide sabayon among 4 bowls. Peel the peaches. If peaches are large, cut them in half and arrange rounded side up on the sabayon. If they are small, serve them whole. Spoon a little raspberry sauce over each peach and sprinkle rose petals or candied flowers on top.

YIELD: 4 servings

# FALL/WINTER

## Apple Charlotte

Really nothing more than crisp buttered bread and thick applesauce, apple charlotte is nevertheless an all-time favorite—truly a case of the whole equaling more than the sum of the parts. The crème anglaise given here is optional, but its cool, sweet creaminess sets off the dessert to perfection.

Crème Anglaise

**⅓ cup sugar**
**5 egg yolks**
**1 cup milk**
**¾ cup heavy cream**
**½ teaspoon vanilla extract**

**1 lemon**
**4 pounds tart apples**
**12 tablespoons butter**
**3-inch piece vanilla bean**
**½ cup apricot preserves, approximately**
**1 ounce Calvados *or* applejack, optional**
**12 slices white bread, approximately**

**PREPARATION:** FOR THE CRÈME ANGLAISE: With electric mixer or whisk beat sugar into egg yolks. Beat until mixture is pale yellow and slightly thick. In a saucepan heat milk and cream until almost boiling. Add to yolk mixture slowly, whisking constantly. Return mixture to saucepan over very low heat and cook, stirring, until thick enough to coat back of a spoon lightly (170°F.), about 10 minutes. Do not allow to boil. Strain into a clean bowl, add vanilla, and chill.

Grate 1 tablespoon lemon zest. Peel, quarter, and core apples and cut them into ⅛-inch slices.

In a large heavy pot melt 6 tablespoons butter. Add zest, vanilla bean, and apples. Cook, covered, stirring occasionally, for 10 minutes, uncover, and stir frequently until apples are tender, about 10 minutes. Sweeten with preserves to taste. Return to high heat and cook, stirring almost constantly, until mixture is very thick, about 10 minutes more. Discard vanilla bean. Add Calvados if desired.

Meanwhile, clarify remaining 6 tablespoons butter. Remove crusts from bread and cut 5 slices into 3 triangles per slice to fit exactly into bottom of a standard charlotte mold (like pieces of a pie). Dip triangles in clarified butter and fit them into the bottom of the charlotte mold. Cut remaining bread slices into 1- to 1¼-inch strips. Dip in butter and arrange upright around sides of mold, overlapping slightly.

Fill mold with apple mixture. Trim bread so that it is flush with the top of the filling.

**COOKING:** Heat oven to 450°F. Bake in preheated oven for 15 minutes. Reduce heat to 350°F. and bake 30 minutes more. Let sit for 15 minutes and unmold.

**SERVING:** Serve warm or at room temperature with chilled crème anglaise.

**YIELD:** 6 servings

# Cranberry Bread Pudding with Whiskey Crème Anglaise

Homey and unusual at the same time, this is an ideal holiday dessert. Plain old bread pudding is updated with tart cranberries and given punch with a whiskey-flavored sauce.

**Crème Anglaise (page 231)**
**¼ cup bourbon *or* blended whiskey**
**1 1-pound loaf sliced raisin bread**
**3 cups half-and-half**
**1 orange**
**¾ cup sugar**
**3 eggs**
**1 tablespoon vanilla extract**
**1 cup chopped cranberries**
**1 tablespoon confectioners' sugar**

**PREPARATION:** Make the Crème Anglaise, add the whiskey and chill.

Cut bread slices into 6 to 8 pieces each. In a large bowl soak bread in half-and-half for 1 hour. Heat oven to 350°F. Generously butter a 6- to 8-cup baking mold.

Grate zest from orange into a bowl. Add sugar, eggs, and vanilla and whisk together. Pour mixture over soaked bread and mix well. Stir in cranberries.

Pour into prepared mold and bake until pudding is browned on top, springs back when touched lightly, and a skewer inserted into center comes out clean, 1 to 1¼ hours. If your mold is deeper than it is wide, bake 15 minutes longer. Cool on a rack for 10 minutes and unmold onto a serving platter.

**SERVING:** Sift confectioners' sugar over pudding and serve warm or at room temperature with whiskey crème anglaise.

**YIELD:** 10 servings

# PEAR MINCEMEAT TART

Both lighter and more attractive than the usual mincemeat pie. You could use apples instead of pears if you prefer.

PEAR MINCEMEAT

**2 firm pears, such as bosc**
**¼ cup raisins**
**⅓ cup firmly packed brown sugar**
**½ cup dry white wine**
**¼ teaspoon cinnamon**
**⅛ teaspoon ground cloves**
**¼ teaspoon ground nutmeg**
**¼ teaspoon ground ginger**
**2 tablespoons butter**
**1 tablespoon brandy**

PASTRY

**1¼ cups flour**
**1 teaspoon sugar**
**⅛ teaspoon salt**
**¼ pound cold unsalted butter**
**3 tablespoons cold water**

**4 to 5 firm pears, such as bosc**
**½ lemon**
**2 tablespoons sugar**
**¼ cup strained ginger preserves *or* apple jelly for glaze**
**1 cup heavy cream**
**½ teaspoon brandy**
**Nutmeg for sprinkling**

**PREPARATION:** FOR THE PEAR MINCEMEAT: Peel, core, and chop pears. In a saucepan combine pears, raisins, brown sugar, and wine. Bring to a boil and simmer, partially covered, until pears are tender and liquid is reduced by half, about 40 minutes. Add cinnamon, cloves, nutmeg, ginger, butter, and brandy. Cook 5 more minutes. Mincemeat can be made ahead and stored in the refrigerator for at least 5 days.

FOR THE PASTRY: Combine flour, sugar, and salt. Cut in cold butter or work with your hands until mixture is the consistency of meal with some pieces of butter still the size of peas. Sprinkle in the cold water and stir until dough just begins to clump together in the bowl. Turn dough onto a sheet of plastic wrap and pull it together into a mass, using plastic wrap and your hand to help gather dry parts of dough and press them into moistened dough. Wrap dough in plastic and chill at least 20 minutes.

Peel and core pears and cut lengthwise into ¼- to ½-inch slices. Squeeze lemon juice over slices and toss.

On a floured work surface roll out pastry. Fit dough into a 10-inch tart pan with a removable bottom and chill 10 to 15 minutes.

Heat oven to 375°F. Prick bottom of tart shell thoroughly and spread mincemeat over it. Arrange pear slices in concentric circles, starting from outside edge and overlapping slightly to form 2 or 3 rings of pear slices, using smaller slices toward center. Sprinkle with 1½ tablespoons sugar.

Bake in preheated oven until crust is golden brown and pears are tender, 55 to 60 minutes. Cool.

Melt ginger preserves or apple jelly and brush over cooled tart. Whip cream with remaining 1½ teaspoons sugar and brandy until it holds soft peaks. Refrigerate cream if not using right away.

**SERVING:** Serve each slice with a dollop of whipped cream sprinkled with nutmeg.

YIELD: One 10-inch tart

# SPICED PUMPKIN CREAM ROLL

If the crème fraîche needed for the filling is not available, you can use 2 cups heavy cream whipped to stiff peaks with 2 teaspoons lemon juice.

CAKE

**¾ cup sifted flour**
**1 tablespoon ground coriander**
**1 teaspoon ground mace**
**¼ teaspoon allspice**
**½ teaspoon ground ginger**
**Pinch salt**
**¾ cup ground pecans**
**6 eggs**
**½ cup firmly packed brown sugar**
**½ cup granulated sugar**
**3 tablespoons butter**
**Confectioners' sugar**

PUMPKIN CREAM FILLING

**2¼ cups crème fraîche**
**¼ cup honey**
**¾ cup puréed pumpkin**
**1 tablespoon rum**

**Pecan halves for garnish**

**PREPARATION:** FOR THE CAKE: Heat oven to 350°F. Line bottom of a 17- by 11½-inch jelly-roll pan with parchment, and butter and flour the paper and sides of pan. Sift flour a second time into a bowl along with spices and salt. Mix in pecans and set aside.

Separate eggs. In a mixing bowl beat egg yolks and brown sugar until slightly thickened and set aside. In another mixing bowl beat egg whites until they hold soft peaks. Add granulated sugar, 1 tablespoon at a time, and beat to stiff-peak stage. Fold ¼ of the whites into yolk mixture. Sprinkle ⅓ of the flour mixture over yolks and fold together. Continue to alternate folding meringue and flour mixture into yolk mixture. Melt butter and fold in.

Pour batter into prepared pan and bake until cake begins to pull away from sides and springs back when touched lightly, 12 to 15 minutes.

Sift a light coating of confectioners' sugar over top. Cover a baking sheet with parchment and put it, parchment side down, over cake in pan. Quickly invert and lift off cake pan. Peel parchment off cake. Sift 1 tablespoon confectioners' sugar over cake and roll up still-warm cake and the clean sheet of parchment lengthwise. Wrap in plastic and set aside until cool.

FOR THE FILLING: Beat crème fraîche until it holds stiff peaks. Fold in honey, pumpkin, and rum. Unroll cake and spread with ⅓ of the filling. Reroll cake and chill 5 to 10 minutes. Frost with remaining pumpkin cream, garnish with pecan halves, and chill.

**SERVING:** Just before serving, sift confectioners' sugar over the cake.

YIELD: 16 servings

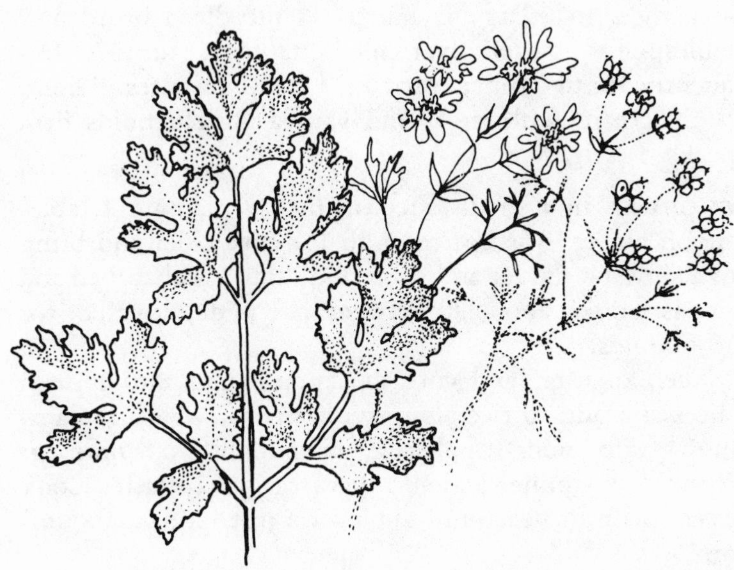

# APPLE AND CIDER SOUP WITH RAISINS

Warm soup for dessert is a novelty we think you'll like. This doubly apple-flavored soup has sweet raisins, whipped cream, and crunchy croutons as well.

**3 slices white bread**
**3 tablespoons butter**
**½ cup heavy cream**
**1 teaspoon sugar**
**¼ teaspoon vanilla extract**
**¼ cup uncooked rice**
**2¾ cups apple cider**
**2 cooking apples, such as McIntosh**
**½ cup raisins**
**¼ cup water**
**2 tablespoons applejack *or* apple schnapps to taste**
**¼ teaspoon cinnamon**
**¼ teaspoon nutmeg + more if desired**
**1 tablespoon brown sugar, approximately**

**PREPARATION:** Trim crusts from bread and cut into ¼-inch dice. In a large frying pan sauté diced bread in 2 tablespoons butter over medium heat, turning frequently, until golden brown, 1 to 2 minutes. Drain. Whip cream with sugar and vanilla until it holds firm peaks. Refrigerate.

**COOKING:** In a small saucepan melt remaining 1 tablespoon butter. Stir in rice. Add 1¾ cups cider and bring to a simmer. Cover and cook until liquid is absorbed and rice is tender, about 20 minutes. Set aside, covered, for 10 minutes.

Peel, quarter, and core the apples. Cut into ⅛-inch slices and add to rice along with raisins, water, remaining 1 cup cider, applejack, cinnamon, and nutmeg. Bring to a simmer and add brown sugar to taste. Cook over medium heat until apples are just tender, about 3 minutes.

**SERVING:** Ladle soup into 4 warm soup bowls. Top with a dollop of whipped cream and sprinkle with croutons and a pinch of nutmeg if desired.

**YIELD:** 4 servings

## WALNUT CRÊPES WITH CARAMELIZED APPLES

Alice Waters of Chez Panisse fame makes crêpes more delicious than ever by adding finely chopped walnuts and crisping the edges in the oven for a few minutes before serving.

CRÊPES

- **1 cup + 1½ tablespoons milk**
- **⅛ teaspoon salt**
- **¼ teaspoon sugar**
- **2 tablespoons butter**
- **¾ cup flour**
- **2 small eggs**
- **1½ teaspoons walnut oil**
- **¼ cup beer**
- **¼ cup minced walnuts**

- **4 small flavorful apples, such as Gravenstein, *or* 3 larger apples**
- **4 tablespoons butter**
- **½ cup sugar**
- **Splash cognac**
- **1 cup crème fraîche**

**PREPARATION:** FOR THE CRÊPES: Heat milk, salt, sugar, and butter until butter is melted. Put flour in a bowl and make a well in the center. Lightly beat the eggs. Put eggs and oil in the well and mix with a whisk or electric hand mixer until flour is incorporated and mixture begins to thicken. Add warm milk mixture, little by little, beating until smooth. Stir in beer. Strain and chill at least 2 hours.

Add nuts, bring batter to room temperature, and stir.

Heat a crêpe pan or small nonstick frying pan over medium heat. Lightly butter the pan. Pour in 2 tablespoons batter, tilting pan so that batter covers bottom evenly, and cook, turning once, until both sides are browned, about 30 seconds per side. Make at least 12 crêpes. If not using immediately, stack separated by plastic wrap and cover tightly.

**COOKING:** Heat oven to 375°F. Put crêpes in a single layer on a rack and set on a baking sheet. Heat in preheated oven until edges are just crisp, 2 to 3 minutes.

Core and peel apples and cut them into ⅜-inch rings. In a large frying pan melt butter with sugar. Turn heat to high and add apples. Cook, shaking pan to keep apples from burning, until sugar just caramelizes and apples are tender, 2 to 3 minutes. Add cognac.

**SERVING:** Top the crisped crêpes with apple filling and serve warm with crème fraîche.

**YIELD:** 4 servings

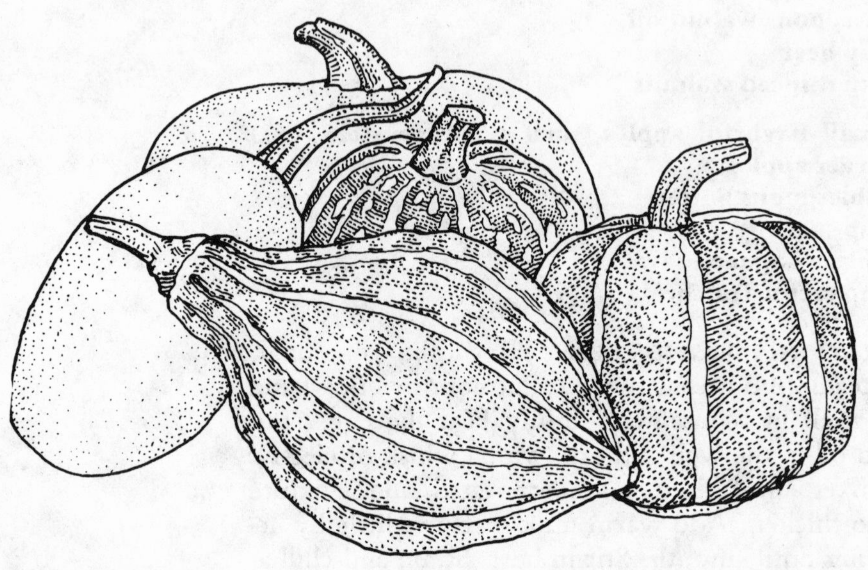

# Maple-Rum Squash Soufflé

The sweet kabocha (or Japanese pumpkin) squash is specified here, but another sweet variety such as sweet dumpling could be used—or even acorn or hubbard squash sweetened to taste. You could also make the soufflé with pumpkin.

**2 pounds kabocha squash**
**½ cup hazelnuts, optional**
**1 cup heavy cream**
**1½ tablespoons dark rum**
**1½ tablespoons maple syrup**
**4 eggs**
**¼ cup firmly packed brown sugar**
**1 teaspoon vanilla extract**
**½ teaspoon salt**

**PREPARATION:** Cut squash into pieces and boil until tender, 25 to 30 minutes. Scoop out flesh and purée in a food processor. Toast hazelnuts in a 325°F. oven until golden and fragrant, 10 to 15 minutes. Cool, rub off loose skin, and chop. Butter a 1-quart casserole. Whip ½ cup cream with 1½ teaspoons rum and 1½ teaspoons maple syrup.

**COOKING:** Heat oven to 350°F. Separate eggs. In a large bowl beat egg yolks until thick and lemon-colored. Mix in 1 cup squash purée, remaining 1 tablespoon rum, remaining 1 tablespoon maple syrup, ½ cup cream, brown sugar, vanilla, and salt. Beat egg whites until stiff and fold into squash mixture. Transfer to prepared casserole.

Bake in preheated oven until golden, 40 to 45 minutes.

**SERVING:** Serve soufflé immediately with rum/maple whipped cream. Sprinkle on optional hazelnuts.

**YIELD:** 4 servings

# ALL SEASON

## ORANGE SHERBET

Plain orange sherbet is a treat when it's homemade. For the best texture, sherbet should be eaten within a day or two of being made. You can, however, melt over-the-hill sherbet and rechurn it to restore the texture.

- **8 oranges, approximately**
- **1 lemon**
- **1 cup sugar syrup, recipe follows**

**PREPARATION:** Squeeze juice from oranges and strain to make 1½ cups. Squeeze juice from the lemon and strain. Combine orange juice and 1 tablespoon lemon juice with sugar syrup and freeze in an ice-cream machine according to manufacturer's instructions.

**YIELD:** about 1 quart

## Sugar Syrup

**¾ cup sugar**
**¾ cup water**

**PREPARATION:** Combine sugar and water in a large saucepan. Heat over medium heat, stirring until the sugar dissolves.

Cool the sugar syrup to room temperature. Store tightly sealed in the refrigerator.

**YIELD:** about 1 cup

## Lemon Granité

This is a particularly refreshing dessert, both tart and cool. A granité should be rough and icy, something like a snow cone.

**4 lemons, approximately**
**1½ cups water**
**⅞ cup Sugar Syrup (above)**

**PREPARATION:** Squeeze juice from lemons and strain to make 6 tablespoons. Combine lemon juice, water, and sugar syrup. Pour mixture into a shallow pan and put in freezer. Stir after 45 minutes. Repeat stirring after 1 more hour. Return to freezer until serving.

**YIELD:** about 1 quart.

# CHOCOLATE CHARLOTTE

This is a classic chocolate charlotte, beloved for generations. There are two tricks useful to know. First, if the chocolate base chills so much that it is too stiff to fold into the whipped cream, simply melt it down and start again. Second, if the chocolate shows through the ladyfinger shell, pipe the whipped cream garnish over any messy spots. The whipped cream is frequently piped between each ladyfinger to cover any chocolate peeking through.

LADYFINGERS

**4 eggs**
**⅓ cup sugar**
**1 teaspoon vanilla extract**
**2 tablespoons confectioners' sugar + more for sprinkling**
**¾ cup flour**
**Pinch salt**

CHOCOLATE BAVARIAN FILLING

**1 package unflavored gelatin**
**¼ cup cold water**
**¼ pound semisweet chocolate**
**6 egg yolks**
**¼ cup sugar**
**2 cups milk**
**1 vanilla bean**
**1 cup heavy cream**

**½ cup whipped cream, optional**

**PREPARATION:** FOR THE LADYFINGERS: Cover a baking sheet with parchment paper or butter it and coat lightly with flour. Heat the oven to 350°F.

Separate eggs. Beat egg yolks with the sugar and the vanilla until they are pale yellow and form a ribbon when trailed from a whisk. Beat the egg whites until they form stiff peaks. Add 2 tablespoons confectioners' sugar and beat until glossy, about 20 seconds.

Sift the flour and salt over the egg yolks and fold in. Stir in 1/4 of the egg whites. Gently fold in the remaining egg whites as lightly as possible. Gently spoon the mixture into a pastry bag fitted with a 3/4-inch plain tip. Pipe 24 fingers 3 1/2 inches long and 1 inch apart on the prepared baking sheet. Dust with confectioners' sugar and bake immediately in preheated oven until ladyfingers are just colored and firm and dry on the outside, about 12 minutes. Cool on pan for 5 minutes and transfer to a rack to cool completely.

FOR THE BAVARIAN FILLING: Soften gelatin in cold water. Chop chocolate into pea-sized pieces. Beat the egg yolks and sugar until light yellow. In a saucepan bring the milk and vanilla bean to a simmer and remove from heat. Remove vanilla bean and stir in chocolate pieces until they melt. Slowly pour the chocolate milk over yolk mixture, whisking. Pour mixture back into saucepan and cook over very low heat, stirring constantly with a wooden spoon until the sauce thickens enough to coat the back of the spoon lightly (170°F.), about 10 minutes. Do not boil.

Immediately strain into a bowl. Gently whisk in the gelatin until dissolved. Set the bowl into a larger bowl half filled with ice and water. Stir frequently until mixture is cool and begins to thicken.

To prepare the mold, trim enough ladyfingers to fit the bottom of the mold snugly like wedges of a pie and arrange them tops down. Arrange additional ladyfingers upright snugly around the sides, tops against the mold.

Whisk the cream until it holds soft peaks. When the chocolate mixture has almost set, gently fold in the whipped cream. Turn mixture into the prepared mold. Chill until set, at least 6 hours.

**SERVING:** Unmold the charlotte. If it does not slip out easily, dip the mold into hot water briefly and run a knife around the edge. Garnish with whipped cream as desired.

YIELD: 6 to 8 servings

# CAFÉ À LA MOUSSE

Coffee and dessert in one—liqueur-flavored coffee topped with a scoop of chocolate mousse.

CHOCOLATE MOUSSE

**1½ ounces bittersweet chocolate**
**1½ tablespoons butter**
**1 egg**
**1 tablespoon liqueur, such as Kahlúa, Tia Maria, *or* crème de cacao**
**¼ cup heavy cream**

**4 jiggers of liqueur, such as Kahlúa, Tia Maria, *or* crème de cacao**
**4 cups espresso-strength coffee**
**Hot milk, optional**

**PREPARATION:** In top of a double boiler melt chocolate and butter. Cool slightly.

Separate egg. In a mixing bowl whisk together egg yolk, cooled chocolate mixture, and liqueur. In another bowl beat egg white until stiff peaks form. Fold white into chocolate mixture. Whip cream and fold into chocolate mixture. Pour mixture into a container, seal, and freeze 5 to 15 hours.

**SERVING:** Put a jigger of liqueur in each of 4 cups. Pour in coffee and add hot milk if desired. Top with a generous dollop of mousse.

**YIELD:** 4 servings

# RECIPE CREDITS

Some of the recipes in this book have on-page attribution. Additional recipe credits are given below.

Angel Shortcakes with Sliced Strawberries in Raspberry Sauce JEAN ANDERSON
Apple Charlotte DINAH SCHLEY
Apple and Cider Soup with Raisins PAMELA PARSEGHIAN
Asian Pasta and Vegetables with Ham PAMELA PARSEGHIAN
Avocado Soup with Coriander Salsa MELANIE BARNARD
Baked Sweet-Dumpling Squash PAMELA PARSEGHIAN
Banana-Squash/Apple Soup ROSINA WILSON
Bean "Bundles" KATHY GUNST
Beans in Curry Cream Sauce with Curried Almonds KATHY GUNST
Berry Gelato PETE AND JUDY SHEPHERD
Broccoli with Starfruit PAMELA PARSEGHIAN
Brown Rice Mint Pilaf TERRY THOMPSON
Brown-Sugar Angel Cake with Sliced Peaches and Rum Custard JEAN ANDERSON
Bulgur-Stuffed Quail PAMELA PARSEGHIAN
Café à la Mousse JANE STACEY
Cajun Ham and Sausage Jambalaya TERRY THOMPSON
Casserole-Roasted Pheasant with Celery Root and Mushrooms RICHARD SAX
Chicken with Artichoke Sauce PAMELA PARSEGHIAN
Chicken Consommé SALLY BERNSTEIN
Chicken Mole BARBARA SAUSE
Chicken Quenelles with Shallot and Red-Pepper Sauce LONNIE GANDARA
Chicken Soup with Almonds MELANIE BARNARD
Chicken with Tomato Cream Sauce MELANIE BARNARD
Chocolate Charlotte DINAH SCHLEY
Chilled Cream of Chervil Soup ANNE BYRN
Cornmeal and Coriander Quesadillas ANNE BYRN
Cranberry Bread Pudding with Whiskey Crème Anglaise JANE STACEY
Cucumber and Cabbage Slaw with Brie PAMELA PARSEGHIAN
Cucumber and Plum Salad with Goat Cheese ELIZABETH WHEELER
Curried Chicken and Apples with Brandy Cream Sauce MELANIE BARNARD
Curried Eggplant STEVEN RAICHLEN
Dandelion Salad SUSAN HERRMANN LOOMIS
Eggplant Gâteau STEVEN RAICHLEN
Elote con Queso (Corn Custard) JANE BUTEL
Grilled Salad of Pork Chops and Vegetables MELANIE BARNARD
Grilled Salmon with Corn, Tomato, and Basil Relish PAMELA PARSEGHIAN
Grilled Scallion and Potato Salad PAMELA PARSEGHIAN
Ham and Crab Jambalaya PAMELA PARSEGHIAN
Hot Papaya Salad SIBELLA KRAUS
Individual Meat Loaves with Blue-Cheese Butter Sauce MELANIE BARNARD
Individual Salmon Mousse with Cucumber MELANIE BARNARD
Kale Timbales with Sautéed Radishes SUSAN HERRMANN LOOMIS
Lamb with Rosemary Sauce ANNE BYRN
Lobster and Zucchini Consommé PAMELA PARSEGHIAN
Maple-Rum Squash Soufflé ROSINA WILSON
Mozzarella with Tomatoes and Basil PAMELA

# INDEX